Baby
Doll

Baby Doll

AN AUTOBIOGRAPHY
CARROLL BAKER

ARBOR HOUSE   *NEW YORK*

Many thanks to Elia Kazan for his permission to use the *Baby Doll* photographs; David Rosenbaum and Paramount Pictures for the use of the Paramount photographs; Louis Marino of Warner Brothers Television Distribution for the photographs of *Giant*, *The Miracle* and *Cheyenne Autumn*; Paula Klaw of Movie Star News, and Ronald Alter of Ron's Now and Then for lending photographs from their private collections.

Mister Moses © 1965. All rights reserved. Frank Ross Productions, Ltd. & Belmont Productions, Ltd. Released through United Artists Corporation.
The Big Country © 1958. All right reserved. Donald Hamilton. Released through United Artists Corporation.
How The West Was Won © 1962 Metro-Goldwyn-Mayer Inc. and Cinerama, Inc.
But Not For Me © 1959 Perlsea Company and Paramount Pictures Corporation.
Carpetbaggers © 1965. Paramount Pictures Corp. and Embassy Pictures Corp.
Harlow © 1965 Paramount Pictures Corp. and Embassy Pictures Corporation and Prometheus Enterprises, Inc.
Sylvia © 1964 Paramount Pictures Corporation and Marpol Productions, Inc. All Right Reserved.
The Miracle © Warner Brothers Pictures Distributing Corporation
Cheyenne Autumn © Warner Brothers Pictures Distributing Corporation

Contents

I have always lived too much inside my head. Certainly, it always has been through the most vigorous exertion of will-power that I have forced myself to be in any way outgoing. But somehow I managed to function fairly well for some thirty years, until one day my inherent repression suddenly took over and imprisoned me within the confines of my mind.

My brain imploded. I pitched deep inside where I whirled and then floated through an endless, undefined darkness.

I locked myself in a pitch-black room in a strange hotel in an unknown or since-forgotten city and called out for my mother. No one heard me. Like those terrifying dreams when you scream and scream but no sound escapes.

I still don't know how I got into that room or even where it was or how long I was there. To this day partial amnesia blocks me from pinpointing the details.

Dear Mother,

Do you remember the first time I had a nervous breakdown? You and I have never talked about that. Maybe you're shocked that I'm bringing it up now after all these years. Maybe you've put it out of your mind altogether and can't remember it at all any more, like it didn't happen. Remember, I asked you when you went through the change of life and you said you didn't know. So I asked you when you had your last period and you said you couldn't remember. And I said how could you forget something important like that? Well, I don't believe you forgot. I think you always found those things distasteful so you chose not to remember them.

You and I are funny ducks. Most people would have discussed something as earthshaking as a nervous breakdown, but you and I never did. Why do you suppose that is? I guess I'm really curious about my own attitude.

I am writing about that portion of my life now, and I suddenly realized that there are so many blank spaces, so many puzzling things about that first breakdown which I've never bothered to find out.

I recall the second breakdown because it came on gradually and lasted such a long time—1966, '67, and part of '68, nearly three years.

It was the first one that took me by surprise. It happened so suddenly.

There must have been a void, a blackout, when or for how long I don't know. The first thing I remember was waking up in an icy cold bed. I was crying for you. I wanted my mother, but I didn't know how to contact you. I cried for you over and over again, but my cries simply circled the room and bounced right back at me. There must have been a telephone no more than an arm's length from my bed, but I no longer understood about telephones.

I was terrified that I couldn't see. There must have been a light switch nearby, an electric bulb ready to illuminate my space—but I had forgotten such things existed.

It did seem to me that at one time I must have been able to think because I was fretting that I no longer could get my thoughts straight. I was cold and hungry and frightened, but what I missed most was that ability to reason. Yes, probably worst of all was feeling so confused.

I knew I was alive—at least after a while I did because of the intensity of my fear and suffering.

I must have found my way to the bathroom and some water to drink. I couldn't have survived without water.

All at once you were there beside me. I could see you because you knew how to turn on the lights. You were holding my head and spoon-feeding me hot broth. You knew where and how to get that soup. You also knew where to find extra blankets and make me warm again.

I remember that I refused to go anywhere near the telephone. You used to dial numbers. Sometimes I'd wake up when I heard you whisper into it. When it rang I would shudder, then hide under the covers. I loathed that telephone and I was so grateful that you didn't make me talk to it. But I must have used it once, to call you. Otherwise how did you get there?

Love,
Carroll

P.S. If you don't want to talk about it, I'll understand. Maybe I won't even mail this.

Baby
Doll

Chapter One

LOS ANGELES: 1966
THE SECOND BREAKDOWN

What year is this? Oh, yes, it's 1966. Remember you glanced at the top of the newspaper? Was that this week or last? Well, it really doesn't matter.

It must be August. The sun is low and too hot, and there's always this choking yellow smog hanging over L.A. during August. Is there a smog alert today? Never mind, it won't affect me. I won't move around very much. I'll probably just sit here under the shade of the jacaranda tree and stare at that fucking kidney-shaped swimming pool.

Thank God for the wall around this garden. Nobody can see me. I hope they can't see me and wonder why I've been sitting here for so long, and ask themselves: What ever happened to Baby Doll? Maybe I'd better check again? Don't be silly, Carroll, you've checked the eyeline every day; you know you're safe, no one can see in.

Why don't I take a walk today? No, I'm too tired and I don't want anybody to know that I don't have anything to do. There's never anyone on the sidewalks in Beverly Hills! Yes, but they might look out of the windows and see me, recognize me, suddenly remember who I am and wonder why I'm not working anymore. No, I'd better stay here where it's safe.

What time is it? When did I take my last tranquilizers? I'm beginning to feel nervous. Maybe I should go into the kitchen and look at the clock. No, the maid will see me, and I'll be expected to talk. Anyway, I'm too tired to move, I'll just sit here for a while.

I wonder if the pool man has been here yet? Of course he has. Don't you remember? You watched him from behind the curtains until he'd left and locked the gate? I thought about telling him that he always uses too much chlorine. But I don't want to have to talk to him. I don't mind the gardener. He doesn't really speak anything but Japanese. He never looks at me. I don't think he even knows who I am.

The sun seems directly above me. I wonder if it's noon yet. No, mother would be here with a lunch tray coaxing me to eat. She always pretends that we're having a picnic in the garden. She tastes the food first and pretends that it's something special: "Oh, my, I think this is the best chicken I've ever tasted. Here, just try a tiny bit of mine with some mayonnaise." Of course, I know what she's doing, but I pretend I don't. I'm glad mother came to live with us because she takes care of everything. I don't have to worry about anything or see anybody.

Mother is so wonderful, she never seems to notice that I hardly ever talk out loud, but she tells me everything I want to hear, like: "Isn't it wonderful that the children are enjoying their summer camp so much? They both won blue ribbons for jumping! The headmistress told me that Blanche is a born horsewoman. She rides bareback like an Indian, and Herschel for his age isn't far behind." And mother never tells me anything I *don't* want to hear.

Now if Jack would only die. Oh, no, God, please forgive me! I don't wish death on anyone.

Maybe—maybe You could just send Jack away, and I wouldn't have a husband anymore. Somewhere where he'd be happy, but he'd get lost and never come back. I feel so bad! I'm going to have to take some more tranquilizers! If only I knew what time it was. Dr. Finger suggested four tablets every four hours. My four hours must be nearly up. I don't want to take more than the prescription reads.

Jack might come home soon! I'll have to take the tranquilizers now, so that I can only hear him from a long way off. As usual he'll start to talk about the lawsuit again, when I'm trying to forget it. He'll want me to sign things that I don't want to sign, and he won't leave me alone or let me rest until I give in. He'll just keep at me and at me and at me the way he did that night when he sent that disastrous telegram which started the legal battle. I couldn't talk him out of it. He wouldn't listen. Our lawyer couldn't talk him out of it either. Well, nobody could.

If only I hadn't been so tired. If only I'd had the strength left to stop Jack! Why had fighting a battle, which it seemed to me Jack was deliberately provoking, seemed the lesser of two equally exhausting evils? Why didn't I send Jack to hell instead? I wish I had. Oh, God, how I hate him! No, no, I don't. Please forget I said that. I don't hate anyone. I wish I could leave him now. But I'm still too tired. And there isn't any money at all. Oh, I hope Jack doesn't come home with another bank loan for me to sign. I wish we didn't have to borrow so much money. I wish I had the strength and there was enough money for me to get away from him. Forever. Maybe he'll get run over by a car. It wouldn't be anyone's fault, just an accident. Stop! Stop thinking those terrible things. Go ahead and take your pills.

There. You'll start feeling better in a few minutes.

The William Morris Agency was finally forced to admit that I was being blackballed in the industry. Abe said, "You know how it happens, Carroll. These boys all know each other. They all belong to the same country club. They get together over a drink and say, 'Our girl is giving us trouble. Don't use her,' and the word passes on."

I wish I were dead! No, I don't mean that! Please, God, I don't want to leave Blanche and Herschel alone. They need me.

Why didn't I have the courage to divorce Jack years ago before he had a chance to destroy everything? Why didn't I realize the kind of person he was? Or has he changed? Maybe he wasn't always like this? Orson Welles once said, "If there had not been a Jack Garfein, Hollywood would have invented him."

What am I going to do? I can't help myself, I can't stand him.

I hear footsteps! Please don't let it be Jack. Not yet, not until the pills have taken effect. I can't cope with his maniacal determination to impose his will on me.

That's the sliding door! Please don't let it be Jack! No, it's mother. Mother with another tray full of picnic. I'm getting sleepy. I think I might be too sleepy to eat. Oh, well, I'll try to eat something for her sake. If I swallow a few mouthfuls she'll smile for me. I've always loved my mother's smile. She still has those beautiful deep dimples and those startlingly perfect white teeth.

Mother, did you know that you were always Dorothy Lamour to me?

She didn't respond!

Of course not. You were talking to yourself.

I can still see my mother then: Dorothy Lamour in a house-dress, her black, wavy hair cascading to her waist, her hips gently swaying as she scrubbed clothes on a washboard over our kitchen sink. She acted out movie scenes with me while I played Shirley Temple.

Mother, you were such a natural-born actress. You could be Jane Withers or Monty Wooley, and with equal conviction. When I got the notion to turn our dramatic movie into a musical, you could make the transition unhesitatingly. Remember, you could do an entire dance routine without ever leaving the scrub board and interrupting your washing?

There she goes, serving up our picnic. She's holding up a forkful of something. What is it? Christ! It's green! Maybe it's a frog! It looks like a frog. No, it isn't—it's something else—it's broccoli. It doesn't taste like broccoli. But then it doesn't taste like much of anything. I must be chewing and swallowing it because mother looks happy.

I wonder if she remembers the story about the frogs? I'd like to remind her because that story always used to make her laugh. But I just don't have the energy to talk.

Mother, do you remember when I was eight years old and you left Daddy for the umpteenth time? You took my sister Boopie and me and we went back to your mother's house in Turtle Creek. You never wanted anyone to know that you came from a place called Turtle Creek, Pennsylvania. I don't know why they called it Turtle Creek anyway. I can't ever remember having seen a single turtle in the creek that ran next to Grandma Duffy's house. But there must have been millions of frogs.

Boopie was about two years old then, and Grandma certainly

had her hands full looking after us while you went back to work in your old office job. I never made any trouble for Grandma. You asked me to be good, so I was. I never even went inside the house unless Grandma called to me. I used to play out by the creek all day long, and I became a champion frog catcher.

Look, mother is starting to grin as if she heard me! No. She didn't hear me. But no wonder she's grinning, I've let her fill my mouth with straw. It tastes like straw, anyway. It must be one of those bran things she thinks is so good for me.

You chose not to enroll me in the third grade, because the fall semester had already begun. You shouldn't have done that, mother. You shouldn't have kept me out of school. But you thought Daddy would miss us and ask us to come home. I knew you were embarrassed in front of your relatives and friends and unhappy, too. I couldn't help you but I tried to cheer you up by giving you my frogs.

Every evening, when you stepped off the bus, I ran to meet you, took you by the hand, and led you to the back porch so you could see our newest friends. You always hugged and kissed me.

I remember that visit to Grandma's house grew longer and longer until finding enough cans and jars to keep the frogs in became a real problem. One day I thought I might have to put the whole day's catch back in the creek. But I had a real inspiration. I decided to keep it a secret and surprise you.

When Grandma began dinner, you went upstairs to take your bath. I remember Boopie was tearing the stuffing out of her toy dog, Grandma was peeling potatoes, and I was setting the table, when we heard your blood-curdling scream from upstairs. I was much faster than Grandma, and taking the steps two at a time, I reached you first. You were just in a slip, supporting yourself against the bathroom wall, opposite the bathtub. You had seen our froggy pond. Hundreds of frogs! Big fat ones, little tiny ones, medium-sized ones, pale green ones, green-black ones, and even some albinos. When you got over the shock, you hugged me and started crying.

Mother's crying now! At least those seem to be tears in her eyes. What's the matter, mother? Oh, I see. I have spit out the straw. I'm sorry. But my mouth is so terribly dry. I wonder if I can manage to raise my hand and point to the milk?

Wouldn't you think my father would call once in a while to see how I am? He was always a bit of a pennypincher. But a call from Greensburg, Pennsylvania to California for three minutes can't cost that much.

Finally Daddy called. Maybe it was just good luck that his call came when I was there. I remember mother was at work, Grandma was grocery shopping, and I was in the house watching Boopie. The phone rang just when I was totally frustrated. I had finished a beautiful page in my coloring book, and had gotten it perfectly within the lines, when Boopie grabbed my red crayon and made a wiggly line on Cinderella's face. I snatched the crayon from her, and she was still yelling when I picked up the receiver. Daddy wanted to know what was wrong, so I told him. Boopie had a slight fever, but I told him she was very sick and probably dying. I said mother was pining for him, Grandma was going to throw us out in the street, and the police were about to put me in jail for not going to school. So Daddy came for us on Saturday and drove us home.

One minute Daddy would be stern with me, the next minute he'd take my side. Like when the nuns and Father Mullens wouldn't allow me into the third grade because of the two months I'd lost, and wanted me to repeat second grade. Mother was intimidated by them, but not Daddy. He'd never approved of Catholic school in the first place. So Daddy took me to see Mr. George, the principal of the public school. At first Mr. George was also reluctant, but Daddy really convinced him that I could make up the studies I'd missed by doing extra homework assignments.

I wonder if I ever told my father how much that meant to me. Probably not.

Gosh, I feel drowsy. Oh, mother is gone. Well, you are boring to be around, Carroll. God, life is boring! Try to think about something nice.

Oh, William Watson Baker, you must have been the handsomest father in the whole world. You were as handsome as Spencer Tracy, maybe more handsome than Spencer Tracy.

I mustn't sleep now or I won't sleep tonight. I must keep on thinking about lovely things.

Daddy made me a toy merry-go-round one Christmas. It was

so beautiful! It was what—two feet high? And as big as the card table it stood on. There was a concealed motor that made it go around, and a music box coordinated with the motor. The lever to operate the motor and music box was in Donald Duck's hand. Goofy was poised at the steps to collect tickets. The horses and zebras and lions moved up and down on their poles, and the roof was decorated in bright red oil cloth. Daddy had carefully hand-painted each two-sided animal and figure.

But then Daddy's skills were endless, weren't they? Don't forget he could repair our old rattly Plymouth and make it purr like a pussycat, could even sew tailor-made-looking suits and invent wondrous gadgets. Daddy must have acquired—what— as many as fifteen or twenty patents while I was still in grade school. Too bad one of those inventions didn't make us wealthy. Poor Daddy, he had to stay on the road selling washing machines. Christ, and we couldn't even afford to own one!

Stay awake! Keep thinking. You've got to sleep tonight.

Please don't let me wet the bed again. I've already done it three or four times. It's disgusting! Imagine wetting the bed at the age of thirty-four! I used to wet the bed every night when I was little.

If only they hadn't fought so much! No, it wasn't that. It was just that I never understood what they were fighting about. I could never hear any actual words, just angry tones, occasional screams, and muffled sobs. Mother had to get out of bed and change everything, sometimes twice! But she never scolded me, and she always changed my clothes so sweetly.

There were so many horrible things to be afraid of—God, the Easter Bunny, the nuns, and that "Grand Master of the Inquisition," Father Mullens. Why did they say God was kind if he got angry at every single thing you did! At confession I made up sins. Remember? I wanted to do penance and try to protect myself in advance.

I hated Easter. I didn't want God to get himself crucified all over again—certainly not for my sake! I just wanted Him to leave me alone and not be everywhere, watching everything I did. I thought the Easter Bunny was a monster ten feet tall, wearing a man's dress suit, and carrying a basket full of presents. No wonder I lay there, not daring to breathe, trying not to sweat, listening to every tiny sound until morning came. Then mother would come into my room cheerfully announcing that the Easter Bunny had been there and left me a present. No amount of chocolate eggs was worth the suffering.

The afternoon sun is in my eyes. I better try to move my chair.

I've often wondered if mother knew that I tried to kill my sister. I don't think I've ever admitted it. In a way it was their fault, not mine, because they never explained anything to me. I had no idea that mother was going to have a baby. As far as I was concerned, she just showed up with it one day. I thought her big belly was because she was sick. When she went to the hospital, I was afraid she might not ever come back.

She's left me some water. Good. Now if I can just push my chair a little further out of the sun.

I was totally ignored. I wanted to kill the baby. They thought she was so adorable. They cooed and gurgled over everything she did: "Did you hear Boopie laugh?" "Listen, she said D-Da!" "Look, look, she's going to sit up in her crib!" Big deal! I'd been doing all those things for years.

"Boopie," "Woopie," "Poopie"—"Poopie," "Woopie," "Boopie." They christened her Virginia after my mother, but the name Boopie stuck. I'd never heard of such a ridiculous name!

At first I thought that they might one day take her back to wherever she came from. But they didn't, so I tried to figure out a way to kill her.

When I came down with the measles, mother told me, "Stay away from the baby. If she catches your measles, she could die." Mother was scalding my dishes and silverware at the time, and when I asked her why, she told me the germs were in my saliva. So I prepared a spoonful of that deadly germ-saliva, waited my chance, crept into the baby's room, and offered her the poison.

I remember how Boopie opened her mouth wide and swallowed every drop. It crossed my mind to spit some more into the spoon, but I decided not to risk it.

Soon afterward she did come down with the measles. But she didn't die.

Two

ANOTHER DAY: 1966

You must sleep tonight. It's such torture to lie awake and think! I don't believe I dream any more, do I? When I was six I had a recurring nightmare—a cruel Father Mullens would make me kneel and choose between my mother and father. He'd scream at me, threaten me, and insist that it would have to be one or the other—until finally, I was forced to choose. I always chose my mother, and woke up soaked in perspiration, crying at the thought of losing my father. How strange that, years later, when my nightmare turned to reality and my parents actually did ask me to choose between them, I chose to stay with my father.

Boopie was a delicate, sickly child at the age of five, so mother was planning to raise her in the Florida sunshine. I just couldn't face changing my school or moving away from Greensburg, Pennsylvania, and my friends. I wonder if mother understood?

Oh, God, she looked so hurt! I never want to see that look on her face again! But I didn't mean to hurt her. I just couldn't help it. And it didn't really dawn on me at the moment of our parting just how much I was going to miss her.

When all the girls in our home economics class were talking about their menstrual periods, I couldn't wait to have mine. I didn't want to be a "retardo." When it happened, I was impatient to get to class and brag about being normal, but the night before, when I saw the blood—I wanted only my mother.

Those were the years of the first higher heels on my shoes, and listening to the "Hit Parade" on the radio, and pajama parties, and endless hours of gabbing to my friends on the telephone. Those were the years of growing up during the Forties when mother wrote me lots of letters. Those were the years of missing her.

Grandma Oline had come to live with Daddy and me. We managed very well together and got along just fine. So I didn't understand why my father found it necessary to remarry. And why did he have to marry a twenty-four-year-old for Christ's sake! That Virginia Freeman was only ten years older than me! And when I think of the way that flat-chested Virginia Freeman used to flaunt her body, it still makes me shudder!

Grandma Oline, Daddy and I had always been strictly private people. For example, some families leave their bathroom doors open. I remember being shocked by that at some of my girlfriends' houses. We Bakers never did. Our bathroom was "off limits" to everyone but its occupant. In our house a closed door meant "do not enter," certainly not without knocking, and only knock if absolutely necessary. Before my father's remarriage, I'd never even looked inside his bedroom. Then, once Old Titless moved in with us, my father's bedroom door was always open, and Virginia Freeman was always sitting *naked to the waist* in front of the dressing table mirror! I couldn't believe she'd do that, considering the way she looked. Why, until I noticed that there were no scars, I thought she'd had a mastectomy! There was nothing there except flat nipples and taut skin over protruding ribs!

She used to hang those Fully-Padded Bras of hers everywhere like route indicators pointing to where that hideous sight could be seen. But if the bras or the open door failed to snare her prey, there was still no escaping. Daddy's bedroom was on the landing, so you couldn't get upstairs or downstairs without passing the door. Old Titless had moved the dressing table to the far corner of the room, with the mirror angled, so that she could see anyone attempting to creep by, and summon her quarry. Grandmother Oline, Aunt Alice, my cousin Little Jeanne had all systematically been trapped and horrified. My father's brother, Big Gene, actually stopped using the bathroom when he visited our house so he wouldn't have to pass that door.

My father had lost his head over her. She managed to transform him from a once-decent man into some kind of a pervert.

When I tried to sneak past on my way to church on Sundays, my stepmother would lure me into that bedroom to witness not only the everyday grotesque sight, but also the Lord's Day grotesque sight of Daddy lying there with a silly grin on his face and the covers hiked into a tent over his morning hardness!

I wanted to be out of that house and as far away from them as possible.

I guess that's why I threw myself with a vengeance into nearly every activity Greensburg High had to offer. I liked twirling the baton and marching with the school band, but I never enjoyed being a member of the debating team. I only stuck with it because of the away days. Ironically, the one area I couldn't break into was drama. The drama society constantly rejected me for dramatic plays; but because I had taken dancing lessons from the age of nine, they used me for musical productions.

Lord, it was absolutely sickening the way I calculated and schemed to cultivate my popularity. I think every student, every single time they passed, no matter how often during the day, got a "Hi, there," from me. I must have said "Hi, there" about twelve hundred times a day. But it paid off when the votes were counted. First, I was elected secretary to my home room and then, later, secretary of the entire student body.

In my senior year my name appeared in the school newspaper exactly forty-seven times. I was always in the gossip column's "Hot Line." "Who is the lucky man in Carroll Baker's life this week?" Then, once branded as fickle, I had a reputation to live up to. So even if I liked a boy, I couldn't possibly date him twice —until Johnny Cook, and once I fell in love with him, I think I even forgot to read the school newspaper.

In the beginning I guess I was attracted to Johnny because he was our number-one basketball star and because he fit my girlish image of what was utterly adorable: tall and thin, with a crew cut, perfect white teeth, and that cutest of all imaginable grins. But before long I fell madly in love with him. It was my first time and it was heavenly. But I couldn't possibly have permitted myself to fully express my love for him physically. Oh, we kissed and petted but never dared remove our clothes. Too bad I wasn't seventeen in the Sixties—we were restricted by the moral code of the Forties which considered "going all the way" a girl's ruination. I wish Johnny had been my first lover.

The night of the Senior Prom, when Johnny came to pick me up, my father and Virginia were in the living room. I didn't want to have to introduce my stepmother and she knew it, and I think she deliberately made sure they were there just to spoil my evening.

I was so nervous that when I brought Johnny in to introduce him I said, "This is my father and mother." Well, I had never intended to call that bitch "mother," and it threw me completely.

Blushing, I continued, "Daddy, Virginia, I'd like you to meet my date. This is . . ." I couldn't remember Johnny's name!

"I'm Johnny Cook. Pleased to know you."

My dad said, "Be sure you bring her back by midnight, Johnny. Have a good time."

Johnny had handled himself very well. But when we got to the front porch, I knew that he was nervous, too, because his hands were trembling when he gave me my corsage of gardenias. And then neither one of us could pin it on my blue ruffled dress.

The very idea of graduating from high school was unbearable. As far as I could see, my future was going to be a big fat zero. The thought of leaving the glory of my high school days behind and working in a department store, or worse, a factory was shattering. My stingy father wouldn't hear of sending me to drama school at Carnegie Tech, and I flatly refused to go to secretarial school. Thank God, my mother came through for me and saved me from settling down into some lifelong dreary employment.

For a while there I was feeling chilly. Now I'm toasty warm. Oh, I see —mother and I are each snuggled into those overstuffed chairs in the little room off my bedroom. We must be watching television. Yes, the TV set is on. Mother seems to be enjoying the program so I won't disturb her.

Mother, do you remember when I came to St. Petersburg to live with you and Boopie and your new husband? I didn't stay very long, did I? How long did I attend St. Pete Junior College? Was it three months or four? I had gotten that engagement to do my two specialty tap-dance numbers at the Lions Club. And

I'd been paid twenty dollars for that first dancing engagement. Twenty dollars! Well, that was it, wasn't it? Anyone who could earn that much money in one night definitely had a future in show business. Once I dropped out of college, it wasn't long before my club bookings extended from the Tampa-St. Pete area to all over Florida.

I guess one of the turning points was when I got the engagement to dance for the International Brotherhood of Magicians convention in Daytona Beach. Remember you and I were seated across from the Great Volta that evening. Later we got to know him and his wife very well, and he was really the one who launched me into the business as a professional. That was a super magic act he taught me, wasn't it? I wonder if I could still do it? How did it go—

(Music, lights, up.)

I'm onstage relaxing in a chaise longue. I'm dressed in a short, black-lace slip, flipping through a magazine, and obviously bored. The telephone rings. In pantomime, I answer the phone and joyfully accept a date. I stand up and contemplate the short black lace slip that I am wearing. It will never do.

(Idea!)

I approach a large, transparent Lucite cube; wave my hands over the cube; and conjure a beautiful blue, strapless evening gown. Applause. Once I've taken the gown from the cube, and slipped it on, I lift my hands to my throat. I shake my head. This will never do.

(Idea!)

My attention is drawn to an invisible object above my head. I reach for it. A diamond materializes between my thumb and forefinger. Applause. Waltzing from one part of the stage to another, I discover another diamond, and another, and another until I have five. But they are separate stones. I am puzzled.

(Idea!)

From my black velvet dressing table, I conjure up a small, transparent Lucite cube, put the five diamonds inside, and *voilà!*—a necklace is formed.

(Applause.)

I produce diamond bracelets, diamond earrings, a huge diamond brooch, a diamond tiara, and finally a diamond-studded fan. I flick the fan open and curtsey.

(Applause.)

Volta enters in tuxedo, cape, and top hat. He tips his hat, bows, and offers me his arm.

(Applause.)

The music reaches a crescendo. We strut off in time to the music, Volta tipping his top hat to the audience, and I looking coyly over my diamond fan.

(Applause. Applause! That glorious applause!)

It must have been around the beginning of summer of 1950 when Volta booked me into the Kemp Time Vaudeville Circuit. It wasn't until I arrived at their headquarters in Charlotte, North Carolina, to begin rehearsals for the tour, that I discovered Volta had contracted me to do not only the Magic Jewel Act and two specialty tap numbers, but also to dance in the chorus line and be the sex object in the burlesque skits!

The first time I rehearsed with that uncouth baggy-pants comedian—and he dropped his baggy pants, exposing his vulgar polka-dot shorts and expecting me to wiggle and squirm at the sight—I fled the rehearsal hall. No one was going to make a silly sex object out of me!

In an emergency meeting with the management, they agreed to let me out of the burlesque skits only if I agreed instead to drive one of the cars. Later I dearly regretted that I had been shy about those burlesque skits, because that year-long tour was nothing but one-night stands, and every midnight I had to steel myself to drive two or three hundred miles to the next town.

My God, I'm thin! Hey, I don't remember getting in the bathtub. I wonder how long I've been in here, or if I've washed already. I'm going to quickly wash again and get out. I don't want the evening to end. I don't want to have to go to bed. But mother and I always watch the late news, don't we? She wouldn't have gone to bed and left me in the bathtub! Of course not, she always gives me plenty of time to take my bath, dry, and get into my nightgown before the ten o'clock news. I wait and take my last tranquilizers just before the news begins. That's why I'm panicky. The medication is beginning to wear off.

I want to hurry up and get back into the other room. God, it seems to take me forever to take a bath! I take such a long time getting ready for bed!

"I take a long time getting ready for bed, so will you please use the bathroom first?" Samantha said.

In order to save money, the management had booked Samantha and me into that double room with twin beds. Hell, Samantha was tall! When I stood beside her, it was like looking up at a giraffe!

She was a rubbery contortionist, too. She could play that violin while doubled over in any number of impossible positions. As a finale Samantha used to play that flashy, difficult piece, the "Crazy Canary," while standing on her head!

She must have taken a long time in the bathroom because I fell into a deep sleep long before she emerged from her nightly toilet. I woke some time later to see a giraffe in a fatigue suit, with a plastic bag over its horns, gangle out of the bathroom. I screamed.

Samantha apologized for not warning me in advance and gave some weird explanation as to why she always slept in an army fatigue suit, with her hair rollers covered in a plastic bag— something about jungle rot—she had jungle rot or was afraid of contracting jungle rot. . . .

Oh, good, I'm all ready now. Now I can go into the other room and relax and take my tranquilizers and start to get sleepy while I watch the news.

"I'm coming, mother!"

Good. I must have said that out loud. She stopped knocking. How nice. Jack isn't home yet. Maybe I can get to sleep before he gets here.

Wonderful. The commercials are still on, and the news hasn't started yet. Boy, oh boy, this is really my night. Mother has made some hot chocolate. I really feel like having it. Eating dinner escapes me altogether, but I guess I did. Oh, this hot chocolate is delicious. As soon as I've finished it, I'll take my pills. No, I'll take them now and then finish my hot chocolate. Stop talking to yourself and pay attention, Carroll, or you'll miss the news. That's why you never know what's happening in the world. You sit every night and look at the news but hardly ever hear what's being said. You're like some idiot who can only look at the pictures. Which commercial break is this one? I hope it's not the last. I hope I didn't miss the entire newscast again tonight. Oh, it's O.K. It's the weather. Now pay attention. You want to know if there's going to be a smog alert for tomorrow. Look, a girl is giving the weather report.

I was hired by Channel 9 Television in New York as their weather girl! When was that? That must have been one of the very first jobs I landed, shortly after I arrived in New York. God, I was proud!

But the first night I was on the air the prop man dropped my cue cards!

Frantically, I glanced at the weather map behind me. I vaguely remembered something about cold air from Canada meeting a warm front in Texas. I had to have a sparkling personality, so I took a deep breath, smiled brightly, and said, "There is a cold front moving down from Canada. But there is a lot of hot air blowing in from Texas."

That night my landlady knocked on the door with a telegram. It told me not to report for work the next day. One day as weather girl and I'd been fired.

Fired! Oh, God, I was able to forget that for most of the day. Paramount has fired me! I expected the lawsuit, but I never realized that they might fire me. I mean other studios have been in lawsuits with actors without firing them. Haven't they?

Remember when Twentieth Century-Fox fired Marilyn?

She told Life *magazine that "that was not where she lived." Sure, but I knew better. I knew that was right where she lived! Remember how she changed after that? Remember how she looked? Remember how she and Pat Newcomb used to sit at La Scala's every night, and poor Marilyn looked so tired and unkempt and despondent? Remember the night at their table when I told Marilyn, "You don't need Twentieth. You're Marilyn*

Monroe! Go to Europe. Start a new life and a new career. Why, they'll pave the road with flowers!" I'll never forget her answer: "I'm alone, Carroll. I can't go alone."

Why couldn't Paramount have waited until I got back from the Cannes Film Festival before they destroyed my dressing room? The day I went back on the lot, I saw my dressing room gutted. Redecoration was such a lame excuse, and there were dozens of empty dressing rooms; they didn't need mine. What was the rush? They could have let me have one last look at those glamorous silver-papered walls instead of a bare, plaster shell. Why tear those sweet-smelling camellia bushes out by their roots? Where was my golf cart and the silver star that had been on the front door? Why had they been in such a hurry to wipe out every trace of me? I should never have gone back to pick up my things. Anyway, they hadn't bothered to store them. Everything of mine had just disappeared.

I'm so exhausted. I wish I was in bed.

You moron—you are in bed! That's right, I forgot. I must have said "Goodnight" to mother and gotten into bed. Just look at you, Carroll, curled up in the fetal position with your thumb pressed up against your lips! Maybe Baby Doll is closer to you than you've ever cared to admit?

Anyway I feel wonderfully sleepy. I think I'll be able to sleep. If I'm lucky maybe I'll sleep for a long time. But not like Marilyn—not like that —please, God!

What year is this? 1966 or 1967? Oh, yes, it's 1967. Remember you glanced at the top of the newspaper? Was that this week or last? Well, it really doesn't matter.

Chapter
Three

A BASEMENT IN QUEENS: 1952

Life seems to be a never-ending series of survivals, doesn't it? I remember in the times before the breakdowns, before I hated Baby Doll becoming my middle name, when I thought my immediate struggles would be the toughest of my life.

It was the beginning of August 1952, I was two months into my twenty-first year, alone in a dirt-floor basement apartment on Foley Street in Flushing, Queens, and dead broke. My costumes were shabby, my tap shoes were cracked, my makeup jars were caked with dried residue, and if I'd been in an accident I probably would have died rather than let anyone see my tatty, faded underwear.

I'd made it through nearly a year in New York City all by myself. Then what? Go home? Terrific! Where was home? Was home with mother and Boopie and my stepfather in St. Petersburg, Florida? Or was home back in Greensburg, Pennsylvania, where I'd been raised? My father still lived there. But then so did my stepmother, who was to me the Witch of the World, Hag of Hags, Bitch of all Bitches, Stepmother Superior of all Satanic Stepmothers.

The frustrating thing was that I had at last made a foothold in the Big City. I had finally broken through the tough exterior. Jobs were coming my way, two, three, and sometimes even four times a week. How could I give it up? How did other kids manage? How could I possibly have tried harder or lived on less?

How many damn jobs would you have to do a week just to cover barest living expenses?

Shit! All those years of dancing, months of one-night stands on a crummy vaudeville circuit, working my way to New York, pounding the pavement day after day, being humiliated and thrown out of every office on Broadway until I became "that persistent blonde kid who comes in here every day"—and finally they start booking me. After all that, how could I quit?

I did what I promised myself I would never do: I asked my mother for money. There seemed to be no alternative. Every penny I'd saved from the vaudeville tour was gone, last week's earnings had been spent on rent and food, and I was left without even a dime for carfare.

I couldn't have asked my father. He had been dead set against my going into show business. He had wanted me to be a secretary, and then, of course, to marry a rich man. Just like that! Well, it was the cliché-thinking of those times, but God, I used to get sick of him saying, "Remember, Carroll, it's just as easy to marry a rich man as it is to marry a poor man."

Anyway, my mother wired me a hundred dollars. When I collected it, I felt like a thoroughly rotten, good-for-nothing scrounger. I was a Depression baby, so I'd always had this thing about money. I'd felt wicked at the age of five when I had accepted money for an ice cream from my mother's meager savings without telling her it was my second of the day. I'd felt criminal at seven when I had stolen the week's grocery money in order to buy all my friends sacks of candy to prove my claims that my parents were rich.

Maybe if I'd been dealt some swift, sound punishment, I wouldn't even have recalled those incidents. But since my mother herself felt guilt and shame over our being poor, she always sympathized with her deceitful little "Cookie," and what was worse, she always covered up for me. She had said, "It's all right, Carroll, I can manage."

So there I was, adding yet another layer of culpability by not being able to support myself and by taking money from my mother, without knowing how much of a sacrifice it might mean to her. I couldn't help feeling that she'd been covering for me yet another time.

31

There simply had to be a way of earning enough money to make a living in show business!

I began to audition for tours and road companies in search of longer engagements that would bring in weekly checks on a steady basis.

A new hotel, with a nightclub, was opening in October in Windsor, Ontario, Canada, just across the border from Detroit, and the initial engagement was for four months. The man who auditioned me told me that I would be featured in two specialty dance spots, but that if I accepted the job I also had to be willing to dance in the chorus. Because of my vaudeville experience (I'd done everything from dancing, to a magic act, to driving one of the touring cars), it seemed a legitimate demand. But when I went to the agent's office to sign the contract, and I saw that it listed me only as a chorus girl, I thought seriously about walking away from the job. The agent explained, "Hold on, they'll work your specialty numbers in after the first two weeks. And, look, I got you $200 a week because they are 'hot' for you. The chorus girls are only getting $150. What do you think they're paying you the extra $50 for?" (I was to discover that they were "hot" for me to the tune of an extra $50 because I was pretty and could "dress up" the chorus. Apparently pretty girls were not interested in working in such a remote spot.)

Crummy though it was, I hated giving up my dirt-floor basement in Queens. My rent was only $11 a week, and I doubted that when I returned from Canada, I'd be able to find anything that cheap again. Everything I owned fitted into one suitcase and one makeup case, and even those were half empty. Oh, well, it certainly made moving a breeze.

When I got to the Elmwood Hotel in Windsor, I saw that it was a new complex with a coffee shop; three restaurants; an indoor swimming pool; an outdoor ice-skating rink; and a large, modern, wood-paneled nightclub. They had space to burn, so the seven other chorus girls and I were all assigned private rooms on the top floor of the hotel. We had the use of the employees' recreation room, which was also on that floor. It turned out that no one used the recreation room but us, and we would spend all day there because it was so terrific—it had comfortable overstuffed chairs, a piano, record player, pool table, and a well-equipped kitchen.

The management was generous in many other ways. Every day we found bread, butter, jam, coffee, tea, milk and sugar as provisions for our breakfast. When Janet—at twenty-four, two or three years older than the rest of us—discovered that there was virtually no limit to these breakfast supplies, she suggested that we eat bread and jam all day long. It was a sickening diet, but it did save us from buying lunches and dinners.

Harry, the headliner of the show, was an old song-and-dance man whom I'd never heard of—I nicknamed him "Harry Headliner." Since he couldn't move very well any more, he limited himself to one dance routine, supported by us. Actually we worked our butts off to make him look good while he went through the motions. But he did have a strong and often stirring voice. Harry claimed to have first introduced "I'm Putting on My Top Hat," "The Sunny Side of the Street," "The Birth of the Blues," and several other songs which were forever impressed in my mind as belonging to Fred Astaire.

We also rehearsed three strictly chorus numbers, and when I asked the dance director about my featured specialties, the spots I had been promised, he played dumb. So I was to be nothing but a higher-paid chorus girl—well, I'd know better the next time.

The show? It bombed out. The management exercised their cancellation clause, and what was to have been a full sixteen weeks of steady work suddenly became a skimpy four. Poor old Harry Headliner took the brunt of the blame, because as it turned out it wasn't only me—most of the audience had never heard of him either. But the biggest insult was leveled at the chorus line. The customers complained that the show girls were a "bunch of dogs." Christ, that really hurt! Each of us began applying thicker rouge and darker lipstick and doubling the beading on our eyelashes (beading was a wax mascara which you heated and it dried on your lashes in fat black beads).

I'd always been led to believe that I was attractive, but I still felt self-conscious at the head of that chorus line of "dogs." I thought Janet, who was on the opposite end of the line, was quite pretty. But, as I glanced at the six others in between us, I had to admit that if the customers were expecting the well-built showgirl type, these skinny little kids were rather unfortunate choices. At least they were all well-trained dancers. So after the first three nights of "dog" complaints, the dance director called us back into rehearsal and changed our slow walkabouts to flashy routines which never let us pause long enough to give the audience an opportunity to scrutinize our shortcomings.

We did a country hoedown, a Russian dance, and a can-can. I can think of no other dances so totally exhausting—but, even so, every morning at 2:00 A.M. when the nightclub closed, the eight of us would go ice skating. All the waiters and busboys were also in their early twenties. They used to join us at that outdoor rink, bringing whatever food or leftovers they could steal from the kitchen. We lit bonfires, roasted potatoes and marshmallows, ice-skated, and played in the snow until the sky turned bright.

It was all innocent fun. None of the girls was promiscuous, thank God, because that would have been very hard for me to have handled. Anyway, in the '50s, any girl who went "all the way" had to have been crazy. Guys thought you were cheap, and if you had a baby out of wedlock your life was literally over. You could never regain your self-respect. That wasn't for me. I was on my own, trying desperately to make a place for myself in the world, and I wasn't about to mess up my future. I believed in my own resolve and willpower, but as long as I could remember, the thought of rape terrified me—because of the violence as well as the disgrace of the act. Thanks to my Catholic upbringing I became convinced that if I were ever raped, the sin somehow would be mine.

I suppose placing myself in situations where I might be sexually vulnerable was my one big reservation about leaving home and entering show business. Boys my own age had often been a temptation but never a threat. Men, on the other hand, had constantly leered at me, and I'd grown up with a grave mistrust of them. I never dated mature men or flirted with them because they frightened me.

This was the first time I'd lived with a group of chorus girls. I had the idea that all chorus girls were wild, and I was greatly relieved to discover that these kids were as cautious about sexual involvements as I was. Actually, I couldn't have sworn that Janet was a *virgo intacta,* but for the rest of us, intercourse was an act strictly reserved for marriage.

The notice to close the show was a terrible blow. Everybody

had counted on those four months of wages. The night the notice appeared on the bulletin board, Harry sensed how depressed we were, and he decided to give us a farewell party the following Sunday. He didn't invite the orchestra, or the female vocalist, or the comic. It was to be a party for Harry and his eight young chorus girls. But, then, Harry had a special affection for chorus girls: scuttlebutt had it that he'd been married to three or four of them.

Harry was staying across the border in Detroit. His Cadillac Suite was in a swanky hotel where all the rooms had been named for cars. For the party Harry had ordered dozens of sandwiches, plates of chocolate eclairs, and two magnums of medium-dry champagne.

The champagne was lovely. None of us had had champagne before except at weddings. Of course, Janet had, but then Janet had done just about everything. That's why we'd made her our leader.

Janet told me I was drunk. The tingly sweet bubbles tasted like soda pop, and I got giggly, but I never would have known I was drunk if she hadn't said so.

During the evening Harry was unusually kind and attentive to me. He'd never shown any interest in me during rehearsals or the weeks of performances, so I was rather flattered by his attentions. Hey, he was still a star, even if he was old and a bit past it!

The girls were playing pick-up sticks, and I was anxious to participate because I was the house champ, but I couldn't stop eating those heavenly chocolate eclairs long enough to join in.

Harry collected our champagne glasses and a full tray of eclairs, and invited me to sit with him on a settee in the far corner of the suite.

"Now, tell me, Pretty Baby, have you ever been married?"

My mouth was full of chocolate and sweet cream so I shook my head.

He patted my puffed-out cheek with one of his huge leathery hands and whispered slyly, "I'll bet you're still a virgin, aren't you?"

I probably blushed, as I always do, and nodded yes.

He asked me what I planned to do after the show closed, at the same time handing me my champagne.

35

"I'm going back to New York," I gulped. "I gave up my place, so I'll have to find an inexpensive hotel room for a couple of nights until I can get another apartment."

"Sweetheart, if I didn't already have a beautiful girl at home, I'd take you back to the ranch with me."

I studied his broad, sun-baked, well-weathered face and his hulking, aged body, and it occurred to me that at this period of his life, he probably looked more natural riding the range on horseback than he did on a glossy, modern nightclub stage.

"My wife was about your age when I married her five years ago. She's still a gorgeous redhead, but she loves the open country now and never wants to go back to being a chorus girl."

I briefly considered protesting his notion about me being only a chorus girl. He didn't seem to realize that I could do specialty tap routines, but just then he offered me another eclair so I let the moment pass.

"Listen, sweetheart," he said, stroking the baby fat of my arm, "you're a beautiful girl and a sweet, lovely child. Someone should be looking after you."

There was a tapping on the door and the room-service captain came in to ask Harry if he wanted more champagne. He took Harry's order for another magnum, refilled all our glasses from the remaining bottle, and slipped out again.

Harry continued, "A friend of mine, Louie Ritter, owns the Wheylan Hotel. I'll call him and ask him to let you stay there. If the hotel isn't full, there's no reason why he shouldn't give you a room free of charge. Louie is one of the nicest, big-hearted guys you could ever meet. He came to this country as an immigrant boy without a cent and worked his way up in the fur business. Did you ever hear of Ritter Brothers Furs?"

"No," I mumbled, licking the chocolate from my fingers. "Why would he want to give me a free room?"

"Because he's a great friend of mine. I'm sure he'd be happy to do it as a favor to me. All of his friends know that if you ever need a favor, you can count on Louie."

"Is he rich?"

"Louie is a millionaire! He got rich in the fur business and eventually sold his share to his brother. Then he bought the Wheylan Hotel and has made a big success of it."

I thought to myself, "Millionaire, hummmm," and the bubbles dancing in my head said to me, "Hey, maybe this is the millionaire that Daddy wants for you?"

Harry was saying, "I feel sorry for Louie because he is such a lonely guy. He's been married five times but he has just never found the right girl."

I almost said, "I don't want some old guy pawing me," but in deference to Harry, I kept it to myself.

But Harry must have guessed what I was thinking because he continued, "And don't worry, Louie is a real gentleman. He'd never touch you. If you didn't want him to. But I think you two might just hit it off."

I was terribly thirsty and didn't feel like getting up for a glass of water, so I downed another glass of champagne and then I began to reel.

Harry didn't seem to notice because he was too fired up by his scheme. "In fact, I'll go into the bedroom and call Louie now. He'll still be awake."

A few minutes later Harry came back into the sitting room to give me what he thought to be his great news, but I was half in a stupor by then and listened without reacting.

"Louie said he is always happy to do me a favor. I knew he would be. There'll be a suite waiting for you at the Wheylan Hotel and you can stay as long as you want without paying. I'm going to be in New York myself in December. I told Louie I gave my word that he was a gentleman, and that if he doesn't behave himself, he'll have to answer to me. But he swore on his mother's life that he'd never touch you unless you wanted him to."

Around five in the morning Harry announced he was going to bed. He invited us to stay, and Janet decided that we were all too drunk to make the trip across the border.

Everybody except Harry stripped. Harry donned his silk pajamas.

There were two double beds in his bedroom. Six "dogs" piled into one bed and Janet and I climbed into the other bed on either side of Harry, who stretched and wiggled and rubbed against us. He probably fantasized that the two lecherous young chorus girls would tear off his silk pajamas and commit delicious atrocities upon his writhing, naked flesh. But the two inebriated young chorus girls fell asleep instantly.

At two o'clock that afternoon, the maid, whose tapping had

gotten no response, entered the suite and found the beds full of bodies. She gasped and ran out.

When we left the hotel, the curious and gaping staff were all craning to get a look at those brazen show-biz tarts who had had the wild orgy in the Cadillac Suite.

The day we went back to New York, Janet urged us to get to the train early. We arrived before any of the other passengers, found our assigned seats, stored our gear above them (every one of us now owned ice-skates which were tied to our luggage), and dashed to the observation bubble in the club car, where we commandeered the choice center booth. As usual, Janet was right—it was the best spot on the train.

It was early in the morning, but Janet ordered a Canadian Club with ginger ale. So we all ordered Canadian Clubs with ginger ale. It was the first time I had ever ordered an alcoholic drink.

Janet got out her identification before the black porter, in his red and gold uniform, had finished asking us for proof of age. Janet asked him to put on Johnny Ray records, and we sang and cried along with "Cry" all the way back to New York.

Every one of us had given up our apartments. Janet was kicking herself because she felt that she should have known better. Now rents were higher and it might take weeks to find another place and another job. Hotels were too expensive. Two of the girls had parents in the New York area, but boarding at home was ruled out as worse than living in some fleabag.

I had $700 hidden in my garter belt. All of us had bought ice-skates, makeup, and some underwear, but little else, so we each had a bundle of dough and we were afraid of carrying large amounts in our handbags. It had been my idea to wrap the bills in cellophane, securing them with a rubber band and fastening the wad with a safety pin to the right front garter. That way you could keep a continual guard on your money by resting your hand on your upper right thigh.

When we got off the train at Grand Central, Janet went to the travelers' information desk and got a listing of the most inexpensive hotels in Manhattan. When Janet stored her suitcases in a locker, we all stored our suitcases in lockers. Then we took a crosstown bus to the West Side and began checking out the hotels near the theater district which were advertising rooms for $8 to $10 a night.

These cheap hotels all proved to be the same—seedy, forbidding, and filled with the most unsavory characters. Only Janet wasn't scared. She registered at the fifth hotel we looked at, figuring that each one was as bad as the next. Two of the girls who were sharing forced themselves to follow Janet's lead, but the rest of us were too chicken. In fact, one of the girls became so terrified at the prospect of spending the night in one of those terrible places she went home to her family in Brooklyn.

It was late afternoon and the four of us still unsheltered were cold and hungry and frightened and depressed. We found a Nedicks, stood at the indoor counter, and had a scalding cup of coffee while we reviewed our desperate situation. It was decided that by now we had worked our way too far uptown, where the rents would be getting higher. The next area to try was downtown, Greenwich Village. I hung back and said "Good-bye." When they were out of sight, I walked east to have a look at the Wheylan.

From across the street, the Wheylan Hotel seemed to be elegant and inviting. Never in my whole life had I stayed in a place like it. What should I do? Did I have a free room waiting for me in there? If so, it was probably a trap, and Ritter was probably an old lech just waiting to pounce on me. On the other hand, if he had vacant rooms anyhow, why shouldn't he just let me stay for a few nights free of charge? A free room in a comfortable, safe hotel like the Wheylan was certainly tempting.

Yeah, sure—how safe? And since when was anything ever free? Who has ever given you something for nothing? You know damn well it's wrong. You know it. And that's why you never mentioned the Wheylan to the other girls.

But I'm tired and scared and I need to find another job.

Wonderful! So go be a whore! That's something you could have done from the very beginning and saved yourself all the struggles of the last two years.

No, I wouldn't do that. But maybe he's a wonderful guy and we'll like each other and he'll ask me to marry him. I don't really want to get married yet, but when will I ever have a chance to meet a millionaire again? Shouldn't I at least meet him and see what he's like?

Marry you? You dunce! Ritter might not even remember that he told Harry you could have a free room. Anyway, why in the world would he be interested in you? You aren't that special, and being a millionaire, he must have his choice of girls. Don't forget that Johnny wouldn't defy his parents and give up college in order to marry you. Sure, he said over and over again that he loved you. Sure, Johnny was dying to get you into bed. Sure. But he didn't want you enough to marry you.

If I cross the street and go in there, Ritter will probably think that I'm just a chorus hussy and a quick lay. That is, if he's interested at all, or even remembers about me. Shit, maybe I should just forget the whole thing!

What should I do? I can't keep standing on the corner forever. It's getting late. It'll be dark soon. Besides, my feet are swollen, there's a nagging ache in my lower back, I'm desperately hungry, and I'm chilled through and through by the cold. I'll have to find a place to stay soon, but in the meantime I just need somewhere warm to sit down for a few minutes.

Well, why not simply say hello to Mr. Ritter. After all, he might be expecting me. I don't have any luggage, so I could always lie and tell him that I'm already living somewhere else. It wouldn't do any harm just to meet him. Surely he'd offer me a cup of coffee, maybe even a sandwich, and I could use the powder room at the Wheylan.

I mustered my courage, crossed the street, walked in and up to the front desk.

The moment I mentioned my name, a tall man in tails slid from behind one of the glass partitions and over to the reception area. Pushing the clerk aside, he loomed over me, bowed, and introduced himself as the manager. The next thing I knew, he had come from behind the counter and was gently but firmly leading me to the elevators, where he ordered the elevator operator to take us to the fifth floor.

The manager seemed suave and controlled, but his breath came in spasms and he spoke without pausing, running one sentence into another:

"Miss Baker it is a pleasure to have you with us. I do hope you have had a good journey. We have been expecting you. Mr. Ritter isn't here at the moment, but your suite is ready. I do hope you will enjoy your stay with us. I'll show you to your rooms and have your luggage sent up. Mr. Ritter may not return in time for dinner, so he has left instructions with the Dining Room. When you are ready, if you will just call the Dining Room on Two and ask for Andrea, he will arrange for your meal either downstairs or served in your room if you prefer. If you need anything, please feel free to call me. I'll leave my card on the desk. Is there anything we can get you at the moment? A cold drink or perhaps you'd prefer a hot drink?"

I heard myself saying calmly, "Yes, thank you, I would like a cup of coffee." But I was totally thrown by this turn of events, and when the manager closed the door behind him, leaving me alone in the suite, I just stood there for the longest time, plonk in the middle of the room, wondering what to do next.

A tapping on the door jolted me out of my reverie. Oh, hell, who could that be? If it was Ritter, I hadn't yet planned what I was going to say to him and it certainly was going to be awkward. It would have been so much easier to have met him in the lobby with other people around.

When I opened the door, the man standing there was dressed in a tuxedo, holding a black-and-gold menu in front of him.

"Miss Baker, I am Andrea, your Captain," he said. "Welcome to the Wheylan. Your coffee is on the way up. May I help you with your dinner order? Mr. Ritter suggested that you try our Duck à l'Orange, the specialty of the house."

He had said "Duck à l'Orange" with a French or an Italian accent, so I hadn't a clue what he was talking about. But it really didn't matter because I was famished, and I hadn't had an honest-to-goodness full meal for longer than I could remember. And since he made it sound like the food was on the house, I didn't have the strength to say "No."

"Yes, thank you."

"Shall I reserve a table in the restaurant for you, Miss Baker, or would you rather have it served in your suite?"

"Yes, thank you."

"Room service?"

"Yes, please."

"As a first course, may I suggest turtle soup, or some smoked salmon, or perhaps some fresh asparagus?"

"Yes, thank you."

Andrea paused, but ever so briefly, while a tiny suppressed smile played at the corners of his mouth. Then he regained his composure, and with a perfectly straight face, said, "That's fine,

Miss, one order of each." I blushed as he intoned, "One turtle soup, one smoked salmon, and one asparagus, followed by the Duck à l'Orange."

A bellboy entered with a set of Vuitton luggage, bearing no resemblance to my battered cardboard case, and I reluctantly sent them away, explaining that my luggage had not yet arrived. At the same time a waiter entered with my coffee in a silver pot, on a silver tray covered by a lovely pink-lace doily. Lord, it was all so elegant! I felt like Cinderella transformed into a princess. But for a moment I flirted with the very un-princesslike thought of stealing that beautiful pink-lace doily and sending it to my mother for her birthday.

Once the bellboy and the waiter and Andrea had left, I kicked off my miserable, pinching shoes, gulped down some hot coffee, and scurried to find the toilet because I was bursting for a pee. The bathroom was fabulous: all black and white tiles, very roomy, and wonderfully warm. There were dozens of fleecy white towels, a terry-cloth guest robe, and lots of free samples of soaps and bubble bath which I couldn't wait to open. I carefully inspected the bedroom. What an altogether sumptuous suite it was, and very, very expensive looking. Shit! What did all of this luxury cost? I really couldn't imagine. I searched every inch of those rooms without being able to find a price list. Now that's class!

Two waiters arrived, each wheeling a table of food—turtle soup, smoked salmon, asparagus, the duck, parsley potatoes, peas, salad, rolls and butter, water, Coca-Cola, strawberry shortcake, and another pot of coffee. It was far too much food for one person, but I just couldn't bear to leave anything. Well, that's not exactly right, I couldn't manage all of the rolls and butter so I wrapped them in a napkin for later. And the meal was better than delicious, it was scrumptious! Since no one was watching me, before I pushed the tables into the hall, I couldn't resist licking the strawberry-shortcake plate clean.

It's a wonder I didn't drown in the bathtub because my belly was as heavy as lead, and I was drowsy from all that food I'd wolfed down. But my, oh my, that hot water felt good on my aching back and feet and my shivering body, still chilled from tramping around in the icy streets.

When I was dry, I snuggled into the terry-cloth guest robe, climbed onto the bed, and turned on the radio. My skin felt dry, and I wished that I had at least brought my makeup case so that I would have had my skin lotion.

Suddenly I remembered where I was! What was I thinking about? Where was my head? What was I doing wearing a terry-cloth robe, when at any moment a strange man could be knocking on the door?

What had the manager said? That he didn't know when Mr. Ritter would return? Knocking on the door? He owned the hotel, didn't he? My God, he probably had a passkey! Why should he bother to knock? He could creep in in the middle of the night and rape me!

I rushed to check the front door, double-locked it, and secured the chain. Then I ran back to the bedroom and jumped into my clothes. Once I was safely dressed, I went around tapping the walls for secret passages. I didn't find any, and anyway, that was crazy. I was just letting my imagination run away with me.

The clock on the mantel read eight-thirty. It was still dinner time. Suppose he was a nice man? He'd call from downstairs and invite me to dinner, and I had made a pig of myself less than an hour ago. How would I explain that? "Well, Mr. Ritter, it was Andrea's fault." No, that sounded dumb. No one had forced all that food on me.

I had a comb and a lipstick in my purse, so I went into the bedroom to look at myself in the mirror. Too bad I didn't have some mascara to brighten my pale, dull eyes. This was no way to try and hook a millionaire!

Hotels didn't have television sets in every room in those days, so for a while I just sat on the couch in the living room, but that was boring and I dozed off.

My head dropped forward. I woke up. It was five minutes past nine. Could he still show up tonight? Well, I might as well stretch out on the bed and be comfortable. I could lie on top of the covers, and if I smoothed out my skirt and jacket underneath me, they wouldn't wrinkle.

The hours slipped by. All the lights were on, and periodically I got up and rechecked the chain on the front door. I did sleep, but fitfully, on top of the covers and still fully dressed.

By five-thirty in the morning, when the first light was streaking the sky, I wasn't worried any longer.

But by 10:00 A.M., when there was still no word, I panicked again. Checkout time was at noon, and what would I do if I hadn't heard from him by then? Well, I'd leave, of course. What if they presented me with a bill? So what, I'd pay it. After all, I had $700. Surely that would more than cover one night. But then there was also the dinner—that gigantic dinner! Oh, the hell with it! Anyway, how much could a duck cost?

Eleven-ten. Fifty minutes before checkout time. I was sure that I couldn't afford to stay for two nights. What would I tell the manager? "I'm sorry, sir, but I must leave immediately for Calcutta." Oh, Lord, why hadn't I braved it out yesterday with the other girls? Still, I knew the hotel where Janet was staying. I could buy a newspaper and begin looking for an apartment, and then if I hadn't found one by evening, I could join Janet.

Eleven-thirty. Time to leave. If I had to wait in line at the cashier's desk until five minutes past noon would they charge me for an extra day?

The phone rang. It was Mr. Ritter inviting me to join him for brunch in the dining room.

Chapter
Four

THE TRAIN

Two minutes later, the headwaiter was leading me to Mr. Ritter's booth.

The man who rose to meet me was only slightly taller than I. About five-eight. He was thin and wiry, with dark hair and a pencil-fine mustache. His cheeks were sunken, and his brown eyes looked enormous behind his steel-rimmed glasses.

He looked dapper and mobile, and while he had the mannerisms of a younger man, I could see that he was old—a lot older than my father, though maybe not old enough to be my grandfather.

When I stepped up to him, he took my hand and kissed it! That was a first for me, but coming from him the gesture somehow seemed perfectly natural. In a charming Hungarian accent, though not as thick as Zsa Zsa Gabor's, he invited me to sit down and asked me to please do him the favor of calling him Louie.

Once we were seated he stared directly into my eyes with such intensity that I was forced to lower my head. He then lifted my chin, and holding my face close to his, he grinned at me. Perhaps it was the soft lighting of the dining room playing tricks with my eyes, but I could have sworn that his grin was menacing, like the hyena's teeth-baring grin the instant before it goes for the jugular.

"Are you feeling better now?" he asked.

"I'm not sure," I stammered. "I mean, I'm not sure what you mean."

"Come on, now," he purred. "Confess. You were anxious all night wondering when I might turn up."

"That's true," I blurted. At least he released my face from his grip.

He suddenly looked smug and began chuckling. "Don't you want to know how I knew that you were anxious all night? Huh? Well, I'll tell you."

He hesitated in an effort to look even more deeply into my eyes. "I knew that you were anxious because I planned it that way."

His huge eyes gleamed. "I played a psychological game on you."

He paused and said the next words with great relish, "You see, I was in the hotel the entire time."

"Why did you do that?" I squeaked.

"Oh, no, first another confession from you. You're a virgin, aren't you? I want to know all the thoughts that went through your mind during the night."

I was very confused by this psychological game he was playing with me—he appeared to be so deadly earnest about it. Was it supposed to be fun or was it meant to intimidate me for some sinister purpose? I was so uncomfortable and I thought about making some excuse to leave.

In that instant his voice, in fact his entire demeanor softened. "You don't want to play, do you? No, you don't. I can see that from your expression," he said kindly. "I'll tell you what, let's have a lovely brunch. Do you like Eggs Benedict? How about Eggs Benedict and champagne?" And he snapped his fingers for the waiter.

I was suddenly very hungry, and with the peace offering of food, Louie could count on me to be a captivated audience. Carroll, you whore! I thought to myself. They say that everyone has their price. Yours is obviously food.

And sure enough, the moment I began stuffing my face, I relaxed and went along with his idea of an entertaining conversation. "Yes, I was frightened. I thought you might have a way of sneaking up on me during the night. I even looked for secret passages, at one point."

Louie thought that was the funniest thing he'd ever heard. "You mean you were afraid all night long that I was going to get

46

into your room and take advantage of you?"

He croaked with laughter. The more I explained my terror, the more he laughed. And when I also admitted that I'd been very concerned about checkout time and frantic with worry over how much the hotel bill might be, tears rolled down his face. I thought that he was going to have a fit and choke to death, as he repeated my words, "And how much could a duck cost?"

When he'd dried his eyes and composed himself he turned deadly earnest. "I'm sorry that I played a psychological game on you. But how else could I prove to you that I'm interested in more than just pouncing on you?"

He called for the headwaiter to bring him some Wheylan stationery. When it arrived, he began writing.

"I'd like you to stay. I promise you I won't come anywhere near your room. Stay and be my guest. We can get to know each other, be friends. At my age, I'm no longer interested in hopping in and out of the sack for a fast screw. I'm looking for friendship and companionship." His eyes danced with mischief as he added quickly, "I'm also interested in screwing, but only with someone I love."

The word "screwing" embarrassed me and I couldn't think of anything to say. He didn't seem to notice my silence because he'd gone back to his letter. After signing it with a great flourish he called to the headwaiter, "Joseph, take this to the manager and have him witness my signature."

When the headwaiter had disappeared with the letter, I said, "Look, I don't think I should stay here. I don't mind getting to know you but. . . ."

"I own the hotel," he interrupted. "As far as the room goes, it doesn't cost me anything. Besides I promised Harry you'd have someplace to live. And it would give me great pleasure to be able to do something for you. Now, you won't deny me that pleasure, will you?"

"Well, I'd feel funny about it." (Funny, indeed! What I felt was like a rabbit transfixed and confused by the hyena's smile, unable to hop in one direction or the other.)

"Nonsense, you'll never have cause to worry. You won't have to worry again about the bill. You won't have to be afraid that I'll change my mind because I've written out a guarantee stating that you're my guest and that, as the owner, I've invited you to stay free of charge. It will hold up in any law court in the country. No one can come along later and demand payment."

I tensed as he took my hand and held it. "Please stay. Let's get to know each other."

He sensed that I was still uncomfortable, which of course I was, so he placed my hand back in my lap. "O.K., I won't take your hand again. The next time I hold your hand it will be because you've given it to me."

The headwaiter returned with the letter and laid it on the table. Louie looked it over and then handed it to me. "I'll tell you what, I'll make a deal. You stay for ten days. We can have dinner together and sometimes when I'm not too busy, we can have lunch. We'll just talk and get to know each other."

I suppose I must have looked at him with my mistrust showing because he smiled knowingly and said, "You can meet me downstairs, and when I bring you home at night, I'll leave you at the elevators." (All right! That's exactly what I wanted to hear!)

But I still didn't reply, so he raised his right hand and said solemnly, "I swear, on the life of my mother, that I'll never touch you during those ten days."

At that point I was convinced of his sincerity. I wasn't sure if I'd ever have any special feelings for him but he was certainly tolerable. Maybe I should get to know him better. After all, it wasn't every day that I got to meet millionaires. And being his guest in the hotel? Well, what the hell, it didn't cost him anything and at the moment I had no place to put my head down. Okay, so maybe his generosity was his way of trying to seduce me. But whether or not he succeeded was up to me, wasn't it?

"Well, what do you say? Is it a deal? A ten-day trial period? Shall we shake on it? If it's a deal give me your hand."

I extended my hand but instead of shaking it, he kissed it, brushing his lips sensuously over my skin, and looking up at me sheepishly, like a naughty boy who'd played a trick on me. But I had given him my hand voluntarily. His mustache tickled and I shuddered.

Louie sent a bellboy to pick up my luggage at the train station. Once I'd unpacked, I took a long, hot, bubble bath, and then without the least bit of concern, I climbed into bed and took a long peaceful nap.

That night, Louie took me to the glamorous Copacabana

nightclub for the dinner show. He was obviously a regular customer because the headwaiter bowed and called him by name. We were led to one of the best tables in the house, and I was terribly impressed by the number of celebrities there, some of whom spoke or waved to Louie. Even the star of the show, Joey Lewis, joined our table for a few minutes.

I ordered Chinese food, which I love, and it was the first time I'd ever had one of those delicious Polynesian rum drinks. The dance band was superb, and Louie turned out to be a terrific dancer. During the slow tunes he didn't hold me too tight or try anything funny, so my evening was perfect. Well, it was marred a bit, but only slightly, by the fact that I had nothing decent to wear except my traveling suit, which looked out of place among all those delicate cocktail dresses.

At 2:00 A.M. when we arrived back at the Wheylan, there were no guests in the lobby and I began to worry about what would happen next. I tried to say goodnight to Louie the moment we'd come in the front door, but he laughed at me. "No gentleman leaves a lady in the lobby, let me see you to the elevator." When the elevator door opened, he kissed my hand and stood smiling at me as I backed in and the elevator doors closed between us.

The next morning a dozen red roses arrived with my breakfast, and when the telephone rang it was the boutique in the lobby, saying that Mr. Ritter had purchased a blue-silk cocktail dress for me, and would I try it on at my convenience and select the accessories.

That first week was like living in a dream come true, like winning the national lottery. Each morning I woke up to find another present—real gold earrings, a beaded evening purse, a pure cashmere sweater, a dainty wristwatch, and on the seventh day, a white mink jacket from Ritter Brothers Furs.

When I opened the box and saw that gorgeous white mink jacket, I thought I'd faint. I should have telephoned Louie immediately and thanked him for it, but for the moment I'd forgotten all about him. I'd never seen anything quite so beautiful or stroked anything quite so soft. I put it on over my nightgown and pranced up and down in front of the mirror playing out imaginary scenes. At one moment I remembered the old joke about girls who get minks. I giggled and said to myself in the mirror, "How did you get your mink, Dearie? Well, certainly not the way minks get minks, Dearie." I froze, suddenly hit by the sobering reality of my situation. "No, Carroll, that's not how the joke goes, the punch line is: 'The *same way* minks get minks, Dearie!' Oh, God, this is going too far, and you, like a greedy idiot, haven't even bothered to face the truth. You're in very dangerous territory. You really cannot go on accepting his hospitality and his presents. One of these days you'll have to pay the piper."

I sat and stared out the window and tried to analyze my feelings for Louie. Was I attracted to him? It was so difficult to know. My feelings were all mixed up with my desires for security and comfort. How could I divorce him from his money, or the things he could give me, or the life I'd be able to lead? Did I love him? Would I ever be able to love him? Did I want to share my life with him? Was I willing to give him my body?

"A virgin!" I said out loud, still staring out my window. "A virginal piece of meat! That's all he sees when he looks at you. And he hasn't asked you to marry him, has he? No! He's just waiting to get you into bed, once. The minute he has that cherry, out you go on your ass into the street!

"My God, it's all so sordid! He's never once shown any interest in your career. Does he care anything at all about you as a human being?

"And what about you, Miss Goody-two-shoes? Let's be fair. Aren't you leading him on? Aren't you taking everything you can get and giving nothing in return? So far he's kissed your hand and your cheek. You haven't shown him any affection. Do you really care about him as a human being?

"Stop it, Carroll, you're being overdramatic again! You've only known the man for one week. Why in heaven's name would he ask you to marry him in just one week? Why would you want to have to make that decision after such a short time? Anyway, the ten-day trial period had been his idea. He made a deal.

"And so did you. You made a deal. The deal is for three more days, but if your mind is made up, wouldn't it be fairer to break this thing off right now?

"Yes, give him back his presents and tell him you're leaving. You don't want to be a kept woman—not even a married kept woman. You want a career in show business. One day you'll be able to buy yourself a dozen white-mink jackets, if that's what you want. So get this thing over with. Tell him right now that you're leaving, and then do it. But not over the telephone, that would be cowardly. Tell him over lunch, and then get out of the hotel and take up where you left off a week ago."

The telephone rang, and I jumped a mile. Oh, boy, what would I say? I'd have to say something to him about the fur jacket. But I'd save everything else until lunch.

It was Mr. Ritter's secretary on the phone to tell me that Mr. Ritter would be unable to keep our luncheon date, but, please, to meet him in the bar at six o'clock.

I had decided to tell him everything the moment I saw him that evening, but when I arrived at the bar, Louie was with a group of people whom he had also invited to dinner.

I walked in wearing my new blue-silk cocktail dress and the white-mink jacket. Louie kissed me on the cheek and then introduced me to his friends. Once the drinks had been ordered and the conversation was in full swing, Louie leaned over and whispered in my ear, "You look beautiful. How do you like the jacket?"

Oh, shit, I hadn't even thanked him for it!

That night when he brought me home, as we were standing waiting for the elevator, he again kissed me on the cheek and whispered into my ear, "I've kept my promise about never coming to your room. But if you wanted to, you could always invite me."

I caught my breath. I turned hot and cold and a wave of nausea swept over me.

The elevator had arrived, and I got in without saying a word to Louie. Once I'd opened my front door, I made a dash for the bathroom, but I wasn't quick enough. I threw up all over the new white-mink jacket.

The next day when we got together for lunch, I told Louie that I was leaving. His presents were all in my room. I'd only packed what I had come with. The white fur jacket had been wiped clean, and I hoped that he could get his money back for it, and the jewelry, and any of the other things he had bought me. I liked him well enough, but not enough to go "all the way." I could never live with myself knowing that I was nothing but a kept woman. Anyway more than anything else I wanted a career in show business.

Louie said, "You want to be in show business? Why didn't you say so? I know everybody in show business. What do you want to do? Do you want to be in movies? Joe Pasternak, the biggest producer at MGM, is a Hungarian. He is my dearest friend. I'll call Joe and ask him to put you in his next picture, if that's what you want."

If that's what I wanted? To be in movies? The movies! MGM!

Louie left me in the booth with my mouth hanging open, staring into a cup of consommé. Half an hour later he swaggered back, thumbs in his vest pockets, and a devilish grin on his face. "You didn't think I could do it, did you? Well, Miss Carroll Baker, Miss Movie Star, we are booked on the Super Chief to California tomorrow. Joe starts filming a movie soon, and if the director agrees, there is a part in it for you. Don't worry. The director will agree because I'll take along a mink coat for his wife."

"The Super Chief train?" I asked. "Doesn't that mean days and nights?"

A look of deep hurt clouded Louie's face and I suddenly felt guilty, although I wasn't quite sure why.

"My God, you still don't trust me?"

"Well," I stammered, "the fur jacket . . ."

"What about the jacket? My brother is in the fur business. I get them wholesale. I give away furs the way you give away pencils."

"Yes, but . . ."

"But, what?" he asked angrily. "Oh, I see—you thought that what I said to you at the elevator—that I'd said it to you because I'd just given you the fur?"

"Well, in a way, I suppose."

"You silly, provincial little girl. I'm attracted to you. That's only human, isn't it? The last thing on my mind was the stupid fur jacket. Throw it away! Burn it! As a matter of fact, as you hadn't said anything about receiving it, I thought you didn't like it. I was going to ask you today if you wanted me to exchange it for another color or another style."

"No, I'm sorry, I do like it. . . ."

"I don't want to buy you. I could buy whores around the clock, if that's what I wanted." His anger had subsided and he looked wounded again. "What did I say that was so terrible? I merely suggested that you could invite me to your room if you wanted to. You didn't want to, so that was that. Did I follow you, or make a fuss? No. As far as I was concerned the matter was over."

I felt about twelve years old. I knew I was blushing but I couldn't stop, and I couldn't think of a single thing to say.

"You want to call it quits? Fine. That's up to you. Now that the arrangements are made, I'm going to California, anyhow. I've been meaning to do some business out there. You have your own compartment on the train. If you want me to, I'll cancel your reservation."

By that time I was choking back tears. Louie put his hand on the table in front of me, palm up, and I placed my hand in his without looking at him. He said gently, "Look, Carroll, I care for you a lot. We've only known each other for a short time—not long enough, yet, for me to ask you to marry me. But if you want to try this arrangement for a little longer, I like being with you and doing things for you."

I took my hand away to get a handkerchief because I was crying and my nose was running.

"Carroll, darling, have I told you a lie so far? Don't you think you should trust me by now?" He raised his right hand and said, "I swear on my mother's life, that I won't touch you until the day comes when you want me to."

My own poor mother hadn't heard from me since Canada. I sent her a birthday card, enclosing a pink-lace doily Louie had given me, and briefly scribbled something about going to California to audition for a film. Of course, I never mentioned anything about Louis Ritter.

Once again Louie was as good as his promise. When we boarded the train, there were two separate compartments, one beside the other. The porter asked if he could make up the beds while we were in the dining car and if Mr. Ritter wished to keep the two compartments separated or did he wish to have the dividing wall rolled back in order to have one large compartment? Louie said, "Keep them separate tonight, and during the day we'll have one large compartment."

We had a delicious meal with champagne. Louie kissed my hand and said goodnight outside my compartment door.

Once inside, I fastened the lock and slid into place the little red bolt which registered "Do Not Disturb" on the outside of the door. Then I played with all the light switches. The different combinations of illumination were marvelous! It would be more fun, though, to be in the dark with the blinds up, and mark the progress of the train by the towns and stations speeding by.

What an ingenious design modern first-class trains were: everything so functional and compact, hidden away when they weren't in use. What had been the long, upholstered carriage seat was now a bunk bed. I investigated all the surfaces and found a tabletop which opened up to reveal a sink. The inside of the lid was a mirror! The toilet was totally concealed in a closet which didn't appear to be a closet: but for the handle, it seemed to be a part of the wall leading to the corridor. The partition between the apartments seemed so solid and sturdy that I wondered if it could possibly be coaxed into an accordion shape, or if it had to be carried out in one piece for the daytime.

How absolutely luxurious to have this comfort and privacy instead of sitting up all night in a crowded coach! I felt so elegant and important. I undressed very carefully and even folded my underthings neatly before placing them in my case. After gently washing and patting dry my face, just like those girls in the Lux soap commercials, I massaged it with twice the amount of cream I normally used. After all, who knows, I might just be a movie star soon. I slipped into my nightgown and switched out the lights before pulling up the blind. Then I turned down the covers and lounged back onto the cool white sheets and pillows of the bunk, to watch the magic of the night outside flashing by.

There was a loud snapping sound. In the next flash, I saw the wall opposite me vanish. In another flash, I saw a skinny, wrinkled, hairless ape leaping toward my berth.

In the instant he sprang, a brilliantly lit station sped by and I could see him suspended over my head like a spider ape. His erect penis was not like an ape's but it was like a stallion's. As he dropped on top of me there was darkness and suffocation and pain.

The train was wheezing and hissing as it thumped and humped and roared and wrenched toward a tunnel.

No clearway.

Oh, God, so this was pain. I had never known pain before. Yes, the smart of a skinned knee or the dry burn of a red throat, perhaps. But they were not real pain. Flyover. Don't move, don't breathe, it will stop, the pain will cease, flyover.

What did I know—I had seen photographs and drawings and words. Sure I had seen penises before—an ape's, a stallion's, a pig's—but a man's? Yes, once, we had had an exhibitionist in Greensburg, a crazy old tramp who hid under the bleachers at football games. I had heard about the flasher but had put him out of my mind; then one halftime, on my way to the ladies' room, there he was holding his limp penis in both hands like a dead bird and asking me, "Do you like it?" What did I know? I knew that it should be called making love, it should be exciting and beautiful.

Why was he snarling? Where were the sounds of love?

This is not a man. This is not a lover. This is a beast. A snarling beast. A spider ape with a stallion's penis.

The snarls grew fiercer. A snarl became a growl, a roar, a grunt. The grunt became a gnarr, a croak, a wheeze.

The ape shriveled into a tiny wrinkled old man, who cowered on all fours and crawled to the corner of the bunk, where he huddled and snuffled. "I love you," he whimpered. "I'll marry you."

I lay perfectly still: no movement, no emotion, no breath. I knew that I would have to marry him now.

"Daddy, you were right," came from somewhere deep inside my soul. "It is just as easy to marry a rich man! But tell me, Daddy, since you claim to know everything, is it just as easy to keep your self-respect? Or is it just as easy to be happy and to fall in love?"

Chapter Five

THE HOSTAGE

Louis would not marry me in California because of the community-property law. He promised to marry me in Nevada on our return trip. With this promise of marriage alone, I would have remained his captive. He didn't have to confiscate my money, dispose of my clothes, or imprison me in a hotel suite.

I had become a hostage.

From the moment of the rape, I had become a victim not only of what I came to believe was Louie's insidious madness but also of my own strict morality. The one thing I had always feared as the most shameful act had actually happened to me. I was desperate to regain my virtue, and I thought marriage would do that for me.

The second day on the train, I came out of the toilet and discovered Louie searching through my things. He had found the seven hundred dollars which I had so carefully hidden in my garter belt and he was putting the money in his pocket! He flatly refused to give it back to me, claiming that I didn't need to worry about cash any longer. Before detraining, I opened my purse and found to my horror that even my small change was missing. Louie had seen to it that I arrived in California penniless.

We registered at the Beverly Wilshire Hotel, in Beverly Hills, as Mr. and Mrs. Louis Ritter. When we checked in, I felt that everyone saw me the way I saw myself—nothing but a little tramp with an old Sugar Daddy. My shame glowed above my Kelly green suit (the same one I'd worn on my first TV appearance as "Weather Girl"), and I wished that I hadn't been wearing those telltale gold earrings and that dainty expensive watch.

As I opened my suitcase, I couldn't believe what I saw. It was nearly empty. Everything of mine was missing! I found only the items that Louie had given me: the cashmere sweater, the blue-silk cocktail dress, the evening shoes, the beaded evening bag, and the white mink jacket. My tap shoes weren't in the case, or my sheet music, or my costumes!

Louie said, "I swear on all of my future happiness that I had nothing to do with it!" But I had packed everything into my suitcase before leaving the train. Somewhere between the train and the hotel everything I owned had vanished.

"Isn't it odd," I said, "that a thief would prefer tap shoes to a mink jacket?"

As a reward for my sense of humor, Louis slapped me. No one had ever done that before, and I stood looking at him in disbelief.

The Kelly green suit that I was wearing was my only remaining daytime outfit. I was terrified that he might take that, too. But there was nowhere in the room to hide it and I panicked. Louie was downstairs but he wouldn't stay there forever. Then I saw a notice for drycleaning and rang for the valet. I would have nothing to wear but at least my suit would be safe until I could think of a better plan.

Louie kept promising to buy me some clothes, but every day he had some new excuse. "I haven't had money transferred yet," or "I don't have the time today," or "The way you're behaving, I wouldn't buy you anything." His excuses were all lies. His pockets were bulging with money, he had nothing to do but enjoy himself in California, and as for my behavior, well, I must have been in shock because I didn't really do or say anything.

How nice it would have been to take a walk on Sunset Boulevard. Imagine being near Hollywood and not seeing the Chinese Movie Theater where the famous stars had placed their handprints. This wasn't like being in Southern California at all. Shut in a hotel room, I could have been anywhere. The recreation area, as pictured in the hotel brochure, looked so inviting. If only he hadn't taken my money, I would have bought myself a bathing suit and gotten some sun and exercise at the hotel swimming pool. It never occurred to me that I could charge a costume to his room.

I was still in shock, but Louie had more shocks in store for me because he turned deliberately cruel. He didn't seem to care that I had nothing to wear, that I was condemned to the hotel suite with nothing to do during the days but look out the window at the traffic on Wilshire Boulevard. But I just sat and stared and took whatever punishment he inflicted on me. He even began lunching out every day while I was forced to eat in the room. If only Louie's trousers hadn't been too snug, I would have taken a pair and worn them. As it was, when the waiter knocked on the door, I had to let him in wearing only my cashmere sweater with a towel wrapped around my waist. Still, whatever Louie put me through, I hadn't the ability to retaliate.

The hostage was taken out at night to Ciro's, the Macombo, and the Coconut Grove. Nightclubs have never appealed to me, and I began to drink to overcome the boredom. The blue-silk cocktail dress was the only thing I had to wear. Wearing that same cocktail dress, I silently watched Louis spread everyone's palm with green. Wearing that same cocktail dress, I sat quietly night after night listening to Louie's stale jokes and watching him pay huge bills for the new parties of freeloaders.

Louie watched over his hostage jealously. He couldn't tolerate it if any man looked at me. He even interrupted the conversation if a woman spoke more than a few words to me. If I dared to speak, he embarrassed me by cutting me off sharply in front of everyone.

California was a nightmare for me, but I blamed myself. Why had I ever left New York? Why had I gone to the Wheylan Hotel on that fateful day? The guilt seemed mine. Oh, don't you sometimes wish that you could turn back the clock, have the opportunity to erase a mistake, to do things differently? I was tormented by regrets and self-recrimination, incapable of accusing my tormentor.

When I begged over and over again to be taken back to New York, Louie held out the promise of that introduction to Joe Pasternak. But I no longer had the confidence or the spirit to enter into an important interview. I only wanted to be married, to have my honor restored, to find my way back to my self-esteem.

My Kelly green suit was missing! It was as though it had never existed, as though I was crazy. The valet said that he had no record of ever receiving my suit for drycleaning. Louie said, "I swear on the heads of my unborn children that I have never seen you wear a green suit." What could I do? My lovely Kelly green suit was also obviously at the center of a plot. Who could I turn to for help? No one in my family must know about my circumstances until, as a married woman, I could hold my head up again. What could I do but continually beg to be taken back to New York?

Once Louie was thoroughly convinced that I no longer had any desire to go to MGM, he arranged the interview. When the day arrived to meet Pasternak, I still had nothing to wear. Louie insisted that I go to MGM at eleven o'clock in the morning wearing that blue-silk cocktail dress. Suddenly, something inside of me snapped. "Never!" I screamed. That indignity touched me where I lived! And for the first time I stood my ground. "You'll never get me to walk into MGM, in the bright morning sunlight, wearing a cocktail dress!"

Louie shoved me roughly into a chair, but I remained undaunted and said with deadly calm, "You have humiliated me for the last time. I am not taking any more."

As I rose from the chair, he slapped my face with all his might.

That slap struck a chord which reverberated at once to the depth of my sense of injustice, revealing my savage feelings. Suddenly, I wasn't afraid of anything he could do to me. I went berserk!

I whirled on him and fought back. Every object in that hotel suite became a weapon. The furniture flew! I managed to hit him several times on the arms and chest with a straight-backed chair. When he wrested the chair from me, I aimed a vase at his head.

"Stop hitting me!" I screamed. "While I draw breath, I'll never stop fighting back. You will either have to stop or kill me."

My physical strength may not have been a match for his, but I was the trapped one with nothing left to lose.

He stopped.

Brandishing a poker, I yelled, "I am walking out on you! I am going with or without clothes, with or without money, and with or without the help of the police!"

He didn't move a muscle. I put the poker down. I was far too angry to calm down instantly, so I took my anger out on that hateful blue-silk cocktail dress. I ripped that damned blue-silk cocktail dress to pieces, and then I tore the pieces into shreds.

Louie seemed to switch personalities. He crumpled to his knees. He cried. He pleaded. He begged my forgiveness. He implored me not to leave him. He lay moaning at my feet.

When I saw that tyrant groveling at my feet, that was the moment my innocence left me. I suddenly realized that I too had power, the power a desirable woman has over a man—the power of my sex.

My psychological warfare began. First, I never let him out of bed. (What a way to go, you may say!) Louie was a bull of a man, but I had my unwavering urge for revenge and the limitless energy of a twenty-one-year-old. At his age, it took no time at all to demolish him. I reduced him to a state of total exhaustion. In fact, he began taking sleeping pills most nights in order to escape me. It was delicious to be the aggressor.

Knowing his perversity, I feigned indifference to all of his presents, so that he had to buy me more and more in a vain effort to please me. He bought me clothes until the wardrobe bulged. He bought me lingerie until the dresser drawers overflowed. He bought me shoes and makeup and perfume until our suite looked like a boutique and there was no space left anywhere, so he bought me a complete set of Vuitton luggage in which to store my gifts!

Because of the bruises I had received during our brawl, my appointment with Pasternak had to be postponed for ten days. When I did arrive on the MGM lot, I was sitting in my brand new, baby blue, red leather· upholstered, convertible Cadillac!

Pasternak was genuinely pleased when he saw a pretty blonde in a chic white suit entering his office. (I think he was relieved that Louie hadn't sent him a two-headed monster.) He thought I looked a bit young for the part and that I needed to shed five pounds in deference to the weight that the movie camera adds, but when the director heard me read and felt I gave the character enough bitchiness, Pasternak saw no reason not to do his friend Louie a favor.

The small part of Clarise (about eight words) was mine. Shortly after the beginning of the new year, 1953, I played my first movie role in *Easy to Love,* starring Esther Williams, Van Johnson, and Tony Martin.

My brief appearance in *Easy to Love* was filmed in one hour of one afternoon. Everyone involved with the filming was polite. They were also indifferent to me, which made me feel very small. There was no joy in being handed a movie role. Ironically, when the company moved to location shooting in Cypress Gardens, Florida, my sister won a part in the film, on her own merit, doing some spectacular water skiing.

The day I returned to the hotel after the filming at MGM, I couldn't keep up my usual phony happy-go-lucky attitude. My letdown was too severe. In thinking over what I had done on the set, I felt that I had given a strained, unnatural performance.

Louie asked me, "Well, can you act? Do you have any talent?" What could I say? I really didn't know.

"Let's find out from an expert," he chided. "I'll arrange an audition for you with a great director, Gabriel Pascal. He's my friend and a fellow Hungarian. He won't lie. He'll tell me whether or not you are wasting your time."

Pascal was the brilliant film director to whom George Bernard Shaw had entrusted his plays. Pascal and his beautiful blonde wife, Valerie, lived in a dark Gothic mansion in Brentwood. Pascal, himself, was in a dark, intense mood the evening Louie and I arrived for dinner. He scowled at me from across the dinner table and I knew he thought that I was just a vapid, silly little girl who was imposing on his time and genius. The evening was painful. Why had I agreed to audition? Why had I allowed myself to be put in a position where a true artist could destroy my ego?

After the meal, we retired to the living room. Without any instructions as to how I should read the part, Pascal told me, "Look at these pages. You will read for me the part of the stepdaughter in *Six Characters in Search of an Author*." At that moment his lovely, sensitive wife turned pale and left the room. (She is too kind to remain here while he crucifies me, I thought.)

Six Characters in Search of an Author, by Pirandello, is a difficult classic play. I wasn't sure what I was reading. All I could gather from those few pages in front of me was that the stepdaughter was emotionally upset.

"Begin, please," Pascal said gruffly.

Trembling from head to foot, I began to read, endowing the stepdaughter with whatever emotion I was feeling.

I must have gotten to my feet and walked around the room during the reading because when I had finished, I had to stagger back to my chair through a wall of stinging silence.

Pascal rose and tossed his long black hair out of his eyes. "You are a very unlucky child," he said. Striding toward me, he repeated, "You are very unlucky."

He stood in front of me and took my hands. "You are very unlucky, poor child, because you have a great talent. So great a talent that it will forever make you unhappy."

Louie interrupted, "So, then, Gabby, you think that she has talent?"

Pascal snapped at him, "I didn't say that she has talent. I said that she has great talent. Great talent is very rare. It is not a blessing. It is a curse. Great talent is restless, always unsatisfied. She will never find peace."

Louie tried to question him further, but Pascal became impatient and called the evening to an end. At the front door, Pascal told Louie, "You will lose her, Louie. Don't even try to keep her. It is her talent that will take control. Good-bye, my friends, I cannot tell you more."

Louie and I were both stunned and spoke very little on the drive back to Beverly Hills. That phrase, "great talent," kept running over and over again in my head. Just let it be there, as Pascal had said, and I would take my chances with the rest of the prediction.

We were going back to New York. Louie had promised me that we would take the train and stop over in Nevada for three days to get married. But, when the day came to leave, he notified me that we were flying home. "I swear on my dead sister's grave," he said, "that I must get back immediately because I have business that can't wait." Louie was terrified of flying. He must have been very anxious to avoid marriage if he was willing to suffer the nerves of a flight. He was pale and breathless as he fastened his seat belt. When the engines started, his hands gripped the armrest so tightly that his knuckles turned white.

Once on the runway, I asked sweetly, "Are you going to marry me?" He began to say, "I swear—" when I interrupted him by holding his raised right hand. Our plane roared down the runway for takeoff. I said, "Now swear that if you break your promise to marry me, may this plane crash."

Back in New York, the incessant tedium of nightclub life was breaking down my resolve to "stick it out" until marriage. Mother sensed that something was wrong. My letters gave nothing away but still she knew somehow that I was in trouble, and she had been urging me to come back to Florida. On the one hand, I had gotten myself into this mess and I wanted to be grown up enough to find my own solution; on the other hand, I wanted very much to run back to Mother and let her solve my problems.

Night life seemed to be taking its toll on my career, too. I couldn't get up before noon and then I often had a headache and couldn't manage to drag myself out of the hotel suite at the Wheylan until well into the afternoon. I began making the rounds for only two hours a day and looking only for television work. Two and a half months passed without success and then it happened—I clicked in a reading with a comic for the female lead in a running television comedy series! I could hardly believe my good fortune. In fact, I didn't believe it until I had the signed contract in my hand.

The day rehearsals were to begin, I walked into the rehearsal hall and knew immediately that something had happened. The assistant director told me that I was wanted in the producer's office. I had been let go! I was in a flood of tears outside the producer's office when the star of the show came up and put his arm around me. He was boiling mad and told me what had really happened—Louie had bought off the producer, given him a large sum of money to drop my contract. That was it! I couldn't take any more. I wanted more than anything in the world to get married—but Louie Ritter had put my need for security to the final test.

The Cadillac had arrived by train from California. I sold my white mink jacket at a second-hand fur store for about a third of its value to get some spending money, collected the car at the garage, and drove nonstop to St. Petersburg.

Louie began telephoning and pleading with me to come back. Even though I wanted to believe him, I said, "You're a liar. You have no intention of marrying me. You were even low enough to make me lose a wonderful job that could have made me a star. I never want to see you again." He sent me an air ticket for Canada, and we were married in Montreal by a justice of the peace, who looked very disapprovingly at the union of such an old man and a young girl. He nearly refused to perform the ceremony, but I think he saw the desperation in my eyes.

Chapter
Six

DROP DEAD!

Louie and I had endless rows. He wanted me in nightclubs, and I wanted a career. For a time we came up with a silly solution. Louie got me a job in the chorus at the Riviera nightclub in New Jersey. What an odd arrangement! I paraded in the chorus, Louie had his usual night out, and around four in the morning we drove back to Manhattan in the Cadillac to our suite at the Wheylan.

When I got fed up dancing at the Riviera Club, Louie came up with another idea to keep me occupied. He signed a lease at 945 Fifth Avenue for a two-bedroom apartment with a view of Central Park, thinking that I would be busy for months decorating and furnishing the place. Actually, I had no interest at all in making a home, and I told him so.

My thoughts were still on that missed television series. Writing about it now, I can't help but wonder what would have happened had I done the series. My career would certainly have been different; perhaps I would have even been happier in comedy. Who knows?

At the time nothing nearly as good came my way, and I was totally frustrated. Louie nagged me to decorate the apartment, and I kept telling him to hire a decorator. I wasn't going to let him trade that off for something I really wanted, but he wore me down with his insistence. "Can I fix it up any way I want?" I asked. "Do you promise to let me decorate it on my own and keep it a surprise? Do you promise not to look at it until I have finished?"

For once, he kept a promise and waited for the unveiling before seeing his furnished nest. At last the apartment was ready. I could hardly wait to see his reaction!

There couldn't have been another living room like the one I created—at least not on fashionable Fifth Avenue. It had wall to wall carpeting the color of sickly pea soup. (Not an easy color to find!) The couches were glaring orangey-red. No other colors would have clashed quite so astonishingly. The draperies were canary yellow with swirls of other colors in a splashy pattern. (I had to have them woven especially because the material I had in mind didn't exist.) The standing lamps set off the entire decor. They were my finest acquisition. Framing the windows on either side and making even that glorious view of the park seem tawdry were a huge pair of electrically wired red-and-white striped barber shop poles.

When Louie opened his eyes and saw his "home," I wanted to burst with glee. He was totally shocked and deflated. It took every ounce of my sternest concentration to keep from laughing out loud, but of course I couldn't. I had to pretend that this was my ideal home, or he would never have lived there. If I had revealed my true intentions, it would have been just a fleeting practical joke. I wanted this monstrosity as a permanent source of merriment. That apartment cheered me up endlessly. I couldn't wait to invite Louie's friends and business acquaintances. In fact, I began inviting everyone we met to our apartment for a drink. We had nowhere to put drinks or ashtrays because I refused to buy end tables or a coffee table. No matter how much Louie coaxed, I staunchly claimed that tables were old-fashioned. Alone in my room, remembering the looks on people's faces and Louie's embarrassment, I would scream with laughter.

From the moment I had the security of that marriage license, Louie grew progressively restless and discontented with our relationship. It was as if he missed the game of keeping me dangling. But it didn't take him long to invent new games.

Any type of intrigue excited Louie. He even knew small-time hoods and low-life private detectives who allowed him to experience danger vicariously. Other people's problems and marital situations were Louie's specialty. He could spend an entire day listening to a man wail about his wife, egg him on by agreeing that the woman was the world's worst bitch, and then advise a private detective to spy on her. Louie would offer to make all the arrangements, have her movements followed, hidden photographs taken, and her apartment and telephone bugged. The private detective always brought the evidence to Louie first. He reveled in the gory details and dirty pictures, and drooled over the secret conversations. At the same time, he pretended to be a friend to the wife in order to gain her confidence. Then, when he had a firsthand account of how she felt—as well as the evidence—he would proudly present it all to the husband. Most husbands were sorry that they had permitted the situation to get so far out of hand, but by then it was too late. Louie, in the meantime, beamed as he saw other peoples' lives smashed.

Most of Louie's friends were middle-aged. What a surprise when one night our party was joined by an extremely handsome 24-year-old boy. (I'll call him "Boy" because I have no wish for this story to hurt him so many years later.) Boy was supposedly the son of one of Louie's friends. Boy was encouraged to sit by me through dinner, and we were permitted to laugh and talk and even dance. Louie seemed approving of the attention that Boy paid me. Later that night Louie asked me all too casually if I liked Boy. My reply was, "Very much."

Boy began spending every evening with us and then he began showing up at the apartment during the day. Something was fishy. Why wasn't Louie jealous? Why were he and Boy such great chums, endlessly whispering secrets to each other? Could it be that I was being molded into the most recent "bitch" to be spied upon? Even with all these questions and suspicions racing around in my mind, I couldn't ignore Boy. He was so beautiful and such fun to be with.

In the evenings I danced with Boy to my heart's content, and I spoke to him freely and childishly. In the daytime, when he arrived at the apartment, I was extremely cautious. Louie was conspicuously absent from home during the times when Boy arrived. Boy began making passes and asking me to sleep with him. I answered carefully, ever mindful of possible hidden microphones. Boy was nearly irresistible, despite the possibility of a trap.

One day when Boy arrived, I met him at the front door in my coat. I placed my hand firmly over his mouth and silently led him out. We went down to the garage and took the car and drove to Coney Island, where we sat on the almost-deserted boardwalk near the chilly spring beach. Looking out at the ocean, I took his hand and told him that I knew what he was doing. At first he tried to deny it, but when he realized that I really was wise to what was going on, he admitted being part of the plot. Louie was paying him to seduce me.

"You'll be a hero and no doubt get a big bonus, if you try your best to seduce me and fail," I said. "Have you stopped to think how Louie would take it if you succeeded?"

He smiled sheepishly and answered, "He would get a divorce and throw you out without any money." He went on to admit, "Louie coaches me about what to say and do."

I replied, "Well, you are off to a smashing beginning if your ambition in life is to be a gigolo."

"What happens now that you know?" he asked meekly.

"I have no intention of letting Louie know that I know. Once this game is over he will only invent a new one. Frankly, I feel easier coping with this situation than trying to figure out some new deceit. So, if you want to keep your job, I won't give you away and we can have fun." I went on to warn him, "Be very careful—if Louie thinks you have failed, it will be a tremendous boost to his ego and he will reward you handsomely, but if he thinks that you have succeeded, I am afraid of what he might do to you."

Boy only laughed.

I dropped Boy off at a corner in Manhattan and around six o'clock drove the car back to the garage and went upstairs to the apartment, where Louie was waiting for me. He was pacing up and down in a fury. Since he hadn't been able to spy on me that day his imagination had gone wild. He screamed abuses at me and beat me. This time I didn't fight back because I saw a maniacal look in his eyes that terrified me.

We didn't go out that evening. It was the first night that we had ever stayed home. Louie raved on for hours and hours. When he went into the bathroom, I rushed to the kitchen and hid all the knives and sharp objects. I thought he might kill me. However, Louie suddenly turned his hatred toward Boy. He made a series of secret phone calls and I suddenly feared for Boy's safety. There was no way that I could warn Boy to disappear because I didn't know his address or phone number. I was powerless to help him.

I never saw Boy again. I heard a rumor some time later that he had been beaten up by thugs, and my heart went out to him.

I was now convinced that Louie was more than just perverse. He was dangerous. I had to find a way to get away from him.

I knew that Louie was obsessed by money. He made a point of buying friendship and love, and then suffered from the thought that people only wanted him for his money. He constantly accused me of marrying him for his money and then saw to it that I never had any. Even if I needed some small thing like a pair of stockings, I had to call Louie and wait until he arrived with the money to pay for them. It was tiresome to be so dependent. When I went to the hairdresser's, I had to fix a time so that Louie would come and bail me out. He enjoyed keeping me waiting and then magnanimously arriving with a large wad of bills in his hand. His obsession over money was the key to my freedom.

"I know you are worried that I married you for your money. Well, I didn't. Why don't you have your lawyers draw up divorce papers. Draw them up so that I don't get a cent, and I will sign them. I don't want any money from you. You keep telling me that we were happier before the wedding. Let's get a divorce and then continue to live together."

Louie jumped at the idea. He was so thrilled I didn't want any money that he granted me my freedom. He actually believed that I would stay with him after the divorce. Maybe I was a good actress. Maybe I was simply dealing with a totally bent mind.

A divorce, mutually requested, with no alimony or property settlement, can be obtained quickly and with a minimum of fuss. But I didn't get away from Louie so easily.

After the divorce was granted, we were still living together, and Louie was determined that I was going to remain with him. I had to have a small amount of cash to get started with, but Louie disclaimed all knowledge of my original seven hundred dollars. My only assets were the presents Louie had given me— clothing, suitcases, some jewelry, and in place of the white-mink jacket, I now owned a small stole and a beaver coat. They would all have to be sold, but I knew Louie would destroy them before he would let me sell them. The Cadillac was too big an item to take. Basically, what I wanted was the seven hundred dollars that I had started out with eight months before. Eight months? It seemed more like eight years.

My plan was to get away from Louie first and then inform him when it was a *fait accompli*. I had to be absolutely certain that Louie would be away from the house for a couple of hours, so that I could make my move undetected.

At last, three nerve-wracking weeks later, he had a three-hour appointment, from 9:00 A.M. until noon. From our front window I watched him get into a cab and pull away. I dashed into the bedroom, dressed, and threw everything into the suitcases. I stole down the back stairway to the garage, hid the luggage, and asked for the car. Once the car was running, I grabbed the luggage from the back hallway, loaded it and drove away.

Within an hour and a half, I had sold my clothes at a thrift shop, my furs to the second-hand fur store, my jewelry in a discount jewelry store, and my Vuitton luggage to a junk shop. The total price for everything was eight hundred dollars and some change.

While at the junk shop, I bargained for a cheap suitcase and beauty case in which to keep the handful of things I'd kept for myself. The owner of the junk shop agreed to look after my belongings for a few hours.

It was now eleven-thirty, and I was shaking as I drove the car back to 945 Fifth. I left the car in the garage entrance for the attendant to park and ran to the side of the building to hop in a cab. Once I was away from the East Side, I began to breathe again. Only one last sticky thing to do—call Louie and tell him that I wasn't coming back. Shortly after noon I rang. Louie asked me where I was, but I told him not to look for me because I wanted a clean break.

By afternoon, I had my very first checking account and a furnished room on the Upper West Side of Manhattan. All I needed was a cot, a sheet, a blanket, a towel, and a few utensils for my kitchenette. The sun came streaming in the high front windows of my brownstone, and with outstretched arms I whirled round and round to greet its rays. It was a dance dedicated to spring and a new life.

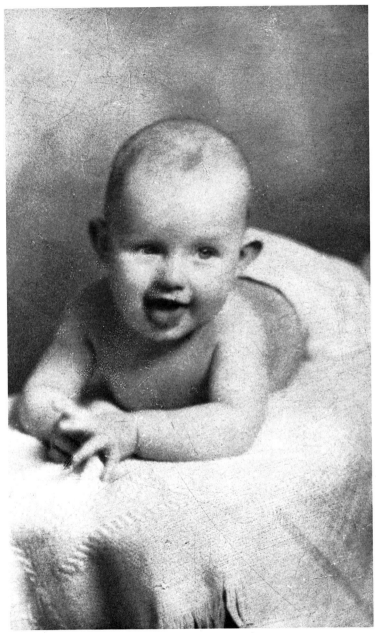

Carroll at 6 months!

Me at three, with my parasol and
Chou-Chou

With Daddy

With Boopie and Daddy

That's me at the far right as flower girl to the May Queen

Mother, 1937

Missing Mother at age eleven

A serious Carroll at eight

Boopie waterskiing in *Easy to Love*

Before Hollywood: At the Actor's Studio, 1953

April 3, 1955: Jack and I make it official

"Baby Doll" has her own two baby dolls

With Herschel, age five, and Blanche, age six

Louie, however, set his bloodhounds on me. The second morning in my new home, I raised the window blinds facing the street and recognized the private eye waiting across the street.

When I came outside, I waved to him, but he pretended not to notice. As the fool followed me all day on my rounds, I waved and made faces at him, but he refused to look me in the eye.

Around six o'clock, when I entered my room I realized that an intruder had been there. The door had been opened by someone, but the apartment had not been broken into. The kitchen cabinets were open and the drawers were pulled out. Nothing was missing—I owned next to nothing, anyway. The telephone rang. Telephone? I hadn't ordered a telephone! Louie was on the line. He'd had the phone installed so that he could talk to me. (Also, where was the fun, if I had no phone to bug?)

Louie called me at all hours of the day and night begging me to come back. He had his friends call and plead his case. I had no peace. Finally, I did what I'd seen people do in the movies —I cut the phone wire.

The next afternoon I came home to find my cot, kitchen utensils, and suitcases piled on the sidewalk. My landlady had thrown me out. My copy of the lease and my rent receipt were the only things missing from my suitcase. That old witch of a landlady wouldn't admit that she had been paid off, but I knew very well that this eviction was Louie's doing.

That ridiculous detective was standing across the street grinning, so I walked over and confronted him. "You stay here and don't you let anyone walk away with my possessions. I'll be right back. And don't forget that I know who you are and where you're located. If any of my belongings are stolen, I'll report you as the thief."

At the police station, they told me that eviction was a legal matter and that I would have to take the landlady to court. They also advised me to get my cancelled check as proof of payment. I hurried to the bank to ask for my cancelled rent check. After getting out my file, the teller looked at me strangely and asked me to step into the manager's office. Inside, the manager told me that my bank account had been frozen. There could be no transactions of any kind until the matter was settled. A Mr. Ritter had obtained a temporary injunction against my account.

71

Louie must have assumed that if I was out on the street with no money I would be forced to come back and live with him. Never!

In my haste, on the day of my escape, I had not left behind, as I had intended, the car papers and the extra set of keys. They were still in my purse. I marched into the garage at 945 and took away the Caddy, despite the protests of the attendant.

The first used-car lot I drove into offered me only a thousand dollars for that fabulous convertible, but the offer was in cash, so I sold it to them on the spot. Next, I had to find an apartment that Louie couldn't get me thrown out of. I went to my union, AGVA (variety artists), which had a list of landlords who were union members, and I was able to arrange a room by phone.

The silly detective was still at my old address, slumped on the steps of the brownstone guarding my things. "Have you got a car?" I asked. When he pointed to it, I told him, "Drive me to my new apartment." He hesitated, and I added, "You won't have to follow me, you'll know exactly where I live."

In the car I told him, "By the way, my new landlord knows the entire story and he can't be bought. No one will be allowed into my apartment. If you break in, it will be a police matter. The landlord also knows that I won't be getting a telephone."

When my few possessions were unloaded on the sidewalk in front of my new address, a brownstone on the Upper West Side almost identical to the previous one, I thanked the detective for his help. I added, "When you see Louie, tell him from me: drop dead."

Chapter
Seven

NEW YORK CITY: 1953

Under the oppressive heat and humidity of August, days in the city are sluggish, and there isn't even the hint of a breeze to relieve those nights of restless tossing in twisted, damp sheets. I had been married to a rich man and had owned a hoard of treasures. Now, in August of 1953 I was back to where I'd been the previous August: alone and broke in New York City—with one big, big difference: I'd learned what it means to lose your liberty and then to have that priceless right once again as yours. Oh, to turn twenty-two and be free! You don't feel, at that age, that you have to pick up the pieces, you just march unhaltingly into the next episode of your life.

In my own little apartment, free at last from Louie's harassment, I had the peace of mind to think again about my career. Unlike my deliberate decisions to give up vaudeville and then magic, my ambition to dance simply faded until I no longer thought of myself as a dancer.

My only source of income was a Coca-Cola commercial that I did once a week. The commercial didn't pay much, but it was regular and helped to keep the wolf from my door. I was one of five girls dressed like bobby-soxers sipping Coca-Cola at a soda fountain. The commercial was staged at the beginning and at the end of a television play, so I was able to observe the actors at work. (In the early days of television, the entire broadcasting day, including commercials, was done on the spot and transmitted live.)

Frankly, while watching the dramatic programs, I got the feeling that acting was a cinch. Most actors seemed merely to imitate one another, characterizations fell into set patterns, and line readings were predictable. There was no reason why I couldn't do the same thing, if I was willing to settle for "sameness," but maybe I could be more than that. Maybe I could fulfill the ability that Gabriel Pascal had predicted. If I wanted to be special, I would first have to have the best acting training available. That would have to wait until I had the funds.

In the meantime, could I get some experience in the legitimate theatre? But what nerve I would need to go to theatre auditions—going up against the most qualified and skillful of actors! Well, why not? Nothing ventured—right?

Just as I had expected, most stage managers took one look at my résumé and refused even to let me into the reading. However, once again, the law of averages worked for me. I went to so many play auditions that now and then they allowed me to read. I struck it lucky. I was hired for a walk-on role in a play starring Brian Aherne, *Escapade.*

This letter, which I found among my Grandmother Duffy's souvenirs, expresses how I felt at the time:

Boston, Mass.
October 28, 1953

Dear Grandma,

You won't believe this—I am so thrilled—I have copped a small part in a Broadway play! I am thrilled to death to be a part of the legitimate theatre.

It makes me proud to think that I belong to all the theatrical unions now. I have worked in vaudeville, radio, television, movies, and now the theatre!

We are on the out-of-town try-outs for the play which is called "Escapade." Last week we played Hartford, Conn., and we will be playing here in Boston for the next two weeks before opening on Broadway.

There are so many things to learn about the theatre. Do I feel green! However, I am watching and listening and gathering so much valuable knowledge and experience for the future. Can you imagine how terrible it would be to be green like I am and have an important role?

I don't have any lines but I'm seen taking shorthand all through out the first scene of the third act.

We didn't get very good write-ups here or in Hartford, and my name wasn't mentioned, so I didn't bother buying the newspapers.

"Easy to Love" should be in Turtle Creek in about two weeks. Watch the movie section of your newspaper!

Love,
Carroll

Easy to Love played at Radio City Music Hall, but whatever thrill I might have gotten from that fact was diminished by the appalling shock of watching myself in the film. My performance wasn't just bad—it was agonizing! My résumé has never listed *Easy to Love* as a credit. Some years later I met Esther Williams again at a party in Hollywood. Esther taunted me about my boyfriend bribing everyone with fur coats in order to get me the part in her film. She reproached me in front of Louella Parsons, so I think she was really looking for a gossip item rather than a discussion. Fortunately, Louella was not interested in the story. Early in my career, I would have been horribly ashamed for anyone to know that I had been in that film—especially under those circumstances.

Escapade only lasted a few weeks in New York, and, since I was working for scale, I wasn't able to save any money; but it was a Broadway credit that I included on my résumé with pride. While we were at the theatre in Hartford, I uncovered what I took to be a good omen. There was a shortage of dressing rooms in that particular theatre and, as the least important member of the cast, I was relegated to dress among the wardrobe in a crowded prop room with no mirror or vanity table. There was a tarnished, illegible star high above my door frame, and one day, out of curiosity, I climbed on a chair and polished it—it read *Jeanne Eagles!*

Backstage at *Escapade,* the conversation was often about the Actors' Studio. Someone called it the "dirty T-shirt" school of acting. Someone else said that the instructor, Lee Strasberg, was a phony who turned out mumblers. But having seen *A Streetcar Named Desire,* and Marlon Brando's performance as Stanley Kowalski, I realized which side I was on! Although *Streetcar* had been a disturbing film, and even difficult for me to fully understand, its new realism was exciting in such a vibrant, unique way that it had changed the way I had looked at films. Brando's performance was one of the finest I had ever seen and if Brando's style of acting was what they taught at the Actors' Studio, and Lee Strasberg was the best instructor of this new "method," then that was where I wanted to study.

Would the Actors' Studio accept me? After all, my only real experience was in vaudeville. If they did accept me, how could I pay for the lessons? It took me weeks to muster up enough courage to go to the loft near Ninth Avenue where the Studio sessions were held, and inquire about membership.

What I found out amazed me. The Actors' Studio was free of charge! They required no qualifications whatsoever! It wasn't necessary to have acting credits, or experience, or looks, or even money! The only criterion was talent; the only admittance was by audition. Elia Kazan, the director of *Streetcar,* was one of the artistic directors who watched over your progress. Big names in the theatre like Eli Wallach and Anne Jackson were willing to work alongside promising newcomers. Karl Malden or Lee J. Cobb might moderate at a session. Geraldine Page, Kim Stanley or Maureen Stapleton might be experimenting on some new characterization. When you did a scene, maybe Julie Harris would give you her comments. Maybe you would look up one day and find Marlon Brando looking back! It was too good to be true. What a fantastic opportunity for a young actor—but you had to pass that audition first. I trembled just signing my name to the waiting list.

Apparently the Studio operated on contributions, and while Lee Strasberg volunteered his teaching skills, the members themselves took turns with the administrative work.

The first person I spoke to at the Studio was a boy named Jack Garfein. He had very kindly and patiently explained the rules to me. I didn't know then who he was, or, of course, how important he was to be in my life. When I had walked up the stairs to the loft, I had seen Jack in the hallway sitting on a folding chair with his feet propped up on what looked like an old kitchen table. He was a short boy and oddly disproportioned. Although big-boned, he was small and had the hands and feet of a not quite fully grown child. Moreover, his head appeared to be too large for his body. True, he had an exaggerated amount of wild, reddish-brown hair, but it was more than that. It was as if his head had developed while the rest of his growth had been somewhat stunted. Still, there was a haunting look in his eyes that fascinated and disturbed me.

It was a look I had never seen before, and little wonder, for Jack Garfein had walked through the vale of hell. He was a Czechoslovakian Jew born in Bardejov, a small village in the Carpathian Mountains. When Jack was nine years old, the Nazis rounded up the Jews of Bardejov, including Jack and his younger sister and his parents, and transported them by cattle car to Auschwitz.

Auschwitz was the clearinghouse of concentration camps, where human beings were separated into categories according to their usefulness to the Third Reich. Babies, young children, the old and infirm were eliminated from further consideration by being marched immediately to the gas chambers. It was there that Jack's mother refused to allow her little girl to be taken from her—and they were both gassed and cremated in the ovens.

Jack's father was lined up with the strongest, healthiest men of the village and marched to the awaiting trucks for transfer to a distant concentration camp devoted to hard labor. He was led away believing that his son Jack was doomed along with the other children. He eventually succumbed to dysentery, starvation, and a broken heart.

Jack was saved by a family friend who took him by the shoulders and said, "Stay by me. I will be sent with the craftsmen. Tell them that you are my apprentice."

At the end of the war, having been shifted from one concentration camp to another, thirteen-year-old Jack, weighing less than forty pounds, was carried out of Bergen Belsen on a stretcher.

Jack was liberated by the British and taken by the Red Cross to a rehabilitation center in Sweden. An uncle, who had immigrated to the United States before the war, contacted the Red Cross and arranged for Jack to come to New York and live with him and his wife. Studying at the New School for Social Research, Jack developed a passion for the theatre. When I met him in 1953, he had the year before, at the age of twenty-two, directed *End as a Man* in an off-Broadway house with a cast of unknowns from the Actors' Studio. The production had received rave notices and had been successfully moved to Broadway. Ben Gazzara had become an overnight star in the leading role; the entire cast had been hailed for their fine ensemble work; and Jack Garfein had been dubbed the new Orson Welles, boy genius of the New York theatre.

All this I learned later. All I knew then was that here was a fascinating and disturbing boy.

When my interview was over, Jack asked if I would like to join him and some of his Studio friends that evening at Pete's Tavern near Gramercy Park. It wasn't a date, just a casual get-together with everyone going "Dutch."

Pete's is the oldest pub in New York and to this day has remained a favorite hang-out of mine. I adore the old wood paneling, the atmosphere, the Italian food, and the people who work there and run it.

That first evening, excited at the thought of meeting more Studio kids, I arrived at Pete's long before Jack. I had to walk around the block for twenty minutes. It was an enchanting evening for me because of the surroundings; the privilege of hearing the kids from the Studio discuss the theatre; and also because I found myself attracted to the wild, Bohemian, intellectual, twenty-three-year-old Garfein. I'd never before met any one even remotely like him.

My audition at the Actors' Studio six weeks later was a thoroughly traumatic experience. I have no memory whatsoever of having done the scene itself. I just remember how numb I felt when it was over, sitting there on a folding chair on that brightly lit stage of the loft, peering into the audience, trying to make out the faces of the judges. The auditioning board sat twice monthly and consisted of five members (out of a possible fifteen whom Lee Strasberg had designated as qualified to judge). Paula Strasberg, Lee's wife, was one of the judges I recognized. I was sure I had never seen three of them before. I gasped audibly when I suddenly made out the face of Jack Garfein. Oh, no, it hadn't occurred to me that he might be there! If I had made a fool of myself, did it also have to be in front of Jack?

Paula Strasberg stood up. She asked me incredulously, "Was that scene from *Gulliver's Travels*?"

I blushed. *Sullivan's Travels.*

None of the board had seen the movie *Sullivan's Travels.* Personally, I thought it was a good film, I chose the scene because it had been given to me to use for an audition at a movie tryout. Now, I could have kicked myself—choosing a movie script—they were probably too highbrow to even go to the movies. They must have thought I was very corny.

The judges went into a lengthy huddle.

How could I have made such a stupid mistake and blown my chances of belonging to the Studio? Finally the muttering stopped, and it was Paula who spoke to me again, "We have had a difficult time deciding what to say to you. You seem to show some natural talent, but at the same time your scene was conventional; perhaps it was the material. We are willing to give you the benefit of a doubt and let you audition again with a scene from a contemporary play." Well, at least I hadn't been flatly rejected. There would be another chance, but I had to find out which plays to read in order to find a part that was right for me and acceptable to the Studio. God! I felt like such an ignoramus!

Jack Garfein was a good person to ask for advice. I also wanted an excuse to see him again, so I waited downstairs in the hallway for two hours until the auditions were over. Fortunately, Jack wasn't rushing off to an appointment. He seemed pleased to see me, but he didn't invite me for a cup of coffee, as I had hoped. Maybe he didn't have the money. I would have offered to buy him coffee but all I had was the ten cents for the bus ride home.

We sat on the steps in the hallway and talked for a long time. I kept thinking how brilliant and interesting he was and wished that we had been in a more comfortable place. Jack gave me a list of plays to get from the library, and he suggested that I study with Lee Strasberg in one of Lee's acting classes that was outside of the Studio. Jack felt that these private classes were even more valuable for a beginner than the Studio because they dealt with exercises and basic foundation work.

We were about to part without any mention of meeting again. While I knew that he wasn't married, the thought crossed my mind that he might have gotten involved with some other girl since that time we'd been together at Pete's.

"Do you still go to Pete's?" I asked.

"Only when I have the money," he replied. "I'll tell you what, the next time I get a job, I'll invite you on a date."

I said, "Okay," but I thought to myself, "and if I get a good job, I'll invite you."

At the time I went for an interview, Lee Strasberg was in the process of putting together a new beginners' class. I was worried that he might be snobbish about my background, but, to my amazement, Strasberg was fascinated and wanted to know all about my experiences in vaudeville and magic. When I discussed my Actors' Studio audition, Lee said that he, too, had enjoyed the film *Sullivan's Travels,* and my self-assurance was restored. He told me on the spot that I was accepted into his new class, and I was thrilled.

Now, I simply had to find the money for the classes. They were to begin in three weeks, which didn't give me much time. Cigarette commercials paid a lot of money, but I didn't smoke. I had heard that the same agency that handled my Coca-Cola commercials was putting together a commercial for a new cigarette. Maybe they would let me try out for the job.

When I went to inquire, the agent said to me, "But you told me that you don't smoke."

"How many days before the auditions?" I asked.

"Two."

"Well, in two days I can learn to smoke."

The new cigarette was called Winston and was made by the makers of Camel cigarettes. The agent laughed and gave me a carton of Camels to practice with. "Remember, you must be able to inhale deeply," he said. "This is Tuesday. Come back at ten o'clock on Thursday, and if you can smoke by then, I'll send you on the audition."

My room was full of smoke and I felt deathly ill, but by Wednesday night I had smoked a full carton of Camels. By Thursday morning I still felt dreadful, but I was at least able to hold down some food and the natural color had returned to my face.

The client's representative liked me right away. He thought that I looked just right for the part and that I read the lines well. The preliminary audition won me a place in the finals, to be held that afternoon. It was lunchtime but I still felt queasy so I made the mistake of not eating.

At the finals, I got the feeling that I was the representative's first choice. He was very encouraging and asked me to read the lines exactly as I had done before, but to inhale more deeply and allow the smoke to linger in my lungs before exhaling.

Somehow, I managed to get through it without anyone realizing how sick I was feeling. But even though I was overwhelmed by dizziness and nausea, I still hadn't inhaled deeply enough for their liking. I unobtrusively found my way to the ladies' room, where I heaved.

I returned to the rehearsal room and was confronted by the sight of the other six contestants all relaxing with a cigarette! Fortunately, a break was called, because I couldn't have remained in that room. I went outside, bought a quart of milk, and drank the whole thing. It steadied my stomach, and I felt much better.

When I returned, I was asked to do the commercial again. This time the smoking was going very well and I felt sure that I was going to be all right. At the very last second, as I had nearly finished exhaling, big tears welled up in my eyes.

The filming was to take place in another three days. My smoking hadn't been good enough, but the representative liked me so much that it was agreed that two girls would be filmed and then the best film would be chosen. Before I left, I was asked to practice and given another carton of Camels.

There were two more agonizing days of continuous smoking until I had finished my second carton of Camels. The day at the film studio was more torture, smoking over and over and over again. The filming fee was only a flat one hundred dollars and I was sure that would be my only reward.

However, we repeated the filming so many times that one of the takes must have been perfect because it was my footage that was selected. My paycheck was for one thousand dollars!

First, I went to Strasberg's secretary and paid my class tuition for six months in advance. Then, I went to the Actors' Studio to find Jack Garfein and invite him for a celebratory meal at Pete's Tavern. He had also just finished a job, and we both said at once, "Can I take you to Pete's?"

After a glorious evening, Jack took me home in a taxi, which was very grand because we were at Irving Place near the Lower East Side and I lived way uptown on the West Side. When we got out of the taxi, I felt shy and awkward and wasn't sure what to do next. Jack suggested that we go inside and make coffee.

There was only one cup and one glass in my kitchenette. Jack said that in Eastern Europe they drank tea from glasses, so he wouldn't mind using the glass. The only place to sit down was on my cot. We sat down in unison in order to keep the cot balanced, but the moment our combined weight hit the frame it snapped like a twig and sent us to the floor with the hot coffee flying. We sat there giggling like two idiots, trapped in a maze of canvas and bedclothes, soaked in coffee and holding an empty cup and an empty glass.

Still giggling, we ran a bathtub of water and got in with all of our clothes on. We washed our clothes, ourselves, and even each other. Our shyness had vanished by the time we had taken off our clothes and hung them up to dry. We ran another bath using dishwashing liquid for bubbles. We laughed and played and made love in the warm, soapy water. The lovemaking seemed natural and so loving. My first experience with a young man was all I had ever hoped it would be.

FAMOUS PEOPLE WHEN THEY WERE STUDENTS

Only twenty applicants had been chosen for Lee Strasberg's new class. Two of my fellow students were Inger Stevens and Mike Nichols.

It was obvious from his very first scene that Mike Nichols was exceptionally gifted. While the rest of us were making an effort just to place one foot in front of the other without tripping, Mike was showing signs of being a brilliant comedian. He could make even a simple exercise hysterically funny in an absolutely genuine way. (Recently, when I asked Mike why he has never used me in any of his films or stage productions, he told me it was because I had refused to do scenes with him when we were in class together.)

It was also apparent that Inger Stevens was star material. She was beautiful and graceful, as well as talented. We were friends despite the jealousy that naturally exists between young actresses. When she moved to California, I lost track of her for a time, but in the late Fifties we had two wonderful weeks together when we both attended the Catregna Film Festival. Inger was a sweet, kind, wonderful girl, and I shall never forget her infectious laughter. When I heard about her suicide, I went into deep mourning.

Fame, it seems, is not an answer in itself. Inger chose not to go on at a time when she was making one film after another and soaring to the heights of her career. She left a suicide note in which she said that she could "no longer endure the loneliness."

At the time I began studying in Lee Strasberg's private classes, Jack had not only become my lover but also my Pygmalion (which makes for a precarious relationship, because the day comes when the sculptor refuses to acknowledge that his work is completed, and the statue insists upon her independence). Even in that early stage of our relationship I began to feel stirrings of resentment.

Jack guided me in everything: the books I should read, the theatre I should see, the way I should look at religion and politics. He bought me a record player and records and introduced me to classical music. Although I was a good pupil and was anxious to learn, there were times when I tired of trying to be so intellectual and would sneak away to hear pop music or read a mystery novel.

One of the fellows Jack introduced me to was a guy named Rod Steiger. He was putting on a workshop production of Ibsen's *Peer Gynt* at the Actors' Studio, and Jack and I went to see it one evening. Rod was fine, I'm sure, but I could hardly sit through that play. Afterwards, when I dared to suggest that I didn't care much for Ibsen, Jack and I had our first big fight. Jack had given me all of Ibsen's plays to read, and while I enjoyed *A Doll's House,* on the whole I found them too out of date and heavy for my taste. But it was sheer sacrilege to have said so in front of Jack and his friends. (They made me feel that I was stupid and for years afterward I was unsure of my opinion. Recently, I saw one of my favorite actresses, Vanessa Redgrave, in Ibsen's *The Lady from the Sea.* Vanessa was excellent, but I can now freely say that my feelings about Ibsen are unchanged.)

Jack and I used to go to Rod Steiger's apartment once a week for a play reading. Rod was married and more set up for entertaining than most of us. Rod's wife would make coffee, and we would all sit around the kitchen table with our play scripts. Saying that I didn't like Ibsen had made me an outcast and they rarely gave me a part to read. Most of the time I had to sit there and silently follow the text. But it didn't really matter to me that I was looked on as the dumb blonde. I knew that I was learning, learning, learning.

Rod has always been intrigued by accents. He practiced a

different dialect each week whether or not the part called for one. Anyone who has seen Rod's *Napoleon, The Pawnbroker,* or *A Fistful of Dynamite* knows how highly varied and masterful his accents are today. But in those days, when he read Molière, his accent went from northern Spain to southern Italy, with a bit of Yiddish thrown in, before it settled down into France.

Eva Marie Saint and her husband, Jeff Hayden, were also good friends of Jack. A group of us often gathered to listen to classical music, and these evenings were sometimes held at Eva's apartment. The first time I attended one of these musical evenings, I couldn't believe that we did nothing but sit silently for hours on end listening to music. After one record, I was ready for coffee and conversation.

At each of these musical evenings was a small, blond boy who sat in a corner by himself. He never spoke, not even to say hello or good-bye. He would simply wander in and slip out again. Often, he would squat on the floor and quietly tap his bongo drums in time to the music. Nearly everyone at the Studio thought he was strange but phenomenally talented. Apparently, a powerful personality was released when he was able to hide his self-consciousness behind a character. He fascinated me, and I used to stare at him to see if I could read his thoughts. When he caught me staring, he would break into a crooked grin. Being caught made me blush and that in turn made him laugh. His girlfriend, Claire, told me that he loved attention from girls, even though he went to extremes not to be noticed. Behaving as you felt—not according to convention—was Lee Strasberg's attitude and most of us mimicked him. But this kid went further with "doing his own thing" than anyone else in our group.

He and Claire had met while she was raising funds for the Actors' Studio. Their relationship was most unusual because while they spent hours and even days and nights together at her apartment, they were never seen socially. He confided in Claire, and she was careful not to betray his trust, so I couldn't get her to tell me why they never went out together. Perhaps it was because they were so different in appearance and background. He was short with a funny little face and eyes that were a bit too close together; Claire was a tall, unquestionably beautiful brunette. He had been raised by his grandparents on a midwestern farm; Claire had come from a well-to-do Eastern family and had been a debutante. He had a burning ambition; Claire just enjoyed being around the theatre and theatre people. His attitude toward her was somewhat cavalier and at times almost rude. Claire, on the other hand, was refined and gentle and understanding. More than anyone else, she understood the troubled rebel in him. It was those very qualities, together with his extraordinary talent, that later made James Dean such a big star.

Elia Kazan was preparing to do another film with Marlon Brando, *On the Waterfront.* Our friends, Eva Marie Saint and Rod Steiger, were both cast in leading parts! Secretly, I was hoping that when the filming was over, Eva would still be the same sweet, unassuming girl that I knew. If she were, she might tell me about Marlon Brando.

Eva had been working on a project called *A Hatful of Rain.* It was strictly a Studio project, an outline of a play in progress, written by a member, Mike Gazzo. Ben Gazzara, who had the lead; Tony Franciosa and Henry Silva, who had important supporting roles; and Mike Gazzo were all kids I had met through Jack Garfein. They mutually agreed that they would like to have me as Eva's replacement, and to my great surprise and delight, Lee Strasberg gave his consent.

So when Eva left to film *On the Waterfront,* I took over the female lead! It was a wonderful part in a play that had definite possibilities, and I felt honored to have been chosen.

There was one sandy-haired boy who made his presence felt everywhere. He had a vibrant personality. He was not only friendly and sparkling, but he was downright pushy. During *End as a Man,* he continually nagged Jack Garfein to let him replace Ben Gazzara; and although he wasn't a member of the Studio, he kept accosting Mike Gazzo to give him a part in *A Hatful of Rain.* Because he made the rounds as often as I did, we ran into each other somewhere on Broadway almost every day. I thought he was a super guy. We used to stand and gab, laugh and giggle, make silly gestures, and gossip about the kids in the Studio. It was fun to know him because there was nothing introverted or brooding about Steve McQueen.

As warm and close as our relationship was and remained, we never became lovers. Steve got the recognition he fought so hard for. Yet, sometimes, when we got together in Hollywood, I felt that he was forcing himself to carry too heavy a burden. In 1968 I moved to Europe, and I didn't see Steve again during the remaining years of his life. But friendship transcends time and distance. Perhaps I'll meet him on some street corner in Heaven, where we can stand and gab, laugh and giggle, make silly gestures, and gossip about life on Earth.

Jimmy Dean was someone that I came in contact with so frequently that I considered him a part of my community. And there were others whom I also felt close to even though our thoughts were seldom articulated.

There was someone else whom I only stared at. This other fellow had a different aura than Dean, but was just as interesting and mysterious. He was strongly built, exuded masculinity, was dark, and at times even looked menacing. Even today, I am still hypnotized by him.

Every time we meet the moment is suspended, we stare transfixedly like two cobras, and after an indefinable length of time, one of us breaks the spell by saying hi. I think I must always be the first one to break. If not, I should have long ago been drawn into the depths of those eyes and swallowed up. To this day I still experience this sensory tingle which I first responded to years and years ago—and in a less personal way, I feel it every time I see a Charles Bronson film.

The rehearsals for *A Hatful of Rain* were in the late afternoons and evenings in order to leave the days free for job hunting and work. Jeff Hayden had told me that he had never permitted Eva to attend those rehearsals alone, and now I understood why. Jeff has always been a perfect gentleman and with him sitting on the sidelines, the "boys" would have controlled themselves. With me, it was like one woman being thrown into an army barracks. I heard words and expressions that I had never heard before and wondered at the need men have for such extensive ball-scratching.

I was the only woman, the only non-Italian, the only non-member, and the only novice to the "method." In my acting classes, each of us had gotten on the stage and done a sense memory exercise under Lee Strasberg's close supervision. When a student chose an emotional subject and gave signs of getting out of control, Lee would deftly pull in the reins. In the loft, however, surrounded by the Studio "Mafia" (so nicknamed because they were a clique of boisterous, volatile Italians), I often found myself quite unnerved. I was terrified during the fight rehearsals. Violence was the theme of the play and there was a lot of it, but after a few weeks I learned to trust the professionalism of our mafia: Ben Gazzara, Tony Franciosa, Henry Silva, Mike Gazzo, and our director, Frank Corsaro, were all highly skillful and never hurt one another, but in the beginning I feared for my life and everyone else's.

In my acting classes we had only reached the first level of simple improvisations. In the loft I was suddenly required to plunge into the deep end of my darkest, most concealed emotional pool. These improvisations left me unsure, unstable, and very giddy.

Mike Gazzo had sketched the characters, plot, and situations. He didn't want to commit the play to a final draft without the actors' contributions. As we improvised, Mike sat with paper and pencil, making notes of any dialogue or behavior that enhanced the script. Over the months and months of improvisation, we naturally threw away more than we kept, but we uncovered the subtle values. Now and then, not being tied to set patterns led to marvelous, spontaneous moments, moments which we tried to retain with the help of our director, Frank Corsaro.

The object of these exercises was for the actor to be totally uninhibited and allow the make-believe character to fuse with his or her own personality. In this way we hoped to create an authentic character that would be truthful in word, gesture, and movement. The trap for the inexperienced person is in losing the ability to tell where make-believe finishes and you begin. I fell into that trap.

Now it was my turn to unnerve the mafia boys. When I did my crying scene, I worked myself into such a state of hysteria that the entire action of the play ground to a halt. The fellows stood around helplessly until my sobs subsided. Hank Silva was playing the drug pusher who supplied my husband, Ben Gazzara, with his fix, and he was supposed to make his entrance at the end of that scene. He had to wait in the doorway for twenty minutes or so until I regained control of myself. When Hank was finally able to make his entrance, he encountered my next emotion: wrath. It was very fortunate that none of the boys "rough-housed" me because I pulled out all the stops. Poor Hank made his entrance only to be pounced upon, slapped, kicked, and bitten. Hank's character was a thoroughly evil and vicious criminal, whereas in real life he is a gentle person and very respectful toward women. At my onslaught, Hank, who would have killed me had he stayed in character, merely stood there trying to protect his hair and eyeglasses.

My love scenes with Ben Gazzara were improvised with such abandon that I found myself unable to contain my passion.

Against all custom, Mike Gazzo, as writer, and Frank Corsaro, as director, were forced to intervene during my love scenes. They permitted my other emotions to run their course, but copulation on the Actors' Studio premises was forbidden.

In the other emotional scenes, I gradually learned how to keep the intensity, but to harness and curb my reactions to the requirements of the play. But in the love scenes I remained totally out of control. I was shaken so badly that I couldn't recover. It was difficult for me even to hold my cup of coffee during the break.

Normally, off stage, I thought it best to keep my eyes averted, but one evening I was too curious and had to know how Ben was composing himself. I glanced over and noticed that he was trembling so much that his coffee was spilling into the saucer. I then saw that he was looking at me. Neither of us looked away.

After rehearsal he waited for me in the hall. When I came out, he didn't speak but took me into his arms and kissed me for a long time. The next thing I knew, we were running to my apartment to realize what, up to now, had only been make-believe.

Both of us were swept away by lust. It didn't matter that I didn't own a bed. We tore off our clothes, and we rolled on the floor and abandoned ourselves to frantic, passionate lovemaking.

There was never any doubt about our relationship—we weren't in love, it was purely physical. In fact, we were each in love with someone else. Ben was married, and I was involved with Jack. We might have felt guilty but we were on a runaway roller coaster and it was too rapid and too thrilling to stop. Weeks went by before we could even catch our breath. It was a love affair that lasted for months and months, or at least as long as the project. Once *A Hatful of Rain* was over, we drifted out of character and returned to being ourselves. It took a great deal of persuasion, but eventually we were both able to return to our original partners.

When we presented *A Hatful of Rain* in a week of performances at the Actors' Studio, most of the important producers, directors, and agents came to see us. It was at one of these performances that I first met Elia Kazan. He was the director I wanted most to work with, and I was so dumbstruck the night he was in the audience, that I could barely be heard. I gave the worst performance of the week. The agents from MCA (Music Corporation of America)—largest and most influential artist agency around—saw the production, and I couldn't believe my good fortune when they offered to take me on as a client.

There was big excitement at the Actors' Studio when Shelley Winters announced that she wanted to be a member and that she was willing to take the audition. We were all impressed that such a famous star would be willing to risk rejection. It was the first time that a movie star had come to the Studio; all the other names had been students first and then gained their reputations in films.

Shelley is completely down-to-earth. She has such *joie de vivre* that it makes you feel good just to be in the same room with her. I was crazy about her from the moment we were introduced, although I had every reason to dislike her. *A Hatful of Rain* was being produced on Broadway, with everyone from the original cast except me. My part had been given to Shelley! It was a bitter pill to swallow after all the months of hard work, but I had to make myself understand that Shelley Winters was a name for the marquee. Later, when I saw her in the part, I had to admit reluctantly that she was the better choice. (That project, by the way, went full circle; the original creator of the role, Eva Marie Saint, played in the movie version.)

One night after having seen the preview of a new play, Shelley and I were walking down the street. Most of the time, she wasn't recognized because of her odd clothes and the flowered bandana she constantly wore to conceal her hair. Passing an Italian restaurant, we heard lovely guitar music. Without warning, Shelley grabbed me by the hand and pulled me after her down the steps into the place. The guitarist was playing, "Where have all the young men gone?" Shelley tore the flowered scarf from her head, waved it at the patrons, and in a loud, whining voice sang out, "Where have all my husbands gone?" She was recognized instantly by the overjoyed owner. He ushered us in and presented us with a lavish complimentary meal. Shelley, who had been married to the Italian actor Vittorio Gassman, had learned all the romantic Italian songs. Her unique renditions had everyone in the restaurant laughing and crying. By 2:00 A.M. the guitarist had had too much wine to continue standing, Shelley was still in the middle of the room singing, and I had finished two five-course meals all by myself.

One day I was on my way to the MCA offices on Madison Avenue, when a friend of mine stopped me on the corner: "Carroll," he said, "you are just the person I have been looking for!" He then began to tell me enthusiastically about his plans for us to do a scene together and show it to MCA. He was one of the most attractive guys I knew and even if I hadn't gone for his idea, I still wouldn't have refused to rehearse the scene with him and help him in the audition. As it was, he had a terrific idea. He felt that we would be perfect casting for the romantic leads in the movie of *Picnic*. Daniel Taradash was tentatively set to direct it, and MCA felt that they would be able to get him to look at our audition if they themselves were convinced of the casting.

My friend and I worked together and put on the scene from *Picnic* twice at the MCA offices. The agents and Taradash all felt that we were perfect casting for the parts and that we had wonderful chemistry.

The rehearsals had been most enjoyable. My friend was a warm, personable guy who had talent, a special magnetism, and the most beautiful clear blue eyes I have ever seen. He had been signed by Warners to a seven-year contract and felt that Warners had ruined his career by making him appear in a ridiculous film called *The Silver Chalice*.

Josh Logan replaced Taradash, and Logan chose Kim Novak and William Holden for *Picnic*, so Carroll Baker and Paul Newman had to wait for other roles to achieve their film successes.

Picnic was only one of many important projects that I auditioned for, because word was out on the Broadway grapevine that a twenty-three-year-old blonde actress was showing exceptional promise. Instead of straining to get into interviews, I was now being invited to read for Broadway plays and Warner Brothers, Twentieth Century-Fox, and Columbia had all put out feelers about a possible seven-year contract.

My first major break came when I won the ingenue role in Robert Anderson's play *All Summer Long,* which was to star John Kerr. Bob Anderson had previously written the highly successful *Tea and Sympathy,* which had starred Deborah Kerr and made John Kerr (no relation) an overnight sensation.

During the first day of readings, the director, Alan Schneider, made me do the hysterical crying scene about ten times until he was convinced that I would be able to maintain a high emotional level throughout a run of performances. By the end of the day I was totally wrung out, but I knew that the part was mine.

The day I signed that contract for my first major role on Broadway, I got on the bus hugging that piece of paper to my chest as if someone might steal it from me. In celebration, I bought myself my first new dress in ages. In fact, although Jack and I had decided to live together at my apartment and pool our resources, making the rent payments was a struggle. We ate nothing but macaroni-and-cheese dinners because they were filling and cost about ten cents.

The dress I bought was white silk cotton with a floral design. It had a scoop neck, a tight bodice, a large soft belt, and a full skirt that was held out by a crinoline petticoat. I thought it was the prettiest dress I had ever owned, partly because I had bought it for myself and because it was the symbol of a shiny new career. I sashayed out of my apartment and down the streets of Manhattan on that brightest of all spring days, with that beautiful windblown skirt and petticoat swooshing to my step. As I hustled past a black man sitting on a brownstone stoop, he gaped at me and muttered, "Lord save us from sin."

I shuffled up and down Broadway feeling that that magical street in some way now belonged to me. I hoped to run into friends to share my good news with, but it was one of those rare occasions when I didn't see a soul I knew. It never occurred to me to have lunch anywhere but the automat, so I went, wearing my new finery, to have a blueberry muffin and coffee. As I turned from the slot with my cup of coffee, someone bumped into me and the coffee spilled down the front of my lovely new dress. I stood there looking in horror at the stain that would probably never come out.

I heard a man saying, "I'm sorry, I'm sorry," over and over again. When I looked up, I saw that he was a half-starved little tramp. "I'm so sorry, Miss," he said. "Please, I'll give you the ten cents for another cup of coffee."

My reviews in *All Summer Long* couldn't have been better if I had written them myself. Every one of them was glowing and I was flushed with success. The movie studios began to make even better offers but my agents and I were cautious. Paul Newman had had a difficult time rebuilding his career after the disastrous *Silver Chalice*, and Broadway was still lamenting the way Hollywood had misused the talents of that fine young actress Anne Bancroft, by putting her in B-grade films.

Within weeks of my rave reviews, I was offered a starring part in a television show, a half-hour mystery theatre called "The Web." It was the first part I had ever been offered outright without auditioning. The story was about a mentally disturbed girl, which made it a very flashy acting part. The male role went to a dashing, handsome newcomer who, even in the early days of his career, was a forceful actor of considerable talent: Jack Lord.

George Stevens, the great film director *(Shane, A Place in the Sun)*, saw "The Web" the night it aired. George was preparing to make *Giant*, and he asked to screen-test me for the part of Luz Benedict II. Elizabeth Taylor, Rock Hudson, and James Dean (who had made a hit in his first film, *East of Eden*) were the stars. Warner Brothers was anxious to have me if I agreed to a seven-year contract.

While "The Web" also won me accolades, I wasn't so sure of myself. I wanted to stay in New York and continue my acting classes with Strasberg. I had been developing my inner concentration and was able to release emotions more readily, but I was still too shy and frightened and inexperienced to be able to give a relaxed performance. For that reason I had turned down a lovely romantic comedy with Fred Astaire called *Daddy Long Legs*. The offers were coming in just a little too soon. I felt that I needed more time before I could unlock the secrets of the "method" and let them work for me. But my agents were also warning that I dare not let every chance pass me by while I was the "hot new girl."

Jack and I sat up all night discussing the *Giant* offer, and whether or not I should go to Hollywood. I felt completely insecure about myself as an actress in the film medium, but Jack maintained that the best way to learn was to put myself in the capable hands of one of the greatest film directors, George Stevens. And it was Jack who persuaded me not to pass up this splendid opportunity.

Jack and I had also talked many times about some day getting married. If I were to leave for Hollywood, Jack wouldn't be able to leave the stage production he was preparing, and he would have to remain in the East. Realizing that, we both panicked and decided that we had to get married immediately.

The first person I told was Paula Strasberg, and she instantly offered to help with all the arrangements and even to hold the reception for us.

Everything had to be done practically overnight, but I had always dreamed of wearing a white wedding gown. Even with so little time, I set about making one. That meant no sleep from the moment I bought the material, and the morning of the wedding I had to get some of my friends to pin the back of the dress while I pinned the last of the pearls onto my veil.

Paula and Lee Strasberg found a rabbi who was willing to marry us even though I wasn't Jewish, and the ceremony as well as our beautiful wedding reception was held in their apartment on April 3, 1955.

And on April 5, 1955, I was on a plane to California. Jack and I kissed and said a tearful "See you soon," but a leading New York gossip columnist wrote: "Carroll Baker and Jack Garfein, who were married two days ago, have just called the whole thing off, and Carroll is on her way to Hollywood."

Herschel, age five, and Blanche, age six

Jack makes ice cream cones for the kids

The Garfeins with Lord Olivier

The Garfein family

Mother, the children and I visit Rome
in 1968

My first trip to Paris—and haute couture!

The famous transparent dress,
courtesy of Balmain

The Carroll Baker Film Festival in San Francisco, 1979

The stage production of *Motive* with my present husband, Donald Burton, 1978

Chapter Nine

FIRST IMPRESSIONS OF HOLLYWOOD: 1955

All of my life I had had the fantasy that Hollywood one day would demand my presence. Now, here it was! Hollywood had indeed summoned me. But what was my reaction? I was full of trepidation! My husband practically had to push me onto that airplane.

It didn't make much sense. After all, on my first trip to Hollywood, I had been ready to hurl myself into the mouth of the MGM lion without a second thought. But this time I was aware of what was expected of me, of how difficult it was to make good, and of the perfection that I now demanded of myself. Above all, I was dying of homesickness. I didn't want to leave my city or my two-day-old marriage. I loved my new husband, and wanted to be with him.

I was seated in the first-class section of the plane reading *The History of the Jews.* Someone leaned over me and asked, "What's a *shiksa* like you doing reading *The History of the Jews?*" I looked up and saw one of my idols, Danny Kaye!

Danny was traveling with the movie director Mervyn LeRoy. "Mervyn," he called over to him, "come here and see what this *shiksa* is reading!" They introduced themselves and asked about the purpose of my trip. When I told them, LeRoy simply wished me the best of luck, but Danny asked why I wanted to go to Hollywood. We spoke seriously for a long time, and I was touched by his concern for me. (Danny has always had a concern and a compassion for young people. He's given so generously of his time as the international ambassador at large for UNICEF.) He must have sensed something about me, maybe that I wasn't sufficiently mature or experienced to be able to look at things objectively.

"Go back!" he said. "Look, kid, that town is not for you. My advice is to turn around and take the next flight back to New York. Forget Hollywood. It isn't for everybody and in my opinion, it's not for you. Turn right around and go back!"

At the Los Angeles Airport, a bland young man in a Brooks Brothers suit met me with a chauffeur-driven limousine and escorted me to a large commercial hotel on Hollywood Boulevard. Once I was checked in, the bland young representative from Warner Brothers hurriedly departed. My appointment at the studio was not until 9:30 the next morning, endless hours away. I paced up and down the room and looked out my windows at the traffic below, recalling my first experience in L.A., when I had been a prisoner in just such a hotel suite. With that thought, I fled the hotel into the streets and began a very long walk.

Most people visiting Hollywood for the first time are in for a big disappointment: it is not what one might expect—it's totally ordinary! For years the Chamber of Commerce has been trying to correct this impression, but without a great deal of success. I stood on the corner of Hollywood and Vine, that magical-sounding location which stirs the imagination of people all over the world, and was deflated by its utter mundaneness. I could have been standing on a street corner in Greensburg!

The next morning, waiting for me in the lobby was a tall, gaunt man wearing a pin-striped suit, white spats, and a bowler hat. His English gentleman's pose seemed like a facade borrowed from a British play seen in some American school production. In clipped syllables he introduced himself as Jack Warner's personal secretary (his name I vaguely recall as being Charles). He was so fascinatingly false, I had difficulty concentrating on what he was saying during our drive to the studio.

We were on and off the Hollywood Freeway and into Burbank in ten minutes. Our limousine stopped for a red light beside some buildings that looked like airplane hangars. When the light changed, we turned right, into the entrance. It was Warner Brothers. We halted beside the guard's booth for an identity check.

The guard was slumped with his head hung forward, and his cap (which was sizes too large) covering his face. Charles became theatrically indignant because the guard wasn't saluting him and granting us entrance. I heard a voice, a familiar voice that seemed to be coming from under the cap, whispering, "Carroll, Car-roll, CARROLL!"

To Charles's astonishment, I hopped out of the limo and dashed over to the guard's booth.

"What kind of a trick are you playing?" I asked the crown of the cap.

The brim turned upward and a small face peeked out—the eyes a bit too close together, a crooked grin—Jimmy Dean!

The real guard moved into view and over to the limo, saying, "Sorry, sir, Mr. Dean wanted to surprise her, and I knew you wouldn't mind."

Jimmy hissed, "Quick, let's get out of here." Stepping out of the booth, he took me by the hand and pulled me around the barrier to a big silver motorbike. Jimmy climbed on, started it up, and motioned for me to straddle behind him.

"Where are you taking me?" I screeched over the roar.

"Just hang on," he ordered, "don't tense up. I'm good on these things."

"I'm not afraid," I shouted, "but where are you taking me? What about my appointments? I'm supposed to be meeting the big shots at this very moment!"

"You've got to treat these guys like shit," he shouted back. "It's the only thing they understand."

I never should have said that I wasn't afraid, because that challenged Jimmy, and he deliberately stepped on the gas. We flew over a bump and did a dip which took my breath away. My thighs gripped cold metal, my arms tightened around his waist, and I buried my chest into his back. I could feel the heat of his body, the contractions of his muscles, and the wind tearing at every inch of me that wasn't pressed into either him or the machine. The combined sensations stunned me so that when we swerved deeply to one side, I wondered with a curious detachment if my tilted foot and ankle were going to scrape the pavement.

The bike slowed. I slid my head under Jimmy's armpit so that I could see what was ahead. We were entering the back lot and approaching the replica of a small American town. We stopped before entering the deserted tree-lined street. Once Jimmy had cut the motor and braced us, we remained motionless, with me still hugging his back, but now affectionately. There were no people here except us, but it was teeming with ghosts, so we waited and listened, not wanting to impose on them too abruptly. The ghosts dispersed and hushed, so with another squeeze I ended the embrace.

When I released Jimmy, he swung off the bike and sauntered up the empty street to a white frame house. It had a perfect lawn, a big oak tree, and a wide front porch. It even had a white picket fence.

As I approached the sidewalk and then the white picket fence, I began to hum "Tea for Two." Jimmy chuckled and squatted on the porch steps. I waltzed past him and perched Doris Day–like on the front-porch swing.

"Gee, this is nice," I murmured, and swung softly back and forth.

"Yeah," he droned. "I come here often."

There was a long silence. Then he added, "When they're not filming, it's always this quiet."

There was another even longer silence, and I was transported to all the other times from my seat in a dark movie house that I had lived on this same street.

"I must have seen this street in a hundred movies," I whispered.

"Yeah, it's nice. Kinda reminds me of home," he said to the big oak tree.

We became lost in our own thoughts.

I thought about Jimmy. He certainly had changed. He had never been this outgoing before, at least not with me. In fact, this was the first time that I had ever been alone with him. Wasn't it? Yes. I couldn't remember Jimmy's ever having said three words to me before. When had I seen him last? Just before he left to film *East of Eden*. Maybe his success had given him more confidence? Why was I spending so much time thinking about him? What about my appointments? What would Jack Warner think of me? After all, Warners had paid my transportation and expenses. It had been understood that if George Stevens gave the go-ahead after my screen test, I would be under contract to the studio at a salary of $750 a week with an increase every year for seven years. Jimmy was already under contract to them with *East of Eden*. It was all right for him to act the bad boy. He was their golden hope. But what would happen to me? But did I care? Did I really want to stay? How did I feel about Hollywood?

Jimmy intercepted my wavelength. "How do you feel about Hollywood?"

"Well, so far I hate it. I'm in a businessman's hotel on upper Hollywood Boulevard and it's horrible. There'll be a lot of waiting around, and I'll probably go nuts or forget the whole thing and go back to New York."

"Naw, you can't do that," he chuckled. "We need your talent here."

I didn't know how to reply to that so there was another long silence. Did Jimmy think I was talented? Strange, I didn't know he had ever seen my work. Maybe he had. Maybe, as was his habit, he had slipped in unnoticed to a performance of *Hatful* or one of my Strasberg classes.

Finally he spoke again, "Clifford Odets is staying at a place called the Chateau Marmont. That's where a lot of the New York people stay. You'd like it. You ought to move there."

I made a mental note of the name and then began to fantasize about how I would change hotels. Who would I ask for directions? Who would I have to inform at Warners? I thought of asking Jimmy but I didn't. The questions drifted out of my brain and intermingled with the dust that was circling my head in the sunlight. When the dust specks carrying my thoughts rolled into his sphere, Jimmy caught my questions. "Call your agents and have them make the arrangements," he said aloud to my unspoken questions.

A voice in my head replied silently, of course that's what I'll do.

I looked over at Jimmy because he was thinking about me.

Without returning my look, he knew that he had my complete attention, so he addressed his boots and the porch steps. "I'm going to do another film before I begin *Giant*. The script is crap but the characters are very good. I think if it is cast right we can make a hell of a film. I want you to play the girl's part. The director, Nick Ray, is a good guy. I'll get him to call you at the Chateau Marmont. Come on, I'll take you back," he said to his blue jeans as they moved down the steps and across the path to the picket fence.

He passed through the gate as I was leaving the swing and asking, "But I'm only here to screen-test for *Giant*. Maybe I won't get it, and maybe they won't want me for any other film?"

Jimmy straddled the bike. "Get on," he said, impatiently gunning the motor. "The screen test is only a ploy so that you won't ask for too much money." Then he continued over the acceleration noise, "Their tongues are hanging out to get you."

He whizzed me back to the guard at the front gate, and when I had debiked, he whizzed away again, throwing over his shoulder the command, "Meet me at the commissary at 12:30."

Good grief, how was I supposed to meet him at 12:30 when the plan was for me to have lunch with someone from the publicity department?

"Miss Baker, Mr. Warner is expecting you in his office!" I turned at the sound of the guard's voice and saw that he was standing with Dean Martin.

I must have paled, because Dean Martin rushed over to hold me up. That only made matters worse. When he took my arm, I was swooning.

"Don't call for an escort, Joe," Martin said to the guard. "I'll take Miss Baker to see Jack."

Dean Martin was one of the most naturally funny men I had ever met. I've forgotten the specific things he said, but I do remember how my awe of him and my fear of Warner slipped away as I giggled all the way across the lot. We burst into Warner's office without giving the secretary time to announce us.

Upon seeing Martin, Warner came from behind the desk and began doing a tap dance! Then they went into a comedy routine! They must have done those jokes countless times before because their timing was faultless. I was never introduced to Warner, and the only acknowledgement of my presence was an order directed at a young man sitting on the sofa: "Take her to see the pictures we're shooting, Bill," Warner slipped in between the gags. Bill and I left the office as Warner and Martin were going into the same routine for the third time.

Outside the office I said, "My name is Carroll Baker."

"Yes, I know who you are. Jack knows, too. Jack knows, too. Don't pay any attention, Jack always goofs off that way. I know, I'm married to his daughter. My name is Bill Orr. I'm a vice president of the company."

Bill Orr took me to watch the filming on the various sound stages. Five films were being made on the Warner lot at that time, and he pointed out with sadness that I had missed the "good old days"—before television when all twenty-some sound stages would have been busy. (Later I was to think of 1955 as the "good old days" because I witnessed the movies dwindle from five on one lot to five on all the lots combined, finally, to one movie in all of Hollywood and to its near demise.)

At noon Bill ended my tour at the publicity department and said goodbye. There I had to sit and wait for someone to take charge of me. At twelve twenty-five, I decided that if I got up and walked out, no one would notice. No one did.

Unlike Metro Goldwyn Mayer, Warners was small, friendly, and easy to find my way around on. Jimmy was waiting on his motorbike outside the commissary building, surrounded by a group of extras who were obviously fans. Added to my joy of having a friend in this strange place, I was proud that James Dean was waiting for me.

Jimmy took me through the large cafeteria where the crew members, supporting actors, and extras were eating. My previously shy buddy greeted scores of people, many of them by name. We approached the glass doors to the Green Room where the leading actors, stars, and executives dined. It seemed quite formal as well as small and exclusive, and I suddenly felt out of place. I asked Jimmy if we couldn't eat in the cafeteria. He laughed at me, then he marched us straight in, and we took a center table without allowing the hostess to do her job of seating us.

I ordered a Betty Grable salad, but Jimmy didn't bother to order lunch and spent his time table hopping. (Was this the same boy? Was this the Jimmy who normally appeared and disappeared without so much as a word?) Hedda Hopper entered from the street door and Jimmy leaped up to greet her. She swept in with a flourish, her flowered chiffon dress and enormous picture hat fluttering in the crosscurrent of the warm outside breeze and the cold of the air conditioning. It *was* a dramatic entrance that deserved recognition, but for a moment I was afraid that Jimmy was going to throw himself on his knees in front of her. All attention was focused on her conspicuous arrival and his extravagant greeting, so that when they both turned and looked at me, every head in the Green Room followed suit. At this rush of instant notoriety the blood surged in my cheeks, and I raised the menu to hide the hideous blush. Jimmy then motioned for me to come over, and with acute agony I rose from the table and walked those ten thousand miles from my chair to the doorway.

Hedda spoke loudly enough to inform a football stadium. "So you are the beautiful, talented New York actress Jimmy has been raving about?" Those of you who blush know that the harder you try to stop, the redder you become. I went from red to brilliant fuchsia.

"How charming," Hedda continued. "I didn't know young girls blushed any longer." Fortunately she went on talking, because I was incapable of opening my mouth. "You must see me tomorrow," she ordered. "This is my office number. Call me this afternoon or this evening without fail. We must meet no later than tomorrow."

She thrust her card forward and I took it obediently, but the action was that of a robot who hadn't been programmed to speak.

Jimmy said, "I gave my word that you would let Hedda interview you first—before you spoke to Louella."

The glass doors opposite us opened and mercifully the spotlight swung to Elizabeth Taylor and Montgomery Clift.

With one motion, Jimmy jerked his head and pushed me in their direction. We left Hedda Hopper as though she didn't exist. When I looked back at her apologetically to say something like "Excuse us," Hedda's full attention was riveted on Taylor and Clift. Jimmy and I might as well have vanished.

Jimmy gave me another shove, apparently because I was blocking his progress—and when he spoke it seemed like he was talking to himself. "Elizabeth is here to see George Stevens. Let's go over to George's table and meet her."

"You go. I'll come later." I said it to no one in particular because I had become invisible.

Having turned into a wraith, I next materialized in the ladies' room, where I ran cold water over my face, the back of my neck, and my wrists. It was all too much for one day. My official meeting with Stevens was scheduled for two o'clock and I had no intention of barging in on him during his luncheon with Elizabeth. I waited in the ladies' room for a long time, wondering what I would do if Jimmy again pointed me out and insisted that I come to the table to meet Stevens and Taylor. That worry had all been for nothing, because the moment I re-entered the Green Room, I still felt nonexistent. Not a soul could see me. I was amused, however, because I realized that these people had been raised on *Topper* and *The Invisible Man.* There was only one other person eating alone, a man who faced me—but he too looked straight through me.

My Betty Grable salad had arrived. Upon swallowing a tomato wedge, I must have suddenly reappeared, because the waitress came over to me and said, "Miss Baker, would you like to open a charge account and sign for your lunch?"

The solitary man sprang to his feet and grabbed the check out of her hand. "I'll take that," he barked.

"Miss Baker," he said, with more than a little desperation in his voice, "where in the world have you been?"

He turned out to be the tardy publicity man assigned to me. For the next hour I recited my life story, addressing the account to Elizabeth Taylor six tables away, while the publicity man watched every glittering entrance and swirling exit without even making the slightest pretense of listening or taking notes. Studying Elizabeth those six tables away, I was amazed at how self-conscious she was. She had been touted as the most beautiful woman in the world—imagine her ever feeling uncomfortable? The world had been at her feet since she was a child. George Stevens seemed perfectly at ease and interested in their conversation. It occurred to me that he was an extraordinary man because he was the only person in the restaurant who was paying attention solely to his own table. Even Elizabeth, if she was listening at all, was only listening with half a mind. The other half was concentrated on the rest of us concentrating on her.

I was amazed that she was so overweight. Even that gorgeous face seemed slightly puffy.

The publicity man rose. I thought for a moment I might have been talking out loud about Elizabeth, and he had risen in protest. In fact, he rose to make a point. "Now don't forget what I said!" (Had he spoken? That was news to me.) Seeing my blank look he leaned over, blocking my view of Elizabeth and forcing me to listen to him. "You are to go and visit Louella Parsons as soon as possible. Louella and Jack Warner are very close friends. Louella has always been good to our product. Your first interview must be with Louella. Do you understand?"

Jimmy passed our table, ignoring the publicity man, and asked me, "Where have you been?"

Chapter

Ten

SCREEN AND OTHER TESTS

My meeting with George Stevens was not the interview or audition I had expected. He complimented me on being a fine artist, and told me that the job didn't in any way depend upon the screen test. The part was unquestionably mine. The purpose of the test, he said, was to give him an opportunity to light me and to see my hair, makeup, and costumes. So far he had been very disappointed with the makeup department. They had been making his people look unreal. He cautioned me, "Try to get them to keep you natural. I want to see you just as you are now."

The next morning the head of the makeup department and six other makeup artists held a conference during which they took turns pointing out my defects. They worked on me for hours and when they had finished, I looked in the mirror at an extremely glamorous girl who, from a distance and in shadow, might have been mistaken for Dorothy Malone. Now, there is nothing wrong with Dorothy Malone; she is lovely. It is just that I was a bad copy, and I didn't look anything like my mother's child.

George Stevens was busy all morning and I didn't have any other allies, so I was forced into the still gallery to be immortalized wearing someone else's face.

When George finally saw me, he hit the roof. "Carroll is unrecognizable! The test will be postponed and she will come in to makeup every day until you manage to make her look like herself."

After five more tries, even George Stevens was ready to compromise and agree to my Sandra Dee image. When I realized how clever these people were at re-creating famous faces, I had an inspiration—they could make me look like Elizabeth Taylor's daughter! That solved the problem. They darkened my hair to brown and gave me thick eyebrows and eyelashes. The makeup artists and hairdressers felt that they were being creative, I felt in character, and George Stevens was thrilled at the resemblance.

What a joy it was to move to the Chateau Marmont! It was more like living in your aunt's run-down mansion than in a sterile, impersonal hotel. In fact, there were two little old ladies who ran the place and took a personal interest in me. When I ascended the grand staircase to my rooms, those rooms greeted me with the comforting smell of dust and times gone by.

If I wanted company, all I had to do was to walk down to the swimming pool where it always seemed like there was a party going on. Clifford Odets, Carol Channing, and Gore Vidal, all of whom I knew from New York, were also staying at the hotel.

Nicholas Ray, the director, kept a bungalow at the Chateau. He was a nice guy, very bright, with a sound knowledge of moviemaking. *Rebel Without a Cause* was being rewritten. Although I wouldn't have called the script "crap" as Jimmy had, it did need work. With Nick directing, I felt that the possibility was there for a good film. The character studies were certainly strong.

On my fourth day, after doing an early morning costume fitting, and even though it was only 10:00 A.M., I was finished for the day at Warners. I planned to go back to the Chateau, change into a bathing suit, and relax by the pool. However, when I picked up my key, there were two messages in my box. One of them was to call Louella Parsons. (Oh, no! Now what would I do? I hadn't yet called Hedda Hopper as I had promised. Maybe I had put both columnists out of my mind, thinking they would forget me.) Before I stewed over that any further I decided to return the other call, which was from Mr. Warner's secretary Charles.

I assumed that Charles's message would be some simple request, but what Charles had to say also threw me into a tizzy. Jack Warner was inviting me to a dinner party at his home that evening. My first reaction was that I couldn't go. A party of Hollywood notables at Warner's home . . . I wasn't ready to jump into a glittery social evening . . . I wouldn't feel comfortable . . . nobody knew me . . . I had nothing to wear. But the more I hemmed and hawed, the more insistent Charles became: it was out of the question for me to refuse Mr. Warner's invitation. I was the guest of honor. It would be horrible and rude for me to refuse. The wardrobe department would send a selection of dresses over to the Chateau for me to choose from. One of the guests would be Madame Chiang Kai-shek, and she was anxious to meet me. He, Charles, would escort me. He and the limousine would be at my hotel at precisely 6:45 P.M. I was to be punctual.

Well, the day was totally ruined: a dinner party to worry about and the immediate problem of Hedda and Louella. (Why did other people always force me into these uncomfortable situations and impossible dilemmas?)

Warners had wanted me to talk to Louella first, but I had promised Hedda the first interview. After an hour of agonizing, I decided to try to see both of them on the same day. I called Hedda and she asked me to come right over.

Once the decision was made, I thought the interview itself would be a piece of cake. Not so. Hedda didn't want to know anything about my professional life. She wanted me to say that I was having a love affair with Jimmy Dean. It was so distasteful and unfair! Why should I be put in the position of having to deny such a blatant falsehood? I got very upset because I didn't want Jack to read a stupid rumor in a gossip column that might cause him embarrassment or worry while he was three thousand miles away, trying to put on a play.

Still shaking from that interview, I rang Louella and went to see her. If she asked me about Hedda, I planned to tell the truth.

But Louella didn't mention Hedda. I relaxed much more with Louella because she seemed like such a sweet, motherly type. She wanted to know all the things I liked talking about: my family background, my marriage, my career. But as I was about to leave, she made a threat which revealed her true colors—a threat that hit me harder than anything Hedda, who was tough and straightforward, had said, because I was completely off my guard and because it was so bizarre.

"Dear, I want you to remember something. Marriage is sacred." (I knew that Louella thought of herself as a good Catholic.)

"Yes," I agreed, backing toward the door.

But Louella wasn't quite finished. "I want you to remember something, dear," she continued. "If you ever leave Jack Garfein, you'll be finished in this town."

I stood there with my mouth open, sure that I had not heard her correctly. (Leave Jack? But I loved him. She couldn't possibly have threatened me about leaving Jack.)

"What?"

"Remember, dear, marriage is sacred. If you ever leave Jack Garfein, you'll be finished in this town. I'll crucify you."

Still reeling from my first Hollywood interviews, I had to try to collect myself for my first Hollywood dinner party. Hanging in my room on a portable dress rack were five of the most outrageous cocktail dresses I had ever seen. I suspected that it was a practical joke. No one could possibly have such a total lack of taste. They belonged in some extravagant operetta. What could I possibly wear of my own? Since I couldn't compete with the stars who would probably be there, I opted for simplicity. I chose a plain, grey wraparound dress and a tiny gold choker. With any luck I would match the draperies and go unnoticed.

I remember so vividly the details of that evening because at the time my own reactions and feelings were so very strong. I wonder, in comparison, how I would react today to a similar type of evening? I still wouldn't consider it commonplace, but I believe (and certainly hope) that I would be much more tolerant!

Charles arrived precisely on time and said that we only had a short drive. We exchanged some smaller-than-small talk, and I commented on the beautiful golf course and country club we were driving through. Charles stated flatly that these were Mr. Warner's grounds. Then I saw the colonial mansion in the distance, with its spotlights and fountains and uniformed "slaves."

We found ourselves in a long line of cars in Warner's driveway. It was like a procession timed to arrive exactly at the appointed hour. Parking attendants parked the cars of guests who drove themselves. A butler in full livery was standing at the open front door, and Warner was in the main hallway, ready to greet his guests.

Everyone crowded into the entrance hall until all the guests had been acknowledged and permission was given to adjourn to a sitting room. In the crush I got trapped behind what I thought was a huge Chinese lion. The house was like a museum of fine artworks where the curator had gone mad. Every style, period, and country were thrown together in great confusion. The overcrowding and junk-shot stacking made it almost impossible to isolate an object for observation or admiration. Now the guests were assembled in a body, and we were invited to enter. Warner dislodged me from behind the lion, saying that it was from some dynasty, "Ming" or "Ping."

I was greeted mostly by false smiles and glazed looks. Hardly anyone listened to my name during the introductions. No doubt they felt that there was no reason to remember it or me. I blessed Ireland and heaven for having created the divine Maureen O'Hara and all the powers that be for having placed her next to me at dinner. An interest in other people came naturally to Maureen. Her attitude toward herself was neither studied humility nor aggressive display. She was simply herself, and this was reflected in her choice of a dress. She wore a stylish but not outlandish pale green chiffon.

Madame Chiang Kai-shek, understandably, wore a Chinese dress of silk brocade.

Cyd Charisse was enveloped in what appeared to be white spun sugar. Have you ever been in one of those old-fashioned sweet shops and seen the twisted hard-candy ribbons? Well, this was a large one that had no discernible beginning or end. It whirled around her face and neck, yet somehow permitted the nose an escape route to acquire the necessary amount of life-sustaining oxygen. It wound stiffly and massively around her shoulders, arms, and torso and proceeded to totally engulf those fabulous legs. Her feet padded somewhere underneath, making her motions slow, like a mechanical doll. She said not one word all evening. I assumed it was because she was too busy fighting for survival within all that monstrous taffy. What a relief it must have been to her when she at last arrived home where her husband, Tony Martin, could liberate her by means of a hammer and chisel.

Elizabeth Taylor wore layers of blue cloud with white projectiles. Upon closer observation, I reckoned that the designer was inspired by the dance of the seven veils, but this being Hollywood where everything is bigger and better, it appeared more suitable for a dance of seventy-seven veils. The white projectiles were, in fact, hunting trophies acquired from dozens of ermines who had sacrificed their lives so that the world's most beautiful woman might wear their tails.

Other women wore stark black in order not to distract from their diamonds, which were large enough and numerous enough to decorate a medium-sized Christmas tree. There was much conversation about these diamonds. One woman produced from her tiny evening bag a jeweler's glass, screwed it into her eye, and scrutinized any diamond its owner wasn't afraid of having evaluated. (It now occurs to me that Elizabeth must have resolved to one day outdo them all and become the Queen of Diamonds.)

On my other side was Charles, and since we had already scraped the microbes of minuscular thought in an effort to communicate, we were now obliged to resort to nods and grunts. Madame Chiang Kai-shek was the guest of honor, but I didn't reproach Charles for having pretended that I was the chosen one. Michael Wilding was there with Elizabeth. Gene Kelly was there, but I can't remember if Betsy Blair was with him. The men all wore the standard uniform, the tuxedo, and they talked much more than the women. One actor, who will remain nameless, kept asking Jack Warner, "Jack, how long have we been friends?" Whatever the reply, the actor would continue, "Just think of that, friends all these years, and you know something? I have never worked in a Warner Brothers picture!" This actor could be relied upon to repeat that question and the ensuing astounding revelation every time there was the slightest pause in the conversation.

The cold Dom Perignom was flowing, and I held tight to the stem of my crystal glass for support, resolving to sip slowly and keep track of my consumption lest in my nervous state I should overindulge. But because each time I lowered my glass from my lips a white-gloved hand would swoop in with a bottle and replace the missing drops, this proved to be impossible.

The first course was crab in a cream sauce surrounded by what

I thought was rice, and served on a sea shell. Maureen O'Hara might have saved me from what happened next, since I had planned to observe her table manners and copy everything she did, but Maureen told me that she was allergic to shellfish and she didn't touch her crab.

Jack Warner loved to make toasts. He had already made several, and as we began to eat he also called upon individual guests to propose toasts. When he asked me to rise and say something, I had just forked a large helping of the crab and rice into my mouth. The rice was extremely hard. When I saw that no one else was eating theirs I realized to my horror that it wasn't rice at all. It was a pile of decorative pebbles! How could I discreetly spit the pebbles into my napkin when every eye was on me? I couldn't chew it and I certainly couldn't speak! With one large gulp of champagne, I swallowed the lot, stood, and with a raised and empty glass gasped, "Thank you for this lovely evening."

The toast of toasts was offered by Jack Warner. Near the end of dinner, he rose, raised his glass to Madame Chiang Kai-shek, and said, "Madame, I have only one thing to say to you—No Tickee, No Laundry!"

There followed a deadly silence. Even those who had made the greatest efforts all evening to laugh at Warner's jokes were flabbergasted.

This story has become legend, told to me as a joke countless times. It actually happened.

After dinner it was announced that the men and women would be segregated for the next half hour. The men went to a special smoking room for cigars and brandy, and the women were herded into the powder room. The powder room was perhaps twice as large as my New York apartment and was decorated entirely in varying pinks and gold. It provided conveniences by the half dozen: six vanity tables, puffs, mirrors, sinks, and even six toilet cabinets. The plush pink carpeting had such a raised, thick pile that it was nearly impossible to walk on in high heels. The windows were sumptuously draped in the finest pink-silk damask. The sinks and toilet bowls were of a rare pinkish marble and every inch of plumbing was gold-plated!

We were ushered into an enormous living room, where a full-sized movie screen descended from the far wall and we watched an as-yet-unreleased film from a competitive studio. It proved impossible to follow the story of the movie because the men never shut up. They talked out loud, commenting on every single detail of the film, criticizing each technical effect. At one moment Jack Warner moved onto the couch beside me and put his arm around me. It made my flesh crawl! How dare he take that liberty with me! Not wishing to draw any more attention than necessary to myself, I sat frozen in place until I found a seemingly casual excuse to get up. When I sat down again, it was in a small chair that would hold only one person.

At the end of the movie, everyone, as if on cue, headed into the hallway and lined up to say goodnight, and then made for their cars. I found a place at the end of the line and politely said my thanks and good-bye. But Charles made no move to call for our car or to escort me out. Almost everyone was gone when I took Charles aside and insisted that the evening was over and that I too wanted to go home. He looked at me curiously and then stated matter-of-factly, "Jack expects you to stay the night."

From the open doorway I could see Bill Orr entering his car. I flew out of the house and into the driveway after him. I opened the car door and beseeched him, "Bill, please take me home!" Warner was his boss and his father-in-law, but he agreed to drive me home without a moment's hesitation. That to me is a man!

The champagne had made me sleepy, and I welcomed my dreams, knowing that they could never be half as bad as the nightmare of a day I'd had with Hedda and Louella and Warner and that pimp secretary of his. My last thoughts were that Warners would cancel me out and that I'd have to make my reservation back to New York in the morning. Danny Kaye's words came back to me. Well, I'd be home tomorrow and good riddance to this Hollywood rubbish.

The next morning at six-thirty I was awakened by the makeup man asking me to come in for yet another trial. I was noncommittal because I had no intention of budging until Warner had had time to inform everyone that I was no longer under contract. At eight o'clock someone from wardrobe called about a fitting, and at nine the publicity department wanted to see me, but I continued to stall. By ten o'clock there was still no word about my release, so I telephoned Bill Orr and asked him if I should report to work. He said, "Of course." No one ever mentioned the incident again.

When I arrived at the studio around noon, I discovered that the Hedda-Louella feud had not been passed over so lightly. They both had columns, in different newspapers, but on the same day, each claiming that it was the first exclusive interview with Warner Brothers' new find, Carroll Baker. Louella's was a saccharin article about how I had promised her that I would love Jack Garfein through all eternity and much much beyond. Hedda's column strongly suggested that I couldn't wait to get away from Jack Garfein and run to Hollywood to be with Jimmy Dean.

Louella complained to her pal Jack Warner about her excruciating embarrassment and loss of face over claiming to have had the first exclusive interview with me and then having been proved a liar. Louella demanded blood. Someone's head had to roll. The publicity man who'd had lunch with me was fired. He in turn blamed me. He made a special point of finding me that day and spat "Well, I hope you're satisfied, you little bitch! Was it so important to have your name in both newspapers on the same day? I told you that Louella had to have the first interview. Now I've lost my job because of you, bitch!"

I took his comments personally and was terribly shocked as well as hurt. It would never have occurred to me then that I might have the power to restore his job. (Dealing with this type of situation requires an experience and sophistication which were years beyond me. True, I was caught in the middle of an altogether idiotic Hollywood power play, but if it happened today, I'd go straight to Louella Parsons and Jack Warner, assume the responsibility myself and plead for the man's job.)

While I was struggling to stay afloat on the shock waves, I still had to fulfill my obligations to the studio, and I got home late. In the meantime, Hedda's syndicated column reached my husband before I did. When I tried to telephone Jack that evening after his rehearsal, he had checked out of his hotel. The next morning he appeared unannounced at the Chateau Marmont. We could ill afford his trip or the postponement of his play, and our marriage foundation was now weakened by doubts and this display of mistrust.

So, things got "worser and worser." Someone else might have

fought back. I wish I'd had the wisdom and courage not to postpone these confrontations. I should have made my stand right then and there, but I didn't. When Jack was adamant that I turn down *Rebel Without a Cause* and return East with him, I didn't put forth any argument. The moment the screen test and preproduction were completed, he and I flew home.

In three months I was due to report back to begin filming *Giant.* My second audition at the Actors' Studio was successful, and I was accepted as a member. For those three months, I felt secure and protected being at the Actors' Studio, being in my city, New York, and being in the arms of Jack Garfein. But it was only a delusion—all of it.

Chapter Eleven

JIMMY DEAN

Carroll Baker is destined to become a great star.
—James Dean, 1955

There have been few talents to match that of James Dean's.
—Carroll Baker, 1965

The *Giant* company was in Virginia filming the courtship, marriage, and honeymoon of Leslie Lynton (Elizabeth Taylor) and Bick Benedict (Rock Hudson). Bick, as the story continued, would take his bride to her new home, the Reata Ranch in Texas. There Jett Rink (James Dean) would first appear. As Bick and Leslie raised a family and time passed, we, the next generation, would be introduced into the story: Fran Bennett as the oldest daughter, Judy; then Dennis Hopper as their only son, Jordon Benedict III; and then me as Luz Benedict II (named for my Aunt Luz, as portrayed by Mercedes McCambridge).

I got more and more excited about playing my part in this exceptional family epic. This time, I couldn't wait to get on that plane! Before I joined the unit in Marfa, Texas, the studio wanted me in Hollywood for one week of final costume fittings.

To avoid being dependent upon Warner's transportation department, I hired a car for the week—a spiffy red Ford. I checked into the Chateau Marmont where the two little old ladies, whom I had come to regard as my adopted aunts, greeted me with such warmth that I felt instantly at home.

The next morning on my way to the studio, my thoughts turned to Jimmy Dean. I wondered if he were still in town and how *Rebel Without a Cause* had turned out. Driving my spiffy car, I smiled to myself, thinking of the joke he had pulled on me that very first time I had entered the Warner's lot. How had he known when I would be arriving? I supposed that any of the departments could have told him my schedule of appointments. Still, he had gone to some considerable trouble, and it had been such a funny, friendly, and welcome surprise. Jimmy was certainly full of surprises. It seemed to me that he couldn't be typed or conveniently wrapped into a neat, conventional parcel for storage in the labelled-image depot. Jimmy was Jimmy—maybe impossible to really know well. But wasn't that part of his fascination, after all? I had better start accepting all of his moods and actions as unique and stop trying to analyze him. God knows, I was having enough trouble trying to understand myself. Yet, I couldn't help wondering how Jimmy felt about me. Many times I had imagined that I could read his thoughts, but not too successfully when his thoughts concerned me. And what about me? How did I feel about Jimmy?

"Carroll!" I startled myself by exclaiming in a loud voice. And then quite consciously out loud I said, "Put that question straight out of your head!"

After all—I'm a married woman. Maybe it was a mistake rushing into a second marriage so soon?

I addressed myself in the rearview mirror, "That question, well, forget it altogether! Your status is as it is. Don't go opening any beehives unless you are willing to get stung good and proper!"

My thoughts had taken me all the way to Burbank without my even having been aware of driving, and I wondered if anyone on the freeway had noticed me talking to myself.

I turned into the entrance of Warner's and drew up to the barricade. When I looked at the guard's booth, I thought I must be seeing things! It wasn't possible—I must still be lost in my imaginings! The guard was again slumped over in the booth with his cap covering his face!

I waited a few seconds, but when the guard didn't move, I slowly got out of the car and cautiously walked over to him.

"Carroll, Car-roll, *Carroll!*" came a whisper.

It had to be Jimmy pulling the same stunt again! All this show of attention from him was rather thrilling. Tickled at the silliness of it, I giggled and snatched his cap away. "Oh, no you don't, Jimmy. You don't fool me this time!"

But that round cherub face and those enormous brown eyes with long, thick lashes did not belong to Jimmy.

"Oh, I'm sorry," I sputtered. "I thought that you were some-one else."

The beautiful cherub broke into a radiant smile.

"Come on," I said. "You aren't the guard, are you?"

Then I heard that unmistakable low, devilish chuckle, and Jimmy appeared from behind the booth. "Oh, boy, did I fool you. You should see your face!"

I swung at him playfully but Jimmy ducked, faked sideways, and, gripping me around the waist with his hands, he swooped me off my feet and held me suspended in air.

"Here, stay up in the air, dummy."

I shrieked with delight and surprise. Jimmy had a trim, taut, muscular body like that of a dancer, but the powerful strength of his arms astounded me. His squeezing my waist was rather painful and decidedly sexy all at once.

"Put me down, you idiot!"

"Not till I feel like it, dummy. Oh, man, are you a dummy. Anyone could fool you!"

"Put me down, idiot! You idiot!" I was squealing the only name I could think to call him. In truth, I was really enjoying the play and wasn't in any hurry for him to release me.

The sun had caught Jimmy's gray-green eyes and made them seem almost transparent. I don't know if it was his hard grip on my waist or those magnetic, feline eyes that made me feel so terribly giddy.

"My buddy, Sal, here and me—woo-ee—have we had a good laugh!"

"Put me down!"

"You know my buddy, Sal Mineo?"

Jimmy did put me down but so close to Sal that our noses were practically touching. (I thought to myself, "This Sal Mineo is an adorable little boy, I wonder if his mother knows he's playing with the older kids.")

"Hi."

"Hi."

Then Jimmy clamped a hand around my wrist and began to pull me. "Come on, let's go, we are going for a ride."

"Wait, wait, smarty, I can't leave my car there blocking the entrance!"

"Sal, park the dummy's car," Jimmy said, and Sal obliged. (I couldn't believe Sal was old enough to own a driver's license.)

But Jimmy didn't get on the bike because his attention was suddenly on the girl standing in the shade by the building opposite. It was Natalie Wood. She was watching us and smiling shyly.

Jimmy called out to her harshly, like an animal trainer ordering a dog to heel, "Natalie, come over here!"

Natalie unhesitatingly obeyed. They had recently finished making *Rebel Without a Cause* together, and I wondered if this "macho-versus-helpless-female" relationship was a carryover from the movie.

"This is Natalie Wood," Jimmy mumbled.

"Yes," I replied. "We met at the Chateau Marmont once when you were visiting Nick Ray. Hi, Natalie."

"Hi, Carroll."

Natalie was still moving toward us when Jimmy growled, "Stop. Stop right there!" And Natalie stopped dead in her tracks.

I began to speculate uncomfortably about just how far this was going to go.

Jimmy looked her up and down and then hung his head, shaking it slowly from side to side, his darkish blond hair streaked with silvery ash and gold in the sunlight.

He purred, "Jeeze, Natalie—Jeeze—have you looked at yourself today? Do you have any idea how corny you look?"

Jimmy circled her, still shaking his head, moaning, "Jeeze, are you corny—Jeeze, corny, corny, corny. . . ."

Natalie just stared at him wide-eyed, but I had seen a small look of hurt flit across her lovely childlike face. Still, she stood silently and submissively while he continued to mock her.

By now I was so embarrassed for Natalie that I had to look away, and glancing over at Sal, I saw that he too was ill at ease, shuffling his feet.

I looked back to see tears glinting in Natalie's velvety brown and startled eyes. Jimmy lifted his head with a wicked little grin.

He was being deliberately callous and cruel, and he was obviously enjoying his domination of her because he kept on and on until the tears streamed down her cheeks.

Natalie was wearing a white, off-the-shoulder peasant blouse and a full patchwork gypsy skirt and she looked very young and very sweet (Natalie was six or seven years younger than Jimmy and I, and Sal was even younger.) Perhaps the long pendant earrings and the numerous dangling bracelets were a bit reminiscent of a teeny-bopper who had dipped into her mother's jewelry tray, but that was certainly no cause for the abuse Jimmy was heaping upon her. (Lord, but we Actors' Studio people were all so critical of frill. In striving for a reality we often went to extremes, even in something as superficial as dress. It led us to an intolerance of anything but the starkest simplicity.)

"Look at Carroll," he persisted. "Do you see what she is wearing—a plain simple dress and it's lovely."

Of course, I was fiercely proud of what I considered to be my unconventionality, when in actual fact I was but conforming to what I thought Jack Garfein and Jimmy Dean and the rest of the Actors' Studio would approve of. I hadn't yet acquired that strength of conviction to develop any sort of style of my own. So there was certainly nothing special about my dress.

I was wearing a brown-envelope fold-over number held together by an elasticized belt. It was as simple as they come, but I hadn't purchased it for that reason alone. The sales girl had told me that with an assortment of accessories, I could make it look like a dozen different dresses; so its practicality far outweighed any aesthetic merit it might have had.

"Carroll," Jimmy said, still refusing to let up on his victim, "why don't you teach Natalie how to dress?" Perhaps I was as cruel as Jimmy, because I reveled in his admiration.

Natalie just looked dumbfounded, and little Sal Mineo, not knowing where else to look or what else to do, had by this time dug the toe of his shoe into a crack in the pavement and was having difficulty dislodging it.

That instant Jimmy must have tired of his sadistic game. He grabbed me by the hand and pulled me onto the motor bike. "Come on, let's go," he said, displaying his warmest grin for the benefit of all of us. Suddenly he seemed charming, and I marveled at his mercurial changes and his power over us ordinary mortals.

He started the motor before I had a chance to arrange myself properly into a ladylike straddle on the back. The gunning noise was too loud for me to shout over, so I waved goodbye to Natalie and Sal, forgetting to tuck my dress around my legs. Jimmy took off abruptly. I clung to him for dear life, while my envelope dress split all the way to my waist and flew out on either side of the bike like a pair of large brown wings. My sheer panties were very pretty, in fact they were my best pair, but I hadn't really expected to model them for the entire work force of Warner Brothers.

"Jimmy!" I screeched, "Stop! Stop and let me pull down my dress!"

He looked around at my open flapping tent, which by this time had unfolded all the way up to expose my matching sheer bra, and he convulsed with laughter.

I tried to pinch him, but his flesh was well protected by his heavy jeans and leather jacket. He was laughing so hard that I could feel his lithe body heaving against my nearly bare chest and material-constricted arms. With the back of one hand he wiped the tears from his eyes, and the motor bike weaved crazily.

When we entered the back lot and pulled up to the replica of the small American town, he was still doubled up with laughter. His choked giggles were so infectious that I forgot my state of shameful disarray and joined in with the giggles despite myself. He stopped the bike, reached around impulsively, and hugged my half-clad body tightly against his cold leather jacket. We sat there locked together in what could have been a very sensual embrace while rocking back and forth in uncontrolled laughter.

Suddenly Jimmy turned off the motor and everything went still—because Jimmy went still—motionless and icy. His arms dropped to his sides and I slid off the sleek leather and into an upright sitting position. Something or someone had shattered the moment. Although Jimmy was frozen immobile, I could sense the contained but raging fury inside him. He was glaring toward the house with the white picket fence at the intruder who was sitting on the porch steps. When I saw the intruder, I too experienced a sudden loathing for that interloper who had invaded not only our secret place but our intimate moment.

Jimmy sprang into action, his body tensed; he turned on the ignition and gunned the motor. "Get off!" he snapped. "And fix your dress."

"Hey, wait a darn minute," I protested. "You aren't going to just leave me here, are you?"

"That's Dennis Hopper. Go and meet him. Maybe you'll like him better than you like me."

"Jimmy, are you crazy? It isn't my fault that he's here. I didn't tell him about this place. I don't even know him!"

"That's right. I told him." He lowered his head and for a split second I thought he was going to cry, but when he lifted his head again he said furiously, "It's my fault. I told him. Now he's here all the time!" Then, turning his anger on me, "It's his place now, so go and meet him."

I couldn't believe he was being like this. "Jimmy, wait for me. It isn't the place I care about. It's you!" But he had already roared away without hearing me.

I don't know why I did what I did next. I really don't know why. Maybe it was because Jimmy had told me to, but I walked over to Dennis Hopper and introduced myself. He looked up only briefly from contemplating his boots and then reassumed his "James Dean" attitude. But he was only a mimic. There were no thoughts in his head worthy of boot contemplation. The troubled pose was just that: a pose.

I went over and sat on the porch swing and listened to the ghosts. They, too, were disturbed by this imposter. They were darting and worrying all around Dennis, but he wasn't aware of their presence. I concentrated my thoughts on trying to calm them: Easy, easy, my friends. Jimmy will be back. Shush, shush, go quietly. Rest, rest, this place is yours for all time and any of us who intrude upon you are only here for a few fleeting moments. Rest.

Chapter

Twelve

MARFA, TEXAS

Southern Texas had the wide open country and modern ranches Edna Ferber might have had in mind when she wrote the book *Giant*. But Marfa was the typical old Western town of cowboy films. It was only three blocks long and the main street consisted of a sheriff's office complete with a detention cell, a general store that also handled the banking and postal service, and a tiny, two-story hotel. The saloon was intact, but it was now used as a bingo hall or for any assembly too large for the country church. Everything was of an age gone by, with the exception of a movie house, a gas station, and the paved road.

The hotel had perhaps fifteen rooms, so private accommodations had to be found for our enormous cast and crew. But the housing shortage around Marfa was also acute and oh, dear, oh, dear, did that create problems!

In assigning us our living space, the sole consideration—aside from gender, of course—was billing. Elizabeth, who was terrified of living alone, was the only one to get a house all to herself. The dodo in charge even made the grave mistake of attempting to put those diametrically opposed personalities, Rock and Jimmy, under the same roof! With fourth billing, I was made to share a house with (in order of billing) Mercedes McCambridge, Jane Withers, and Fran Bennett. Fortunately, we got along well together, but the stickler was being stuck in Marfa for six weeks or more without the privacy to invite our our boyfriends or husbands to join us.

Our lonely clapboard house was off the San Antonio highway, in the middle of nowhere. Only Mercedes was brave enough to sleep in the downstairs den next to the kitchen with its broken, whining refrigerator, and the living room with its naked picture windows and flimsy excuse for a front door. Jane and Fran shared one of the upstairs bedrooms and I had the other smaller bedroom for myself. Also upstairs was the only bathroom—to accommodate four working actresses!

When I telephoned Jack and told him that he couldn't visit me because there was nowhere for him to stay, he called me a liar. He flatly refused to believe that such an important, big-budget film would be short of facilities. God, I got angry! Here he was doubting my word again! I slammed down the phone, stamped my feet, and started to howl in frustration and indignation, which brought my panic-stricken roommates tumbling into the living room.

The girls did their best to console me. Then one by one they made their calls home, and each got more or less the same reaction from their fellows. We spent the night in the living room sobbing, listening to loud music, sipping warm beer, and munching soggy pretzels.

It is traditional for film companies to issue each afternoon a call sheet which lists the scenes to be filmed the following day, and the equipment and actors required for those proposed scenes. It is also expedient, because the cost of moving a crane to location, for example, runs to thousands of dollars. George Stevens, however, refused to be bound by this tradition and insisted upon everything from props to horses to cranes being ready and waiting at all times, with each and every actor standing by in full makeup and costume—including the stars. Even though Elizabeth and Rock had by far the largest roles, not even their parts demanded that they be on the set continuously; but they too were made to follow this strenuous and inconsiderate schedule.

At 5:00 A.M. a dozen or so cars would collect the entire cast and transport us to the hotel, where all the rooms had been taken over as wardrobe, makeup, and hairdressing cubicles. Then by 8:00 A.M. sharp all thirty-nine of us were to be completely ready so that we could be driven to the Reata Ranch location for the 8:30 A.M. start. Once there, we were made to stay for the length of the working day whether we were actually needed before the camera or not.

Elizabeth and Rock took this seemingly senseless routine in stride, but after three days of doing nothing, Jimmy blew his stack and refused to report for the fourth. Stevens claimed that Jimmy's behavior cost the company a day of lost production. As no one knew what George intended to film, this claim could have been either genuine or simply meant to teach Jimmy a lesson. Nonetheless, as contracted actors, it was our duty to report to work as instructed.

During the filming of *Rebel* (which hadn't yet been released), the entire production had revolved around Jimmy. He had been the sole star, the center of attention, and Nick Ray's main consideration. On *Giant,* however, Jimmy had only the third part. Elizabeth was the focus of attention, with Rock in second position; George Stevens as the master director was, in fact, the star on the set.

George was a very intelligent man, and he must have realized that Jimmy's behavior was prompted by insecurity and jealousy. But he refused to cater to Jimmy and demanded of him that he act like a grown-up and a professional. There are many directors, even superb ones, who would have been phony with Jimmy in order to get a performance—appeasing him on the set and then complaining bitterly about him behind his back. But George was a straightforward, no-nonsense, ex-Army officer. He told Jimmy what he thought of his conduct to his face and never changed that story when relating it to others. But George was also generous in his appreciation of well-acted scenes, never withholding his praise. Any reprimand was directed only at the misdeed itself and never carried over into the artistic area.

The severe scolding George gave Jimmy came on the fifth day of filming, before work began, and took place in front of the entire cast and crew. It was a lesson to all of us, and except for a few small transgressions which Elizabeth committed unthinkingly, like disappearing to change her stockings when the camera was set for a close-up of her face, every one of us toed the line. Jimmy was prompt from then on, and George's honesty and just punishment must have worked: Jimmy's brilliant performance is now recorded movie history.

I personally didn't mind being called to work every day. There was absolutely nothing to do in Marfa, and I certainly wouldn't have stayed alone at our isolated house. On location we could enjoy the camaraderie of our fellow actors, and each of us had a comfortable trailer where we could rest, out of that broiling sun.

We ate the catered noonday meal at long picnic tables, and that made every lunchtime a party. The buffet was sumptuous: caldrons of stews and curries; serving planks with roasts and fish and chicken; mashed, baked, boiled, and fried potatoes; a wide variety of vegetables and salads, assorted cheese, freshly baked rolls and bread; and dozens of yummy desserts. I had never seen such a quantity of delicious foods! At 108 pounds, I was underweight and could afford to pile my plate high and even make several trips to the buffet table. This incredible lunch was the high point of my day, and, like the starving actress I had too often been, I looked forward all morning to those promised feasts.

The days I didn't work, which were many, I played cards with Earl Holliman, who had become a very dear friend; or I coaxed the cowboys into letting me practice on a horse. It was like the most wonderful paid vacation at an exclusive dude ranch!

After work we were driven back to the hotel to change clothes, and shortly after, dinner was served to the troupe in the hotel dining room—gigantic Texas T-bone steaks! Because we couldn't be supplied locally, our provisions were flown in daily. That original Texas-grown beef had been sold to the West Coast, repurchased by our unit, and flown back to Marfa. Our chartered plane also delivered the previous day's developed but uncut film clips, called "rushes," which we were all invited to view at the local cinema after dinner.

Even though they changed rapidly, friendships, cliques and even territorial battle lines were nonetheless drawn from the outset. Rock escorted Elizabeth to dinner, where they laughed and whispered conspiratorially, excluding everyone else. Jimmy and I sat at a table by ourselves in the corner, where, without being overheard, we could be thoroughly derisive about whomever we pleased. Our main diversion was making fun of Elizabeth and Rock. We played a running word and phrase game, seeing which one of us could come up with the most devastating remark about their clothes or their behavior or their acting. We were occasionally witty, but without fail cruel and cutting.

Rock never left Elizabeth's side during the evenings, but Jimmy always disappeared from our table without a word to me. Dennis Hopper would make a dash for Jimmy's vacated chair, but Earl Holliman always seemed to beat him to it. And then Earl would escort me to the movie theatre. Jimmy would be there already, in the balcony, where he could sit all by himself to view the rushes.

I've told you how we toed the line at work because of George's insistence upon professionalism. Well, the rest of the time we behaved like a bunch of undisciplined, out-of-control adolescents. I most definitely include myself because I threw to the four winds any semblance of being a responsible, reasoning adult, and acted like a silly ten-year-old running wild at a school outing. Despite the fact that we had to get up each morning at 4:00 A.M., we carried on like absolute fools—laughing and crying and partying and drinking, and hardly ever sleeping. On the one hand we eagerly sought pledges of loyalty, while on the other hand we were in a continual process of redrawing the battle lines. We were also petty and jealous and decidedly selfish and spiteful.

At first, as I've said, it was Jimmy and I as a couple "versus" Elizabeth and Rock; but when Jimmy began stealing scenes, that changed. Elizabeth and Rock wanted revenge, so they arranged to meet me secretly after work and enlist my friendship and support. The appointment was set—it was so exciting and clandestine! I hurriedly changed out of my costume and slipped out of the hotel, by the back stairs so that Jimmy wouldn't see me. I went around to the rear of the building where Elizabeth's chauffeur was waiting for me beside her limousine, all the time thinking of myself as Mata Hari! He drove me to Elizabeth's house, where Rock was already waiting with a pitcher of martinis and a glorious big welcome. Elizabeth called out for us to bring the drinks and join her in her dressing room while she did her face. I was so thrilled to be in intimate contact with Elizabeth, so stunned by her extraordinary beauty without makeup, so star-struck, so honored to be taken into Elizabeth Taylor's confidence, that had she asked me to poison Jimmy, I probably would have willingly. Mind you, despite the fact that I had made continuous fun of him, I was also overwhelmed by this nearness to Rock Hudson. He and Elizabeth were the luminous, untouchable stars of the first magnitude, and I was, in truth, an awed fan.

Elizabeth's voice was high-pitched and squeaky because she used too little breath behind her words, but right then it ceased to annoy me. Nothing mattered but the privilege and joy of looking at her and being close to her. I carried her drink into the dressing room in the hope that I might touch her in the exchange. She smiled at me, and I went weak at the knees and nearly tipped the glass. As I handed it to her, her fingers brushed my arm and I collapsed onto the stool beside her dressing table just as she was saying, "Carroll, thank you for coming. Sit down beside me."

Elizabeth had lost all that extra weight and had slimmed down to that trim figure I'd admired in so many films.

I had a close-up view of those violet eyes—they were truly violet, no other color could describe them. They were the most gorgeous eyes I had ever seen, and I had the greatest difficulty in trying to concentrate on the conversation—even though both Elizabeth and Rock had launched into a flow of glowing compliments about my acting ability.

Suddenly those violet eyes flashed and that perfectly shaped mouth puckered in anger. "Dean is an outrageous scene-stealer."

"Yes," Rock added, "and we can't handle him, but you can."

"Yes," Elizabeth hissed (her spittle barely missed hitting me but I wouldn't have minded if it had). "Rock and I aren't good enough to get back at him, but you're from the Actors' Studio, and you're as good as he is."

"That's right," Rock interrupted. "He doesn't get away with anything in your scenes. He can't steal scenes from you."

"So we want you to join us—be on our side, and get even with him for us," Elizabeth said, grasping my shoulder with her fragile little hand. (At that time this produced shooting shock waves of delight up and down my spine, preventing me from answering aloud, but I remember inwardly telling her: "Oh, yes, you divine, heavenly gorgeous goddess, I shall slash my wrists and happily permit my life's blood to gush forth as a tribute to your beauty.")

I loved her! I adored her! I worshipped her! I would have been her slave had she let me, but Elizabeth insisted upon treating me as an equal. I had to force myself to stop behaving like her lady-in-waiting or her trailing, adoring puppy dog.

I went to dinner that evening with her and Rock. I can't tell you how proud I was to walk into that dining room, in front of the entire company, flanked by Elizabeth Taylor and Rock Hudson! The three of us put our heads close together to whisper and giggle. We three repeatedly glanced at Jimmy sitting alone and then turned back together to snicker. I suppose, now, that Jimmy must have been hurt, but at the time, I couldn't have cared less. I was transported into another world and my head was whirling in sheerest delight.

On the way to the movie house, Rock walked in the middle, with his arm around Elizabeth on one side and me on the other. I almost burst with happiness. Earl ran behind and called to me, and even though he was my best friend, I snubbed him.

During the rushes, I sat in the row with those radiant stars and George Stevens, whom I also admired and adored. All three were so kind and friendly to me that I basked in a hot delirium and never actually saw the film clips.

The next day I was invited to join the elite for lunch! A special building had been erected to protect the stars from the brutal Texas sun while they ate. Up to this point only George Stevens, Elizabeth, Rock, and Jimmy had enjoyed the comfort of this cool edifice with its linen-draped table and a uniformed waiter to serve them. Now I, too, was accepted as a member of the aristocracy while the peasants made do with the out-of-doors and the self-service queues. When Jimmy entered and saw me, he stamped out again and didn't return for the meal. (I thought to myself: "Tough!")

As soon as we were seated and the waiter approached, Elizabeth fluttered her rows upon rows of long lustrous eyelashes and shrilled in a nerve-grating voice, "It is so desperately hot, do we have to have those heavy foods? Can't we simply get a ham sandwich and a cool glass of lemonade?"

Well, that was it. The price was exacted for my new exalted position—every day from that squawked demand on, I watched with mouth-watering longing as those outside the palace trooped by with heavy-laden trays of assorted delights while I choked on my dry ham sandwich.

However, my promotion to the higher echelon also brought

constant thrills along with special privileges—all-night parties, every night, at Rock's house, sitting at the feet of the beauteous Liz. Rock and Jane Withers were so funny together, and I believe I was in a never-ending state of continuous, uncontrollable giggles. Rock and Elizabeth were completely sweet and warm and friendly. They got around to inviting all the leading players to one party or another, but I was a constant guest. Jimmy was conspicuously absent from this merriment. By the end of the first week, he had moved out of the house he and Rock shared, and he never showed at any of the parties. Maybe he hadn't been invited. (As far as I was concerned: "Who knew and who cared?")

Then Jimmy struck us a terrible blow—one I took personally. He stole Elizabeth away from us—from me! That dirty rat took Elizabeth for himself, and I think I must have gone into a concealed state of mourning. I continued to spend the evenings with Rock, and I continued to laugh and carry on like an imbecile, but as I recall my heart was broken. True, Elizabeth was just as sweet and friendly as before, but I hardly ever saw her any more. She went off mysteriously each evening with Jimmy, and none of us could figure out where they went. They would arrive for dinner together, she would sit in the balcony next to him during the rushes, and then they would slip away for what seemed like most of the night.

At the time I was determined not only to find out what attracted Elizabeth to Jimmy, but also to destroy his courtship and bring Elizabeth back to us—to me. It had been my guess, and I kept my fingers crossed that I was right, that their relationship was not a sexual involvement. I couldn't have hoped to interfere with or break up lovers.

It had occurred to me that when I'd been alone with Jimmy, I'd never felt that sexual threat a woman instinctively senses. But I never believed that he was a homosexual. There had never been an indication of homosexuality. The guys at the Actors' Studio would certainly have known had Jimmy had that tendency. In fact there were no secrets at all at the Studio. Those guys and gals had made a thorough study of everyone—down to everyone's fillings.

After hours of deliberation, it became my well-considered opinion that Jimmy was, in fact, asexual. It struck me that Claire and other girls I knew who had been close to Jimmy had only spoken about how Jimmy had held their hands, and how innocent and boyish he had been—never touching them. Then when Elizabeth had spoken of Jimmy in the same terms, I was ecstatic, and felt I was right, and free to proceed with plans to win her back!

Elizabeth told me how sorry she felt for Jimmy, how she wanted to listen to his problems and help him. (Ha!) I began at every opportunity, slowly and cunningly, to slide little knives of doubt into her gorgeous head about Jimmy's true motives, his deviousness. It was Jimmy who had provided me with the fuel for my vengeful fire by his obsession with publicity. He had been constantly rushing to Elizabeth's side whenever a photographer arrived on the set. (Oh, what a perfect Iago I made!) "Gee, Elizabeth, look, here is another newspaper picture of you and Jimmy." "Gosh, Liz, you never have any pictures by yourself any more, do you?" "It looks as if the *Life* magazine story will all be about Dean, but you are in the background of some of the pictures." "Dean's publicity seems to be only at your expense."

Then it happened—Jimmy went too far and played right into my hands. The culmination of all those small, shadowy doubts burst into one big glaring stingeroo! In front of the press cameras he had picked Elizabeth off her feet, turning her upside down so that her skirt had fallen over her head, exposing her to the waist.

Ordinarily Elizabeth, who was good-natured, would have overlooked this silly stunt, but by then I had set the stage too well, and I hadn't let up when my opportunity came to strike the final blow. We were having lunch, and with saccharin innocence I said to George Stevens, "Gee, George, do you think you could get the negatives of that photo the photographer took this morning and destroy it—the one where Jimmy held Elizabeth upside down?"

And George said, "It certainly was undignified, Liz. Why do you allow Jimmy to do things like that?"

(Hooray, she stopped speaking to Jimmy. She was mine again!)

Rock's fiancée, Phyllis, came to visit him, and while there were a lot of parties for Phyllis, Elizabeth and I spent more time alone together. I never got tired of looking at her or listening to her talk. For one thing, she had the most fascinating point of view. She never spoke of people, things, or situations as any other person might have. She had a reality of her own, an MGM reality. Her judgments and dialogue came straight out of MGM movies, but she actually meant them. It was fascinating!

Then Phyllis left Rock, walked out in a huff, and Elizabeth felt it was her saintly duty to console and comfort him every night. Their long heart-to-heart talks demanded the strictest privacy, so I was on the outside once again. I ran back to my buddy, who had been waiting for me patiently, Earl Holliman. It was Earl and I from then on, even though Jimmy and I had made up.

Jimmy and I hadn't consciously tried to make up. We did a scene one day in which Luz opens the door to let in Jett. In the rehearsal, when I opened the door and saw Jimmy, I gave him a smile which was genuinely from me to him and he instantly returned it in full measure.

In the beginning Jimmy had spent most days with the stunt-men and cowboys, but he was now spending all his time with them. Perhaps that is how the rumors of homosexuality got started. I don't know. But that was not Jimmy's interest in them— his motive was to copy them and learn everything they had to teach him without making the learning seem deliberate.

In the book, Jett Rink was described as a big burly ranch hand who could ride and rope, out-drink and out-fight any man. Jimmy was cast completely against type and really had to work hard to achieve the character. He listened to the cowboys' speech patterns for hours at a time and mimicked them until he finally sounded like a native. He not only learned to ride, he stayed on that horse and wore those slant-heeled cowboy boots until he walked with the bow-legged gait of a man born in the saddle. My favorite scene is the one in which Jimmy twirls a rope expertly. Jett is playing with the rope as if to emphasize his toying with Bick's proposition concerning Jett's inherited land. It is such a well-acted scene, and the rope was entirely Jimmy's idea (as indeed were so many other wonderful contributions to his character and scenes).

It was a sad day when the Marfa filming was completed. Everyone felt a terrible let-down when "That's a wrap" was called at 5:00. We had a private train which was supposed to pull out at 9:00 P.M. to take us back to L.A., but it didn't leave until well after midnight because of the "farewell" cocktail party. The local people didn't want to see us leave and we were all reluctant to go. I, like everyone else, got soppy drunk, but it didn't ease that melancholy feeling of a very special time passing away.

Chapter
Thirteen

ELIZABETH TAYLOR

Once we got back to L.A., everyone in our troupe went their own way, back to their home lives and responsibilities. It was a difficult adjustment at first, and I hoped that we wouldn't lose completely that feeling of togetherness we had known in Marfa.

Jack had come to the Coast and was at the train station to meet me. Naturally, he blamed *me* for the four-hour delay! It only amused me because I found myself observing him closely and wondering, "Who is this stranger, and why is he making such a fuss?" But by the afternoon I warmed up to him, and when evening fell I remembered why I had fallen in love with him and married him.

Jack was stern—as my father had been—and I respected him and knew that he was right in accusing me of being silly and irresponsible. I loved him so much, and I wished that I could have been as disciplined as he was. But—I don't know, at times I just got the crazies—just couldn't resist being childishly uncontrolled. I admitted that I had run wild on location, but when Jack unjustly accused me of being sexually promiscuous with all the men in the cast, I was so hurt that I cried for hours on end. To be perfectly honest, he didn't include all the men—he forgot to mention Earl Holliman. Earl and I had come close to a serious involvement, but we had made a mature decision, of which I was very proud, not to let ourselves get carried away.

Warner's publicity department went mad in their drive to make up for the time lost while we had been on location. They herded journalists into the commissary every lunch hour, and trying to get a few forkfuls of food between questions became a hopeless struggle. I found these assaults most distasteful because the reporters only wanted to pump me about Elizabeth's rumored romances with both Hudson and Dean. The day I told her about the gist of my interviews, she said, "Come on, let's get out of here. I'm sick to death of these busybodies, too. We can go off the lot for lunch."

Driving with Elizabeth behind the wheel of her white Cadillac was a uniquely terrifying experience. I can't imagine how she ever passed her driver's test! She flatly refused to acknowledge the presence of other vehicles on the road—let alone that they might have the right-of-way. We had only two blocks to go from the studio, but even in the sparse Burbank traffic, we had three hair-raising near-misses. Outside the restaurant she drove directly into a parked car, then backed up and hit the man in the car behind us. The driver was so dumbstruck at the sight of Elizabeth Taylor that he forgot to complain, and when he stepped out of his car, she glared daggers at him for having dared to be in her path in the first place. I went around to survey the dent in her front fender, but Liz waltzed directly into the restaurant, totally unconcerned.

My feelings about Liz probably seem extreme, but to me, at that time in my impressionable young life, she was truly the pinnacle of what being a star meant. I loved her—I adored her —I worshipped her. She was utterly regal!

The diners dropped their forks and stared in open-mouthed wonder at Elizabeth's every movement and gesture, and the poor girl couldn't relax for a second during lunch. With all her fame and beauty, she was so sincere and sweet and charming and had at times such a helpless, little-girl quality, that I had wanted nothing more than to watch over her and protect her.

When the bill arrived, she said, "Carroll, you pay it. I haven't got any money." (I remember wanting to crawl under the table and kiss her china doll feet for giving me the honor.)

Elizabeth, with a yearly salary from MGM of a hundred thousand, was always broke. She was perfectly right about the injustice of it all when she said, "Those bastards at MGM make me do five pictures a year for my hundred thousand, and on this *Giant* loan-out alone they are collecting two hundred and fifty thousand from Warner Brothers." Various charities would come on the set asking for donations, and Elizabeth would answer their requests with haughty indignation, "What! I haven't *got* any money!"

After work everyone made a quick getaway, except Elizabeth, who was always the last person to leave the lot. Out of curiosity, as well as my desire to be near her, I had taken to following her to her dressing room at the end of the day. It was like watching the preening of a magnificent bird! Before the wardrobe woman left for the day, she would assist Elizabeth out of her costume and into a starched, immaculately white surgical-type gown. I would put a selection of records on the stereo and hand Liz her gin and tonic when she was ready to be seated at her vanity. I carefully rehearsed the ingredients:

> 2 jiggers of Beefeaters gin
> A small tonic water
> Serve in a tall glass over
> 4 ice cubes
> Garnish with a lime wedge

Elizabeth would gently brush and then carefully bind those splendiferous blue-black locks into a pink chiffon snood. She would delicately cleanse away her makeup using soft cotton pads, boxes of them, dabbing first with a heavy cleansing lotion, then a lighter one, and finally a scented astringent.

I would wait patiently during her luxurious shower. The freshly laundered surgical gown would be discarded as soiled linen, as would the clean pink snood. She would re-enter the dressing room in a thick and fluffy terry robe and matching scuffs, and cuddle up in an overstuffed chair to finish her gin and tonic. After she felt warm and dry, she would go back into the bathroom suite to apply lotion to her body, while I refreshed her drink and changed the stack of records.

When the terry robe and scuffs had also been thrown on the dirty-laundry pile, Liz would again enter, this time wearing some elegant satin gown and high-heeled slippers to begin her street makeup. Elizabeth was truly a natural beauty, and she was at her loveliest without makeup. I was surprised that she didn't understand that anything artificial only served to detract. But I was full of admiration at the deftness and skill with which she applied the paints (she did her own film makeup, as well, with the makeup man only standing by to keep her cosmetic tray spotlessly clean and tidy, and to hand her each requested brush and pencil).

Her entire toilet was carried out leisurely, pleasurably, and meticulously. It was a ritual, part of her MGM lifestyle, and she followed it faithfully even if she and Michael Wilding were going to spend the evening alone with trays of food in front of the TV set.

The Hollywood filming schedule was a long one. Jack couldn't give up his own career in the theatre to be with me, so he was only able to make a few short visits. When he was in town, Elizabeth never failed to invite us to her house for dinner in celebration. (That's how thoughtful she was!) Dinner at her house was always a cold buffet because, while she had a live-in nanny for her children, she had no other nighttime help. She said, "I can't afford servants who stay after five o'clock. God, how I hate being poor!"

Her ultramodern, four-bedroom house was, from my point of view, a luxury model fit for the pages of a glossy designer's magazine. By Hollywood standards it was apparently a medium-income compromise. Liz spoke of that dream house as if it were a hovel, and Michael was in complete sympathy with her.

He told Jack and me, "I do believe MGM might give Elizabeth a bonus soon, and if they do, we simply must get a better house."

"Yes," Elizabeth pouted, "I'm fed up with working so hard and having to live like this!"

In 1963, during the making of *Station Six Sahara*, in England, I rented the house that Elizabeth and Eddie Fisher had once rented in Englefield Green, near Great Windsor. On the drive from London, as one approaches Englefield Green, Windsor Castle can be seen in the distance. When our mutual agent had made this drive with Elizabeth, it is said that he had joked, referring to the Castle, "Well, Mrs. Fisher, there is your house. How do you like it?" And Elizabeth replied in complete seriousness, "Thank you. That will do nicely."

Her house in the Hollywood Hills was on a steep stretch of unlit road just above the most treacherous of all curves—the same one where Monty Clift, after having visited her, had his severe smashup. The curve sprang out of nowhere! Although I drove down the mountain at a snail's pace (Jack didn't drive), it would catch me by surprise every time. Michael adored rosé wine and kept it flowing all evening, and I never refused a refill. I was fortunate, indeed, with my drunken driving, to have gotten away with just a few minor mishaps—mostly scares—on that deathtrap curve!

Chapter Fourteen

LISTENING TO GHOSTS

Whether it was in Marfa or in Hollywood, it was a great experience to work with Jimmy Dean. He was at once fully committed to the scene, entirely responsive to the other actor or actors, and yet a fierce competitor for first place. He was so driven to be better than anyone else that when it looked like a tie, he wasn't above fighting dirty to regain an edge.

The most important scene we had together was filmed in Hollywood. It was the one in which the older Jett Rink proposes marriage to the now grown-up Luz Benedict II. We did that one scene, take after take, for three entire days! It was incredible. George Stevens believed in extensive coverage, but no other scene had gone on that long. The repetition wasn't because of mistakes, because as far as I could see, there were none. Jimmy and I had rehearsed and were both word perfect. Because we were competitive, there wasn't one take in which either of us was anything less than concentrated and intense; there were no technical hitches because the camera set-ups were simple (the action of the scene took place in a booth of a deserted restaurant in Jett's about-to-be inaugurated hotel). Later I discovered that George Stevens had deliberately allowed can after can of film to be used to record what he was quoted as having called "a great boxing match between actors." George kept the outtakes and played them at home for his friends.

It went something like this: Jimmy sat back in the booth . . . I stretched forward, I sat back . . . Jimmy slumped to one side, I sipped my drink . . . Jimmy rolled his cigarette, Jimmy tossed his head . . . I took the rose out of the vase and twirled it . . . and on, and on, and on, take after take, during twenty-one hours of filming!

Jimmy and I didn't break the mood between the rounds. The challenge was far too exhilarating to deaden with small talk. While the camera reloaded, we each retired to our own corners.

We were well into the third day of this acting marathon when Jimmy suddenly made a foul play. He hit me below the belt, so to speak. He slid one of his hands under the table. He clamped that hand right up between my legs and squeezed with all his mighty strength.

He didn't remove his hand or loosen his grip. He also didn't miss a beat of the scene.

And what did I do? I was so shocked and embarrassed, I didn't know what to do. I gasped. I wiped the tears of pain and humiliation from my glazed eyes. I looked at George Stevens for his help as referee, and when he made no sign to intercede, I finished the scene.

Previously George had praised both Jimmy and me after each take. This time he ignored Jimmy and praised only me. When I was settled into my chair, a few tense moments passed in silence. Then Jimmy walked from his corner over to mine. He threw his arms around my neck and clung tightly to me in a long, sad embrace. I patted his back. No words were necessary. Because it was Jimmy, I could forgive him anything.

As an actor, Jimmy was at an enormous disadvantage in the latter half of *Giant*. While the audience was able to witness the gradual aging of Elizabeth's and Rock's characters, Jimmy's character had, for a long period of time, dropped out of sight. When his character was reintroduced into the story, the audience was suddenly confronted by a startlingly older Jett Rink.

Jimmy himself had great difficulty relating to the older Jett. He agonized over his last scene, the one in which he was alone in the ballroom, making a final drunken speech. During his speech, Luz, who was peeping through the door, brokenheartedly witnessed Jett's symbolic downfall. The evening we watched the first rushes of that scene, Jimmy came up to George Stevens and me with tears in his eyes. "I'll never do that last scene the way it should be done," he said, "but just keep cutting to the close-up of Carroll. Everything that has to be expressed is right there on her face." Jimmy had often said marvelous things about my ability, but that was the finest compliment he or any great actor could possibly have given me.

Although George reshot the scene, Jimmy was never satisfied that he had conquered its depth. I knew on Tuesday evening, the 27th of September, when we left the projection room, that Jimmy had completed his participation in the film with a feeling of desperate inadequacy. There were only the three of us, plus a handful of technicians, on his final night. He huddled briefly with George before departing, and then threw me a large circular arm movement as he slumped away, his sad crooked grin slowly disappearing turtle-like into the collar of his tan leather jacket. "See ya," he mumbled.

There were still about three weeks to go until the end of production. Warners had banned Jimmy from racing or even driving until he had completed his part in the picture. He had told me that as soon as the film was over, he wanted to drive a station wagon cross-country to the East Coast, perhaps enter one race along the way. I expected to see him in a matter of weeks in New York at the Actors' Studio.

On Friday, September 30, around six o'clock, Elizabeth, Rock and I and a small group were watching the rushes. George Stevens was behind us at his desk by the controls. The projection room was dark. The phone rang. The soundtrack screamed to a halt. The picture froze. The lights shot up. We turned and looked at George. The phone dangled in his hand. He was white and motionless. Death was present in that room.

Slowly and with great effort, his voice coming from a long and distant tunnel, George said, "There's been a car crash. Jimmy Dean has been killed."

I went numb. No one else seemed to move. If they spoke, I didn't hear them. I sat silently for a long time. Then I left, silently, and drove to the beach. I sat alone all night long watching the surf and feeling absolutely nothing, experiencing nothing, knowing nothing.

At the first rays of the sun, I jumped up, dashed to my car, and raced to the gates of Warner Brothers. But the guard in the booth was the guard, sitting erect, his cap not too large, nor covering his face.

I sped to the back lot and pulled up abruptly at the small American town. It was deserted.

I walked down the tree-lined street and stood for a time immobilized outside the white picket fence. The lawn was nicely trimmed. The big oak tree stood sturdy and proud. The house gleamed in the early morning sun. Nothing had changed.

I flung open the gate with a crash. I flew at the oak tree and punched it and stumbled backwards clutching my injured fist. I turned, kicked the porch steps, and stamped up them onto the porch. I flung myself lengthwise on the glider, beating its cushions until I was exhausted, drenching them with my tears.

The next thing I remember was lying there face down in silence. The sun had gone behind a cloud. The wind had come up. Long, filmy, chilly fingers were stroking my legs, my arms, my back, my hair, my neck. I didn't stir—I was listening to the ghosts.

Chapter
Fifteen

MARILYN MONROE

Stepping into the terminal building at New York's International Airport, I could see Jack in the visitor's waiting zone. He seemed to be jumping up and down for joy, as if he were about to burst with good news.

The line of people in front of me was moving maddeningly slowly.

"Jack," I called. "Hello, darling, hello!"

"Hello, darling," he called back, "can't you move a little faster?"

I finally pushed past a couple and their children, who were greeting relatives, and ran into Jack's arms.

"Hello, darling," he said between kisses. "Welcome home."

"Oh, thank you, darling. I'm so happy to see you. I missed you."

"I missed you, too," he said, giving me an additional squeeze. "And, oh, baby, have I got news for you!"

"What? What? Tell me!"

"Give me another kiss first."

"Jack, stop teasing me! I could see from the distance that you're bursting to tell me something. What is it?"

"Give me a kiss first."

"Jack, if you don't tell me right this minute, I'll never kiss you again!"

"Gadge wants to see you!"

"What! What! Kazan? Elia Kazan? Gadge Kazan? Are you sure? How do you know?"

"I saw him at the theatre last night. He asked me how your performance looks in *Giant,* and I told him you were excellent in the rushes that I'd seen, but that he should call George Stevens and ask him."

"Did he say what he wants to see me about?"

"Well, why not wait and let him tell you?"

"Jack, I'm going to kill you if you don't tell me everything!"

"Now, Carroll, don't get your hopes up too high. At the moment he is only considering you for a project."

"What is it, theatre or film? Did he tell you?"

"Yes, but why don't you wait and let Gadge tell you himself?"

"Jack, I can't stand it! If you don't tell me right this minute, I'm going to drop to the floor and yell R-A-P-E!"

"Well, Tennessee. . . ."

"Tennessee! Tennessee Williams? It's a play written by Tennessee Williams? Oh, my God, I'm going to faint!"

"Darling, darling, control yourself. People are looking! That's why I wanted you to wait and talk to Kazan. You mustn't get so excited. You must calmly. . . ."

"If you don't drop that silly makeup case of mine," I shouted, "and sit down on this bench and tell me word for word everything you know, I'm going to make such a scene that they'll have to call the police!"

"Well, let's at least wait until we've collected the luggage and gotten settled in the car."

"NOOOOOOO!"

"All right, all right, but just be calm and for heaven's sake, keep your voice down."

"W-I-L-L Y-O-U B-E-G-I-N?"

"All right. Well, Gadge is planning to produce and direct a low-budget, black-and-white film. Tennessee has written the screenplay from two of his one-act plays, *27 Wagons Full of Cotton* and *The Unsatisfactory Supper.* At the moment the movie title is *Mississippi Woman,* but Gadge doesn't like that title. So far Karl Malden and Eli Wallach and Milly Dunnock have been cast. . . ."

"Oh, my God! Oh, my God! Those fabulous actors! Oh,

my God, I'm so excited! I can't stand it!"

"Carroll, you're shouting again. Now are you going to listen calmly like you promised or do you want to wait until we get into the car?"

"No, no, I'm sorry. Please go ahead. Oh, my God, Karl Malden and Eli Wallach and Mildred Dunnock! And Tennessee and Kazan! I just can't believe it!"

"All right, now, Carroll, this is your last chance. Are you going to be calm or do you want me to get up and go for your luggage?"

"No, no, no, I'll be good, I promise. Please continue."

"Now look, darling, I don't want you to get your hopes up too high. There is only a possibility that you might be cast. Gadge is only considering you along with other actresses."

"Other actresses? What other actresses?"

"Well, Marilyn Monroe has said she wants to play the part and she is Tennessee's first choice. . . ."

"Marilyn Monroe! Oh, my God! Marilyn Monroe! Marilyn Monroe wants to play the part? But then I don't have a chance in hell against Marilyn Monroe! Oh, you're mean and cruel and nasty! You should never have built up my hopes! You should never have told me about the film! Oh, I hate you and I'll never forgive you!" And I broke into uncontrollable tears.

"Carroll! Carroll! You're behaving like a hysterical child. You see why I can't tell you anything?"

"I can't help it," I blubbered. "I wanted that part so much."

"But you haven't even read the script!"

"I don't care. Just the chance to work with those fabulous artists and play a Tennessee Williams character. Oh, it would have been the chance of a lifetime!" I sobbed.

"Now, Carroll, darling, you're being totally unreasonable. Gadge wants to audition you for the part."

"He does?" I sniffled.

"Yes, he told me he'd like you to read for him."

"Oh, Jack, I feel so rotten."

"Yes, I know, darling. You're tired. You've been up all night. It's a long trip. And you've been very upset these last few weeks. We all have. You still aren't over the shock of Jimmy's death. None of us is."

"Oh, Jack, I'll never get over Jimmy. Never!"

"I know, darling. It is such a tragic loss. He was so young."

"He was my age. He was my friend. Oh Jack, I'm going to miss him."

"Shush, shush, sweetheart. Come on, let me take you home. You need to rest."

"Oh, Jack, when I think of all the times I was mean to Jimmy —of all the mean things I did to him—I'll never be able to forgive myself!"

"Come on, sweetheart, we all do mean things. Jimmy must have at times been mean to you. He wasn't an angel. He was just a human being like the rest of us. I'm sure you did a lot of kind, sweet things, as well. You were his friend, so you must have meant something special to him and for good reasons."

"Jack?"

"Yes?"

"I'm very tired. Will you take me home?"

I fell into a deep, twenty-four-hour sleep. It was nine o'clock the next morning when Jack awakened me gently, handed me a cup of coffee, and reminded me that it was Tuesday—Actors' Studio day. While I had been asleep, Jack had arranged an appointment for me to meet with Kazan after the class.

We got to the loft at 11:00 A.M. The girl standing by the back row of chairs, dressed in faded cotton trousers, a short pink angora sweater, a patterned head scarf, and outsized dark glasses was Marilyn Monroe.

She was surrounded by all the early arrivals. Two or three girls were trying to ingratiate themselves, while five or six guys were tripping over one another in an effort to get close to her. Damn, I was longing to be introduced, but I certainly wasn't going to compete for her attention, and if Jack dared to become one of the droolers—I'd divorce him! But all at once Jack had assumed a smug pose and with studied casualness waved briefly at Marilyn.

To my total shock and dismay, Marilyn not only shifted her attention fully away from the admiring men around her but turned and directed that attention completely on my man! I was so jealous I could have killed her! She pursed her lips and lisped, "Hello, Jack," making "Hello" sound like a dirty word and "Jack" sound positively obscene!

She undulated out of the row and wiggled down the ramp

toward us. Her pretty breasts plopped in place beneath the toddler-sized angora sweater, and her thin cotton trousers might have been grafted to her flesh.

A turtle would have reached us sooner. Marilyn had on spike heels and her tottering sways from side to side usurped a full nine-tenths of the energy which should have propelled her forward.

Finally, Marilyn arrived, towering over us. She was much taller than I had expected, and she never actually stood still. She was like a perpetual-motion gel. If her hips weren't gyrating, she was winching her shoulders, or swinging her pink fuzzy tits, or making that sucking fish-pucker mouth. Somehow she managed, at times, to coordinate all these movements, and I had to admit she was being deliberately witty.

Everything about her stated: I'm yours. Take me. Use me.

I was already hating her for flaunting her availability at Jack, when she turned to say hello to me—and presented me with that same seductive quality of "come on"! I suddenly felt drawn to her and leaned in a bit closer than necessary to accept her outstretched hand. Her hand was lusciously warm and plump, and I found myself clinging to it that added moment. Maybe I imagined it, but I thought I smelled the fruity aroma of sex.

Since Marilyn let her body language do most of the talking, she had very little use for actual words. At that moment she had asked Jack about Strindberg's *Miss Julie*, hanging on his every syllable. Her attitude was: Oh, you're so smart and I'm so dumb. I'm so excited by your mind. Give me your brilliant words.

And, boy, did Jack give them to her. Straight from off the top of his head, he launched into the most fatuous, far-fetched interpretation of *Miss Julie* that the play had surely ever had. Jack had a tendency to show off his superior mental agility, and he often got carried away. But in this Monroe-induced frenzy, he was spewing a torrent of pseudointellectual crap!

I spied Kazan near the doorway talking to Paddy Chayefsky, and decided to edge toward them. But they, like everyone else, were focused on Marilyn and didn't see me. I was sorry that I had gotten so close, because I overheard Paddy say, "Oh, boy, would I like to fuck that!"

Anne Jackson entered, saw me, came up to me, and said brightly, "Carroll, you're back! How was the movie?" (Well, at last somebody noticed me! After all, I had just completed a major film. Surely I deserved a little of the attention in that room.) Her husband, Eli Wallach, was behind her and he too said something nice to me—before making a beeline over to Marilyn. I watched as Marilyn jiggled her parts away from my Jack and smothered Eli with them. Jack couldn't stop the flow of words immediately, and he was standing there talking to a row of empty chairs. Good! I was glad Marilyn had dumped him in favor of Eli—the silly ass deserved it!

I glanced at Anne to see how she was coping with her jealousy, but to my amazement Anne was only amused by Marilyn's antics and Eli's infatuation. Imagine being that confident and mature! I wondered if I would ever be able to handle myself that way.

I turned in utter delight as I heard Lee Strasberg say, "Carroll, welcome home, darling." I kissed him on the cheek and then clung to him and instantly began to choke with tears.

"Oh, Lee," I whispered hoarsely, "I always thought Jimmy would be here for this session."

Lee shook his head, took out a handkerchief, and wiped his eyes and his glasses. "We devoted a session to Jimmy just after it happened, but now that you're here, I'll talk some more about him today. Also Gadge wasn't here the last time. I'm going to ask him to say a few words about Jimmy."

At this point in the story, my mind plays a strange trick on me. I can't remember the audition for Kazan and Williams the way it actually happened. Over the years I've had a recurring anxiety-filled dream about that reading, and today the dream has won over the reality.

In the dream I am kneeling under a bench, my boobs hanging out of the front of my dress, and I'm very upset because they have shrunk. My eyes are directed upward at Kazan, who is standing erect and leering at me. Tennessee is a gigantic white, round balloon with a pig's head. His hog face is stark white and bloated with two round rouged spots on his puffed-out cheeks. He is saying, "She'll have to be fattened up. She needs to weigh fifty pounds more. Her breasts will have to be globular. She must be whiter. Her cheeks will have to be plumper and painted like mine in two circles of rouge."

Kazan is saying, "But, Tennessee, you've already created a bizarre character, and I want to use a normal girl to bring her to life."

Tennessee says, "But this girl is dull, dreary, and titless. I want a sexy 'piglette.'"

He and Kazan get into a heated argument. Tennessee, being a balloon, starts to bounce out of the room with Kazan following, and I am left under the bench crying and unable to crawl out. I wake up at this point with a feeling of emptiness.

All I remember about what really happened during that audition is that Tennessee did want the fat rouged cheeks and additional weight gain, while Kazan (thank heavens) wanted me just as I was. I was also aware that Marilyn was a hot contender for the part, and I did wish my breasts were as big as hers. I find it extraordinary that I keep having the dream, because, after all, I did get the part.

Kazan never employed the services of a casting agent. He believed that casting the right actors for the parts comprised ninety percent of the director's contribution. Once cast, he began to see the actors as the characters and encouraged this fusion. Nor was Gadge an egotist; he felt the director's place was in the background, selecting, molding, and orchestrating the actors' creations. That is why actors longed to work with him, why he has had so many great performances to his credit, and why, once having worked for him, no other work experience quite measured up.

Tennessee's script was a sheer delight, full of humor and poetry, laced with the serious theme of revenge. Baby Doll Meighan is a child-woman who sleeps in a crib and sucks her thumb. Her daddy had given her in marriage to an older man, Archie Lee Meighan, the successful owner of a cotton gin. Baby Doll's daddy gave her to Archie Lee on two conditions: One, that he provide for her; and two, that he resist consummating the marriage until her twentieth birthday.

The movie begins when Baby Doll is nineteen years old and Archie Lee is consumed with an unfulfilled passion for his child bride. He resorts to drilling peep holes in the walls to try and catch a glimpse of her in her bedroom when she is unaware and, he hopes, nude.

Baby Doll's twentieth birthday, the day Archie Lee is to possess her, is drawing near, but it looks as if he will be unable to meet the other condition her daddy laid down—that of providing for her. A foreigner, Silva Vicarro, has moved into the territory and with his modern, efficient cotton gin has taken away all of Archie Lee's customers. Archie Lee's old mansion has fallen into disrepair, and the furniture company is threatening to repossess the furnishings. Baby Doll is adamant that her daddy's wishes be carried out. That means that if the furniture goes, so does every hope of Archie Lee's to satisfy his carnal lust for Baby Doll.

Tennessee's dialogue was scrumptious. Perhaps my favorite line was the one I said angrily to Archie Lee, after he insinuated that I was dumb: "Listen here, Archie Lee Meighan, I've been to school in my life. And I'm a magazine reader!" Another favorite was when the inept Aunt Rose Comfort serves up a mess of sloppy "greens" floating in rancid oil and Archie Lee says to her in disgust, "Aunt Rose, you been cookin' around here and cookin' around there—how many years you been cookin' around people's houses?"

Archie Lee, broke and at his wit's end, sneaks off and burns down Vicarro's cotton gin. Vicarro then comes to the Meighan house to seek revenge. It is Baby Doll who is there alone at the isolated old mansion to receive Vicarro's hot and unrelenting vengeance. Even if you haven't seen the film, I think you can guess what prize it is that Vicarro snatches from Archie Lee as payment for his burnt down cotton gin!

BABY DOLL AND ELLIE MAY

It was just three short weeks after having finished *Giant* that I was in Benoit, Mississippi, to begin preliminary work on what was tentatively titled *Mississippi Woman.* Gadge had presented us with all the tools of the craft to work with: He took us to the location nearly a month in advance of the filming so that we could get the feel of the South, learn about the local people, and, he hoped, perfect a Mississippi drawl.

I left New York with the idea that Baby Doll Meighan was a totally bizarre invention of Tennessee's. What I learned was that girls like her were far from fictitious. Every element and quality that I needed to justify her was there to be discovered in the women of Benoit. Even the name "Baby Doll" was commonly used! One man told me, "Yeh, we sure do use that name. Why, my sister's name is Baby Doll, and we used to have a pet cow called Baby Doll."

Although I was playing a girl of nineteen, I found the perfect model for her in Ellie May, an eighty-year-old Southern belle. Ellie May spoke in a combination of Mississippi dialect and baby talk. The moment I heard her, I knew that those speech patterns were deliciously right for the part. From then on I spent hours with Ellie May.

My model dressed in the yellows, purples, pinks, and whites of the Mississippi magnolia. Like the magnolia she was a delicate, showy, fragrant blossom cultivated for ornament; but Ellie May's backbone was of steel. She was the matriarch, the ruler supreme, over her children and grandchildren (all male) to whom she referred collectively as "her boys." Individually they were John Boy, Bill Boy, Little John Boy, Little Bill Boy, etc. Even when her husband had been alive, she had wielded all the power. He had been her Big John Boy. Her strength of character was not immediately apparent, hidden as it was behind the veneer of charming Southern manners, feminine graces, and coquettishness. Ellie May was alert, spry, witty and vain. One soon forgot that she was an octogenarian. Although she was flattered by my visits, I didn't fool myself for one second into believing that my motives were anything but perfectly clear to her.

Small towns naturally look upon film units with suspicion and apprehension. And don't forget, we were Yankees! But Kazan was a clever politician. Not one piece of equipment was unloaded until we had socialized with and been accepted by the locals. Gadge gave a party in the town hall and invited all the menfolk to a booze up. Milly Dunnock and I had endless teas with the ladies. The crew extensively courted the single girls, Gadge having impressed upon them the importance of respecting the married women. Karl and Eli hung out at the pool room. So by the time filming began, the town of Benoit knew us, trusted us, and were ready to cooperate in every way.

Before the rehearsals began, Gadge took each actor aside for a long, private conversation. He wanted to know us as individuals. He wanted to know every attitude, hang up, and quirk, what made us tick. He delved deeply into the analogy between the character's traits and our own. "What of yourself can you use?" was one of his main questions. "If you believe that aspect of the character is different from you, what can you bring from your own life which will be similar?"

This intimate session with Gadge, while I wanted to reap every benefit from his tried-and-proved method, nonetheless made me extremely uncomfortable. For one thing, I had always been reticent to talk about myself in any depth, and for another, his reputation as a womanizer made me loath to make myself vulnerable. I told you that there were no secrets at the Actors' Studio—well, we all knew which girls Gadge had laid, and those girls he hadn't laid made a very short list indeed. We all knew that he had had affairs with nearly all of his leading ladies. Eva Marie Saint had told me how relieved she was that she had

151

escaped being an entry on Gadge's roster of screws. Gadge had been quoted on numerous occasions as having claimed, "When they can't give me the performance I expect, I can at least fuck them." I wanted desperately to be remembered as a "good performance" rather than a "consolation fuck."

But don't think for one second that it was easy for me to resist Gadge. He was devastatingly attractive and a master of seduction. My interview took place late in the day, after everyone else had gone home. The room we used in the old mansion was cozy and dimly lit. He was informal and relaxed and had stretched out on the cushions of the couch with his arms resting behind his head and his feet on the coffee table. He was my lord and the master of my fate. I craved his understanding, his approval, his affection. And there he was, for the taking. He had set the scene to perfection, even to the heady, semisweet, thick red wine. Desire was oozing from his every pore, and his eyes were blazing with passion. My curiosity to be near him, to touch him, to feel his arms around me, to cuddle into his chest, was overwhelming. All I had to do was make those few short steps from my chair over to him and I knew that once I was within reach, he would have done the rest. I came within a hair's breadth of succumbing to my curiosity and desire, but I was able to suddenly switch gears. As seriously as I regarded marital fidelity, it was not Jack's face I saw before me at the moment that pulled me up sharply —but Eva Marie's. I knew I had to be able to brag to her, as she had bragged to me, that I was not one of Kazan's screws.

One day Gadge took us all through the house and asked each of us, "Which do you think would be your room? What would you have in your room? Milly, what would you have in the kitchen? Karl, where would you keep your tools and which tools would you have? Carroll, what would you have by your crib and in the bathroom? Eli, what would Vicarro wear?" Little wonder that there wasn't one costume, one piece of furniture, or one prop that wasn't familiar and just right—every detail had been so well worked out. I lived in a hotel I couldn't describe now, but I can recall every inch of that "Meighan house."

In rehearsal Gadge turned me and Eli loose on the grounds of the house and told us, "Use everything, try everything, go wild, don't be afraid to do anything no matter how silly it might seem. Anything that comes into your heads, be courageous—try it. Let me see it. It will be weeks before we set anything, so now is the time to experiment."

Gadge was earthy and completely approachable. He made everyone involved in the project feel like a full participant. His crew would have walked through fire for him, because no other director had ever made them sense that enormous satisfaction of being an equal contributor to the whole. On his sets, everyone was encouraged to come forward with an idea. When Gadge had a problem he discussed it openly. For example, the opening shot of the film was of the old Southern mansion. Gadge was concerned that the audience might get the impression of a period piece. It was a gaffer who stepped forward and said, "Hey, Gadge, why not wait until a jet plane flies overhead?" It was a brilliant idea which Gadge jumped at, one by the way which has been imitated many times since. Imagine the feeling of pride that will forever be with that gaffer!

I had a scene in which I was waiting in the open car for Archie Lee. The script indicated that all of the local men standing outside the store made fun of Archie Lee as he exited the store and walked to the car. Because the whole town knew that the marriage had not been consummated and that Baby Doll was still a virgin, the local men were always jeering. Gadge also wanted something visual to hinge the laughter on. He asked Karl and me, "Can either of you think of something that you might be doing? Something that might motivate the jeering?" I said, "My daddy was a traveling salesman, and whenever I used to wait for him in the car, he would always bring me an ice cream cone." Gadge threw his cap down in the dusty street and stamped and hollered for joy. "That's perfect, perfect," he howled. "It will make Archie Lee feel silly and doubly humiliated having to cross in front of the guys with a dripping ice cream cone. It is a perfect childish prop for you. I'll shoot Archie Lee's reactions and those of the crowd as you lick the cone, and we'll have our sexual connotations there, too." Even now, whenever I remember this, the pride I felt at having my idea accepted rushes back to me.

An "activity" suggestion of mine which Gadge went for in a big way was used during the "bathroom scene." Archie Lee stands outside the bathroom talking to Baby Doll through the closed door while she takes her bath. We had naturally thought of the toy boats and rubber ducks for Baby Doll, but I suggested that, during the dialogue, Baby Doll be washing her laundry in the tub along with herself. It was wonderfully tacky. And Gadge also let me wear a funny, unflattering shower cap halfway down my forehead, with my ears sticking out. What joy it was to work with him on the comedy.

The end of that scene, by the way, is when Archie Lee can't contain his lasciviousness any longer, and we see him rush into the bathroom. Off-camera we hear the sound of his splashing into the tub over Baby Doll's howls of protest.

Before leaving for the location, I had seen my first pair of Baby Doll pajamas in a New York store window. I couldn't resist the tie-in with my character's name, so I bought them on the spot and took them with me to Benoit. Both Anna Hill Johnstone, the costume designer, and Gadge thought that those rompers were perfect for my initial crib scene. Too bad I had no marketing sense then, because I never requested a cent for having made those Baby Doll pajamas so famous.

Other than the pajamas, Anna Hill and I shopped locally for my clothes. They had to be inexpensive and a couple of sizes too small, as if I had grown out of them. We came across a silly little white-satin pancake hat. The moment I saw that ridiculous hat I went mad for it. Anna Hill agreed that Baby Doll would be pretentious enough to wear a hat, along with her best suit, when going for a drive in Archie Lee's rattling, decrepit, mud-caked car. That satin pancake was the most chic and expensive hat in all Benoit. It cost $12.95, and Anna Hill even went so far as to give Baby Doll a pair of short, white gloves to complete her ensemble during her simple outings. What laughs we had while coming up with one outrageous idea after another! I believe Gadge wet his pants when Karl suggested that Baby Doll would be snotty enough to insist upon riding in the back seat of the old Chevy, making Archie Lee chauffeur her to town.

My most difficult acting scene was the one I call the "pig-sty scene." Although I can't remember any longer why Baby Doll was so upset, the scene called for hysterical crying and then laughter and tears together. I knew that if I was to continue fierce crying and add simultaneous laughter, I would have to enter the scene fully sobbing my heart out. I went behind the barn to do my preparation—hours and hours of preparation! I thought of every terrible memory I possibly could, and although I felt like hell, no tears would come. Finally our cameraman, Boris Kaufman, told Gadge, "I'm afraid we will have to shoot it right now or else postpone it until tomorrow because the light is going."

Gadge came to me and said, "We can't wait for you any longer, Carroll. Never mind. We'll do the scene without tears."

I was so humiliated to have kept Gadge and Eli and all the crew waiting all afternoon, and so frustrated over my lack of ability that while running to my position in front of the pig sty I burst into the most gorgeous, sloppy tears. My feelings swelled and overflowed convulsively into laughter, making it my most effective scene. But alas, the audience will never share that opinion. Flushed as I was with my histrionic triumph, I failed to notice that in the background those squealing, snorting, grunting, groveling, farting little piggies were completely stealing the scene away from me.

Gadge never wanted his cast to be aware of the camera. No technician was to worry the actors about a difficulty with the sound or the lights. Our concentration was given the highest priority. During the camera rehearsals, Gadge went so far as to whisper his instructions to the crew, to protect us from any concern about the technical aspects.

No scene was rigidly plotted, so during a take the camera operator was trained to follow the actors whatever they might do, to be alert for any unexpected movement or gesture, and to guide the camera accordingly. If we began to edge out of frame and there was a split-second decision to be made, the operator knew that Gadge relied on him not to halt, but to make that decision. At one moment in the "swing scene," my head drifted sideways and hung over the swing nearly to the ground. It was lovely the way the operator caught that spontaneous dip.

Under no circumstances did any of us, in front of or behind the camera, stop or cut a take. Even if we said the wrong line or there was a technical hitch, we continued until Gadge called out, "Cut." He sometimes loved the effect created by a mistake. He often allowed the film to roll after the completion of the dialogue in order to capture some lingering expression or an added thought.

We had a scene on an outdoor double-seated swing where Vicarro seduces Baby Doll. I doubt that Eli and I could have done that provocative, sultry "swing scene" without the thoroughly professional, no-silly-jokes-attitude on a Kazan set. I certainly would never have had the concentration and courage to allow myself to become so totally passionate, or the security and willingness to reveal the depth of what was happening to me.

Given that ideal working atmosphere, the youthful enthusiasm with which I threw myself into the character, the story, and the relationship, I underwent the emotional confusion often felt by actors. The way I treated sweet, darling Karl Malden must have been intolerable for him. I thought so long and hard about my resentment and physical abhorrence of Archie Lee that I couldn't just turn it off. I'm sure Karl felt some of that attitude unintentionally directed at him. Mildred Dunnock resigned herself to my petulance toward her at one moment and protectiveness the next. I think she understood that for the duration of the film, I was going to relate to her as Aunt Rose Comfort. And gentle, refined Eli Wallach loomed in my imagination as that frightening, callus brute Silva Vicarro, to whom I was also irresistibly drawn. I soon found myself besotted by Eli/Vicarro.

Eli, however, could never quite take me seriously. He forever had a twinkle of understanding in his sparkling, dancing eyes. Whether I was showing an exaggerated fear of him or a scorching fervor, he regarded me quite rightly as an overimaginative, overheated pubescent. But that didn't dampen my ardor or keep me from making a complete fool of myself. I might as well describe how wrapped up I was in the Stanislavski method and how I behaved offscreen during the "unsatisfactory supper scene," because it is no secret any more—thanks to Eli.

In this scene, Aunt Rose Comfort is in the kitchen preparing her unsatisfactory supper, and Archie Lee is at the daft old lady's side, harassing her. Vicarro and I are kissing in the hallway just outside the kitchen. Vicarro and I then enter the kitchen with the telltale smears of lipstick on our faces and our clothes askew.

Although they had finished filming Eli and me kissing, and had moved the camera away from us and into the kitchen set, I didn't release Eli. Since we were supposed to re-enter dishevelled and breathless and flushed, I just wouldn't stop kissing him. All through the lengthy dialogue between Milly and Karl, as well as several takes of that scene, I had Eli pinned against the outside wall of the set in an endless, inescapable kiss. Now another method actress might possibly kiss once again, so as to enter in the called-for emotional state, but no halfway preparation for this method actress. I wasn't willing to let one puff of steam evaporate. It was only the cue to enter the scene that saved Eli from being utterly suffocated by my determined and feverish assault.

Eli must have been surprised at first, then curious to see how far I intended to go, possibly a bit flattered, no doubt somewhat excited himself, and certainly amused. The last must be true, because I have never been able to shut him up about this indiscretion. That devil has told that story around the world, and it has been repeated to me by journalists from Calcutta to Chicago and from Tallahassee to Bangkok. There is no way I can ever hope to live it down.

In my efforts to be real in the sexually evocative scenes of the film, I worked myself into a combustible, near-volcanic state of desire. So much so that it wasn't all released on celluloid. I was still smoldering after the "takes," so that if anyone inadvertently touched me it was difficult to suppress a moan. I got really worried when I couldn't sit in the makeup chair without fear of climaxing . . . it was that powder puff! . . . or was I feeling an overwhelming lust for my makeup man, Bob Jiras? . . . or was it a combination of Bob's gentle touch and that soft, sensuous powder puff? Anyway, he caressed my face and earlobes and neck with that powder puff and drove me totally crazy!

I urgently felt that it was time I telephoned Jack and got him to come to Mississippi for the weekend. I remembered a story that Shelley Winters had told me. She was on location for a film and going mad for the want of sex. The guy she really wanted was 2,000 miles away, but nonetheless she flew off over the weekend to be with him. During the days of the studio system, contract players were heavily insured and not permitted to fly during a production. Shelley's producer discovered that she had violated the travel clause and was waiting for her on Monday morning:

PRODUCER: Shelley, I have a right to fire you. You have no excuse for leaving the location.

SHELLEY: Oh, yes I do. It was an emergency!

PRODUCER: Oh, I'm sorry. What kind of an emergency?

SHELLEY: I desperately needed to get fucked!

Well, I telephoned Jack and told him about my emergency. Here's our conversation as I remember it:

CARROLL: So, darling, can you fly down for the weekend?

JACK: It's impossible this weekend because I have an important script conference, but I'll get there as soon as I can.

CARROLL: Jack, I wish you'd hurry!

JACK: Don't worry, I'll be there in a couple of days.

CARROLL: A couple of days! Jack, I'm going out of my mind. These scenes have me turned on all the time!

JACK: Well, don't do anything you shouldn't. Wait for me. I'll get there just as soon as I can.

CARROLL: Please hurry!

JACK: Yes, yes I will. What else is new?

CARROLL: I don't know. I can't think about anything but sex! What's new with you?

JACK: Well, there is something I meant to call and ask you about. There is an opening this Saturday night and Marilyn is alone and wants me to take her.

CARROLL: What! Jack, you bastard, I'm alone and I want you to take me!

JACK: All right, all right, now don't get excited. I didn't say "yes" yet. I wanted to wait and ask you first.

CARROLL: Ask me what? Ask me if you can get into Marilyn's opening?

JACK: Now, there's no reason to be crude. I didn't say anything about getting into Marilyn's opening, or about taking her, as you meant it.

CARROLL: Well, you might as well have. You don't for one minute think that I'm going to believe that you would pick up Marilyn Monroe, escort her to an opening, take her home, and refuse to go inside for a nightcap if she invites you, do you?

JACK: Now you're flattering me. Why should Marilyn Monroe be romantically interested in me?

CARROLL: Oh, yeah, all you have to do is start in again on your cockamamie interpretation of *Miss Julie* and Marilyn will be writhing at your feet.

JACK: Carroll, you have no reason to be jealous. I love you and you know that I've never been with another woman.

CARROLL: No, I don't know that you've never been with another woman. How would I know whether or not you've cheated me? And anyway if you're seen with Marilyn, it will be in every gossip column, and everybody will think that you're having an affair with her.

JACK: Look who's talking. You certainly can't be trusted. I'll probably never know how many of the actors on *Giant* you got involved with. I've heard about you and Dean, and you and Hudson, and I've just recently learned about you and Earl Holliman.

CARROLL: Damn you, Jack, you know that isn't true. You just want to punish me forever because of Ben Gazzara. But we weren't married then. I have never cheated on you since we've been married.

JACK: Don't think I won't find out if you've had an affair with Kazan because Gadge talks and I'll hear it from someone.

CARROLL: Jack, you're rotten, when you know that I'm trying so hard to control myself.

JACK: Oh, is it such an effort then?

CARROLL: Yes, goddammit, you know it is. That's what I called you about in the first place. You're just starting a fight with me so you'll have an excuse to do what you want to do because your tongue is hanging out for Marilyn Monroe.

JACK: No, but that's why you started the fight because you're hot for someone there on location. Who is it?

CARROLL: Everybody, anybody. That's why I called you in the first place, you big jerk. But now I've changed my mind. I don't want you to come. I don't want to see you. Stay right where you are, but don't you dare be seen with Marilyn or we're finished for good.

JACK: Okay, we are both being silly. I'll get there as soon as possible and take care of your urgent needs, but in the meantime can I tell Marilyn "yes"?

CARROLL: Jack, what you can do is stay where you are and fuck yourself.

Well, Jack did arrive a few days later, and he was not seen with Marilyn, at least not publicly.

Mississippi Woman was a very low-budget film, with none of the luxuries of the *Giant* production. We not only didn't have warm trailers to relax in, but we didn't even have those camp chairs to sit on. The Mississippi nights in November and December were cold and damp, and during the night shooting, between set-ups, I would pull up a wooden crate and, like everybody else, huddle around the huge bonfire which the crew always built in the front yard. The crew were dressed in boots and parkas, and Karl and Eli had on trousers and flannel shirts, but I did one entire week of the night filming in a silk slip and my bare feet. But what good care every one of the guys took of me! After a take, I would rush to the fire and one of the crew would throw a blanket around me, while someone else hurriedly rubbed the circulation back into my frozen feet. I was always offered a hot drink or a shot of whiskey along with a dollop of heartwarming concern. The difficult moment came when the next scene was ready, because that meant not only giving up the blanket and the fire, but chewing ice before entering a shot so that my breath wouldn't be seen on film.

We were in Benoit for Thanksgiving and Christmas, and on both holidays Kazan held a family-style dinner for us. Like a "Big Daddy," he sat at the head of an enormous table and carved a huge turkey. We toasted each other and our absent loved ones. How splendid of a director not to forget the importance of such special occasions, to gather his people around him, and to provide the ceremonies which helped to make being away from home bearable.

When the filming was over, Phil Silbert, the set designer, offered to give me the crib, but I turned it down. Can you imagine how much I would love to have it today and what it must be worth? "Carroll, why don't you take the crib? It is a lovely antique," Phil said. I replied, "No, thank you, Phil. It is awfully large and what would I do with it?" He even coaxed me, "But it would be a nice memento and you could use it as a planter." "No, thanks," I said. "I'm only going to keep one small souvenir, the charm bracelet maybe." Fool!

Kazan gave me the best of all parting presents. On our last day in Benoit, he said, "Carroll, you are so spectacular in the film that I'm going to call the movie *Baby Doll.*"

Ellie May adored seeing herself on the screen as Baby Doll. I corresponded with her until she passed away at the age of ninety-six, and for her funeral I sent a bush of pink and white magnolias.

Chapter

Seventeen

THE WEIRD JAMES DEAN CULT

It was the beginning of 1956, and I desperately wanted to have a child before the year was out. With arrogant certainty, I resolved to make 1956 the most meaningful year of my life. I would be turning twenty-five, and twenty-five had an exaggerated, fatalistic significance for me. Somewhere along the way I had decided that twenty-five was the absolute peak of life.

I also believed the day I gave up contraceptives would be the day I became pregnant. Well, that turned out to be a fallacy. Jack and I tried for three months without success. Lord, it was maddening the way my doctor kept repeating, "Relax and have patience." And after the fourth month of "working on getting pregnant" passed without results, I was convinced something was wrong with either Jack or me or both of us. We were ready to submit to a series of lengthy, disagreeable tests, when at last I skipped a period.

The splendid news that I was pregnant came a few days before my twenty-fifth birthday.

Although I had nowhere in our one-room apartment to store it, I rushed out and bought the white nursery furniture with red apple knobs that I had my heart set on. The nursery would be right for either a girl or a boy, and I didn't care which, because I knew that I would never be able to stop at just one child. Perhaps if work went well, I could manage three or even four. I remembered having read *Cheaper by the Dozen* in high school and seriously contemplating that large a family. Perhaps if I hadn't pursued a career, if I'd stayed in Pennsylvania, maybe lived on a farm, I just might have raised a dozen. My best school chum, Bunny, already had four, with another one on the way.

Bunny was dreaming of owning a washing machine. It dawned on me that now I, too, could use a washing machine. I didn't think of lending her the money because Jack and I needed so many things ourselves.

Imagine—I was under contract to Warner Brothers for two pictures a year for the next six years, had two important films "in the can," and I was worried about washing machines!

I called my dad to see if he could get two machines wholesale, one for Bunny and one for me. My dad had a small hardware store in Norvelt, outside Greensburg, and he told me he no longer had any connections with the appliance company.

I wish Dad had been more enthusiastic about my having a baby, but he couldn't conceal his skepticism over the security of a child's future when both parents were in show business. I couldn't wait to get off the phone, because he lectured me for ten minutes on responsibility, and nagged me for another ten about taking a secretarial course while I was pregnant.

My mother gave the whoops and hollers over my news that I had anticipated, but I got the feeling that she was overreacting slightly in an effort to make me feel special. Right after high school, Boopie had married an Air Force colonel who was stationed at McDill Air Force Base in Tampa, and she had given birth, six months ago, to an adorable baby girl. So, even though I was older, Boopie had beaten me to it and presented Mother with her first grandchild.

I had some other news: Louis Ritter was dead. After the police had picked him up for running naked down Fifth Avenue, his family had had him committed to an insane asylum—or so the story was passed on to me. It seems he had talked his way out of the asylum after a few months, and then had died shortly afterwards of unknown causes.

His family had kept the news from me as long as possible (perhaps in the hope that I would be too late in filing a claim for his estate). If so, they needn't have worried. I didn't feel that on the basis of our brief sham of a marriage, I was entitled to—or even wanted—Louie's money. I felt so blessed in my own life; and I wished only that Louie's troubled soul would at last find peace.

I discovered, to my delight, that after having watched my father when I was a child, I had acquired some of his skills purely by observation. Sewing came easily to me, as did handy work around the house; and once I began to take up cooking and baking in earnest, I was on my way to becoming a well-rounded, talented homemaker. But most of my day was taken up shifting furniture from one end of our studio apartment to the other.

Once we had added a rocking chair and the nursery to our crowded one-room, it became almost impossible to move around in the place. If I came in the front door with groceries, I had to climb over our bed to get to the kitchenette. While I was cooking, I had to push the table up against the bathroom door, blocking the entrance; and to get to the windows, I had to move the nursery furniture. So, the next priority became finding a bigger place to live.

We had a stroke of exceptionally good luck in our house-hunting. We were able to sublease a rent-controlled apartment from a friend. When we moved, we went from the ridiculous to the sublime: a three-bedroom apartment on Central Park West, with a large entrance hall, high ceilings, and a huge living room with a Park view!

In late September, cuddled snuggly in my cozy nest, blissfully content with my big belly, all thoughts of movies or glamour were gone from my head. It was one of those delightful sleep-in Sunday mornings. I was voluptuously nuzzled warm and happy in my marital bed when the sharp, piercing sound of the telephone stabbed my marshmallow visions. I shifted my belly to look around at Jack, hoping that he would put a stop to the clanging, which had to be a wrong number, because nobody calls at dawn on a Sunday morning! Perhaps he would quickly dispatch with the disagreeable noise and then mercifully allow the phone to remain off the hook. But Jack was fast asleep and didn't even stir during the persistent ringing, although the phone was on the floor by his side of the bed. I shook him but he didn't respond in the slightest.

Ring! I couldn't bear to throw off the woolen covers and walk around on that cold hardwood floor. Ring! I couldn't see my robe and I could no longer bend over to put my slippers on. Ring! Well, whoever it was was certainly determined. Ring! I would just have to shake Jack some more. Ring! It was no use, Jack wouldn't budge. Ring!

I managed to roll on top of Jack and then over him to the edge of the bed. With one hand I grabbed the noisy instrument, while trying with my other hand to cover myself with an end of the sheet.

"Hello," I wheezed. "You have the wrong number."

"Good morning," boomed a loud and all-too-cheery voice. "Is this Miss Baker?"

"I think so."

"Is this Miss Carroll Baker?"

"Yeah."

"Miss Baker, my name is Mr. So-and-so of UPI."

"You must have the wrong number."

"Is this Miss Carroll Baker?"

"Yeah, what day is today? Isn't this Sunday?"

"Miss Baker, this is a reporter from the UPI. . . ."

"I can't see the clock from here. Isn't it terribly early?"

"Miss Baker, are you listening?"

"I'm trying to but I'm hanging over the bed and I'm cold. My husband has turned over and taken all the covers and anyway there is no sense talking to me when I'm half asleep. I probably won't be able to remember what I'm saying."

"Miss Baker," he said sternly, as if I had disturbed *his* sleep, "this is Mr. So-and-so of UPI. . . ."

"Do I know you? Ouch!"

"Miss Baker, is anything wrong?"

"My baby just kicked."

He launched nonstop into a speech, giving me no time to interrupt him again. "Miss Baker, as I said, this is United Press International, your film has been condemned by the Catholic Legion of Decency and this morning Cardinal Spellman has denounced it from the pulpit of St. Patrick's cathedral. Have you anything to say?"

Pause.

"Miss Baker?"

165

Pause.

"Miss Baker, have you anything to say?"

"Which film?"

He lost his composure and stuttered, "Wha—whadda ya mean, wh-which film?"

"Which film, *Giant* or *Baby Doll?*"

There was no more peace that morning—or, it seemed, for years to come. The phone continued to ring, and the press continued to badger me with questions about the nature of *Baby Doll.* I needed help, but Jack had a pillow over his head and was refusing to respond, so I had to resort to shaking him violently and assaulting him with my most annoying voice.

"Please, Jack! Wake up! Please! Make some coffee! Please! Give me some covers! Please! Please! Please!"

"What, what," he mumbled, and rolled further away to escape my attack, taking with him the last vestige of the sheet I'd been holding.

"Waaaaaaaa!" I screamed, bouncing up and down with all my might, "Jack! Give me some blanket! I'm cold! Turn on the heat! And get up, it's *Baby Doll!*"

He rolled my way, bringing a remnant of the cover with him, and slurring, "What? Your sister?"

"My sister's nickname is 'Boopie.' Jack, please turn on the heat and make some coffee. It's about *Baby Doll!*"

"Baby Doll who?"

"Very funny. We know dozens of girls named Baby Doll."

"What about Baby Doll?"

Rinnnnggggg!!!

"This call is all yours," I said, handing him the hateful receiver. "I'm getting up to turn on the heat and make some coffee."

The time had come to begin to think about films again. *Giant* was opening in October and *Baby Doll* two months later. I had to find a mother-to-be evening gown and coat to wear to the *Giant* premiere. I probably wouldn't make the *Baby Doll* premiere because my baby was due mid-December. I couldn't ignore any longer the fact that the crib photograph was being painted on the largest billboard that Manhattan had ever seen.

With James Dean in *Giant*

With Elizabeth Taylor and Rock
Hudson in *Giant*

My Elizabeth Taylor "look"

Baby Doll opens in London in 1957

Elia Kazan working his magic with me and Karl Malden in *Baby Doll*

With Eli Wallach in *Baby Doll*

With Eli Wallach in *Baby Doll*

"Baby Doll" beckons Karl Malden

With Eli Wallach in *Baby Doll*

The picture of me—dressed in my rompers, curled in my crib, and sucking my thumb—was above the Victoria and Astor theatres on a sign which was an entire city block long!

Now, also, a controversy was being blown out of all proportion. Why should the Legion of Decency take exception to the film? Was any film important enough to warrant Cardinal Spellman's denunciation from the pulpit of St. Patrick's cathedral? The last time the Cardinal had personally addressed himself to an issue had been to condemn the Communists for the imprisonment of Cardinal Mindszenty. How could a film compare in importance to a human rights issue? But it got even sillier. Dean Pike defended our film and in so doing made the statement that *The Ten Commandments* was a more objectionable movie than *Baby Doll.* Cecil B. DeMille decried such an unfavorable comparison. Once walking down a side street, I saw a church's announcement board list the sermon of the day as *Baby Doll* versus *The Ten Commandments.*

Life magazine had written a glowing advance report about the exceptional artistic merits of *Baby Doll* and called it the "sleeper" of the year. Along with the text were printed the most beautiful stills from the movie. The week the controversy began, another article appeared virtually retracting everything good that had previously been said about the film, completely slanting the new article with sleazy innuendo, all accompanied by murky, insinuating photographs.

In the meantime, a man from Warner's New York office telephoned to tell me that I had been chosen "Best New Actress of the Year" by *Look* magazine. They wanted to take a head and shoulders shot of me for their forthcoming issue, and, since Warner's was the producer of both my films, they preferred that I dye my hair the color it had been in *Giant,* to insure greater identification with my role in *Giant* than *Baby Doll.* He told me the advance reaction to *Giant* made it look like a hot contender for the Academy Awards. Because of the moral ban, Warner's wanted to play down the discredited *Baby Doll* and aim toward every possible award for *Giant.* They wanted to promote me for a "Best Supporting Actress" in *Giant* rather than a "Best Actress" in *Baby Doll.* It was not out of disloyalty to Mrs. Meighan, but because I was anxious that my performance in *Giant* not be overlooked in all the hoopla and controversy of the Kazan film, that I did dye my hair a medium brown. With the more wholesome image I posed for the *Look* magazine photograph and also for *Modern Screen,* which listed me as one of the "ten most promising newcomers of the year." My performance in *Giant* won for me "Best Supporting Actress" from the Film Exhibitors, and also from the Women's Press Corps.

A week before the *Giant* premiere, I bought a black silk-and-lace evening gown. The silk flared from the lace yoke bodice to the ground and hung softly in folds which partially concealed my pregnancy. The evening coat I found was of maroon velvet with gold trim, and it too hung widely from the shoulders. With my medium-brown hair, I looked demure, and certainly a far cry from that outrageous image painted over Times Square.

Accounts were circulating of a weird cult who worshipped James Dean, believing that he was still alive. A group of these fanatics had been camped outside the Roxy Theatre, expecting to see Jimmy arrive at the *Giant* premiere. Two hours before we were due to leave for the theatre, George Stevens had a reception for the cast in his hotel suite. The head of Warner's publicity department gave a speech in which he advised us that there was some concern for our safety. The New York Police Department believed that they were well-prepared, that the wooden barriers would hold back the crowds, and as long as nothing sparked off a riot, our entrance into the theatre should go smoothly. We were instructed not to go into the crowd or reply to any inflammatory shouts. The press would be permitted to photograph us entering the theatre, but in case of a warning from the police chief, we were to calmly but steadily file past the press and into the auditorium.

How delightful it was to greet my Marfa roommates, Mercedes and Jane and Fran. Two hours was hardly enough time to' greet everyone, and yet I wanted to talk at length with all of them, with George Stevens and Rock Hudson and Earl Holliman.

Elizabeth was now married to Mike Todd. She seemed so happy and so much more mature and confident. Mike had presented her with a pair of ten-thousand-dollar diamond earrings as a present for the *Giant* premiere. I hardly had time to admire them properly and say a few words to her, when it was time to file downstairs and into the limos.

There was an enormous crowd outside the Roxy, stretching for blocks in every direction and ten deep. They cheered and waved and leaned over the police barricades to peer into the limos. They seemed excited but friendly.

Jack and I stepped out of our limo and onto the sidewalk immediately behind Elizabeth and Mike Todd. A loud roar went up from the crowd. I had expected applause and cheers for Elizabeth, but something was terribly wrong in the sound of that grating and discordant roar.

Having been first in line, the fanatic Dean cult were nearest the red-carpet aisle leading into the entrance. Those closest to us were thrashing against the barriers, letting out menacing eerie cries; they had red, distorted, lunatic-like faces. The sight of them filled me with revulsion a moment before the premonition of danger gripped me. Jack held my arm tightly. "Carroll, I don't like the look of this. Let's try to get into the lobby."

But the path of entry was narrow and clogged by reporters and photographers who had no intention of giving way. Mike Todd also sensed danger. He turned over his shoulder to Jack and me, observed the hysterical, pushing crowd, and shouted, "You better think about that baby and get inside away from this. I'm going to have to shove the photographers aside and get Elizabeth to safety." As Mike began to tunnel his way through the first group of cameramen, there was an explosion of human bodies across the barricades and a stampede of howling maniacs trampled each other and rushed the actors. Cameras flew in the air along with notepads, policemen's caps, and ladies' handbags. Jane Withers fell to her knees. Millions of hands were tearing at us, our gowns, our jewelry, our hair. Jack threw his arms around me to protect our baby. I could feel the hammering on his back and arms. His pleas of "Stop! Stop! My wife is pregnant!" were drowned in a cacophony of wild, furious raving.

Three girls were hanging on Elizabeth's hair and forcing her into a backbend. Mike threw his body weight against them to dislodge them, and then, putting his arm around Elizabeth, seemed to protectively tuck her head under his arm and onto his chest. Elizabeth was screaming, "My earring, I've lost one of my ten-thousand-dollar earrings!"

"Forget the earrings," Mike said, "I'll buy you another pair!"

The police were regaining their footing and struggling to throw their bodies around us in a cordon. The photographers also backed up against the crowd and gave us enough of an opening to dart into the safety of the lobby.

The actors who had arrived first and missed the rioting were already in their seats. Those of us who had been in the thick of it were ushered into the manager's office and given large brandies. Everyone's first thought was for my baby. George Stevens wanted to call a doctor, but I assured him that physically I felt fine. Jack had protected me by taking all the knocks himself. George excused himself and went to talk to the projectionist.

Mike grabbed the telephone. "I got to call Sam Goldwyn. What time is it in California?"

We were all very dishevelled and a bit bruised, but no one was seriously injured. Jane Withers looked as if she had taken the worst punishment. She had raw, skinned knees and a hopelessly torn evening gown. Rock was bending over her. He had lost his bow tie, his shirt front was ripped open, and one cuff dangled over his hand where the cuff link had fallen out. Jane was forever jolly, and Rock always had a twinkle in his eyes, so they looked as though they'd been costumed for a one-reel black-and-white comedy.

"Oh, your poor knees!" Elizabeth squealed. Turning to the manager, she told him to find a first-aid kit. I could have sworn he bowed before backing out of the room.

Jane protested good-naturedly, "Naw, don't worry about me, Liz, I been livin' on a ranch. I'm used to a few scratches."

But Elizabeth was insistent. "No, Jane, they must at least be cleaned." Then she held up her remaining earring. "What am I going to do with one earring?"

We all sympathized with Elizabeth but Mike, who had confiscated the manager's telephone for nonstop calls, held his hand over the mouthpiece and snapped, "I told you that you'll have another pair in the morning!" And then to the telephone, "That's corned beef with mustard on the side."

The police kept filing into the office with a squashed handbag, or a bent comb, or a cracked compact, or a mangled set of keys, until the manager's desk had a heaped pile of jumbled personal belongings. Every time they came in, Elizabeth would ask,

"Well, did you find my ten-thousand-dollar earring?" And Mike would interrupt another of his phone calls—"Elizabeth, will you shut up, I told you you're getting another pair." Then into the phone, "Yeah, give or take two million, and I want Marlene Dietrich or no one!"

The manager returned with the first-aid kit and said rather timidly, "The audience is just about all seated." Everyone ignored him because a delivery boy had followed him in with a box containing a couple dozen corned beef sandwiches. Mike Todd, holding the phone under his chin, reached into his pocket, produced a wad of money, handed the boy a hundred, and without even looking at the bill waved the boy away.

Surprisingly enough, we were all hungry and dug into the sandwich box; and the manager, whose office was well stocked with booze, produced several more bottles of brandy.

Mike hung up the phone and announced, "Okay, I reached the jeweler at home. He's delivering the earrings first thing in the morning."

Rock handed Jane the Mercurochrome, saying, "I'd put this on for you, but I go wild for knees!"

Jane pulled one of her famous mugs and chuckled, "Stay where you are, boy, we don't want you gettin' all hot under the collar."

Rock pointed to his gaping shirt. "Do I still have a collar?" And we all broke into laughter.

Elizabeth gave a loud squawk.

"I know what I'll do with this one. I'll have them make me a matching brooch!"

Her earring problem solved, Liz remembered that her head was sore where her hair had been tugged. When the manager, who had been mumbling under his breath, "I believe the audience must be in by now," produced a bottle of aspirin from his desk drawer, Rock took the bottle. He dangled it in front of Elizabeth and teased, "Come on, Elizabeth, give the aspirin to the real victim, your wig."

Elizabeth began to giggle, unpinned her supplementary "fall," which was heaped upon her own ample head of hair, held the wig on her upper lip, and bending her knees, slouched around the room in a Groucho Marx imitation.

The manager waited for a lull in the laughter, and clearing his throat, offered apologetically, "Perhaps we should go in now?"

Now that we had regained our composure, we repaired ourselves the best we could and finally entered the auditorium. Since the movie was such an enormous hit, and I've seen it so many times, I recall only vaguely the rest of that evening. (But I loved the film then and still do.)

When the end credits came on the screen, and the name James Dean appeared, someone whispered, or perhaps I just heard it in my head, "Well, that's Jimmy for you—still stealing the show!"

Chapter Eighteen

BABY DOLL'S BABYDOLL

So far, receiving attention from the public and the press was a confusing, disillusioning, distasteful, and even abhorrent experience. The kind of notoriety I had been bombarded with in no way measured up to my childhood fantasy of what it would be like to become a famous movie star.

While I wanted the audience to judge me on the basis of what I created as an actress, torridness and infantilism were constantly being projected upon me as a person. I thought of myself as a private person—an actress, yes—but divorced from my screen image. The press, however, was having a field day describing my sensuous baby face and my nubile body, portraying me as a stupid little piece of baggage. They were intent upon manufacturing a ludicrous, larger-than-life symbol, whether or not it had anything to do with the real me.

Thanks to a tidal wave of "Baby Doll mania," I was submerged in an identification with a fictitious, outlandish caricature.

I was told that if I personally met with the press, they would portray me as I really was. Not so! Interviews were a nightmare. Journalists came to meet me with the imaginary baby doll already firmly in mind, even if they hadn't seen the movie. They knew exactly what they were going to write before they even spoke to me. They used the interviews to seize upon any slip that would confirm the image of the infamous Mrs. Meighan. I loved that character. She was as real to me as my sweet Ellie May, and misrepresentations of her hurt me nearly as much as misrepresentations of me.

They wanted a freak, so my quotes were slanted, distorted, and used out of context. They used the ploy of asking a question and then turning it around as if it had been a statement. "Are you from the South?" became, "Carroll 'Baby Doll' Baker is a Southern girl." The constant use of Baby Doll as my middle name drove me to distraction. And I avoided photographers altogether, once I realized they were only interested in getting a picture of me sucking my thumb.

I was comfortable only in my homespun cocoon. Outside of it, I no longer had any privacy. I began to dread even walking to the corner store. People stopped and stared at me, sometimes pointing and snickering and called out things like:

"There goes Baby Doll."

"Hey, Baby Doll, did you just get out of your crib?"

"Hey, Baby Doll, suck your thumb for us!"

I really didn't have the courage or the desire to attend any openings after *Giant*. Jack did talk me into one opening night; I don't remember now what the occasion was, but I was so anxiety-ridden over the thought of being accosted by the journalists and photographers that I took hours getting ready. We missed the film or play and only arrived at the tail end of the late night party that followed. Jack and I met Marilyn Monroe and Arthur Miller in the coat room. They were leaving as we were arriving.

Marilyn looked gorgeous. She had a black-satin sheath, daringly low cut, with her bosom precariously held up by thin spaghetti straps. The attendant was helping her into a full-length white-mink evening coat. Jack remarked on its beauty, and Arthur Miller told us that a New York furrier lent Marilyn furs for special occasions. Chalk up one for the positive side of being famous!

Marilyn turned to me and said, "Carroll, congratulations on your Baby Doll film."

I snapped "Thank you, but I'm not so sure congratulations are in order."

Marilyn looked puzzled, then hurt, then suddenly distant.

I suppose I was still jealous of her, but when I realized how hurt she was, I felt guilty about my selfish, insecure attitude.

And, oh, God, I could have bitten my tongue. Why couldn't I simply have accepted her congratulations graciously? It had been kind and generous of Marilyn, particularly in view of the fact that she had wanted to play the part. She must have been hurt far too often, and I hated myself for being guilty of adding to the many offenses she must have suffered. I tried clumsily to explain the difficulties and controversy arising from the film, but Marilyn had retreated somewhere inside herself. There was no penetrating her glazed expression.

A few days later, Marilyn again demonstrated her generosity. The *Baby Doll* premiere was to be a benefit for the Actors' Studio. Marilyn agreed to be an usherette and to launch the ticket sale by posing for a publicity shot holding a huge photograph, in the form of a ticket, of me in the crib. The newspaper captions read:

> 12-4-56 ** New York ** MM launches ticket sale for "Baby Doll" premiere ** Marilyn Monroe (Miller), in her first public appearance since return from England, is shown as she launches sales of tickets for Warner Brothers' gala Actors' Studio benefit premiere of Elia Kazan's *Baby Doll* on Dec. 18th at the Victoria Theatre. Proceeds will go to the Actors' Studio.

My obstetrician, Dr. Mintz, declared me to be healthy and strong. He saw no reason to anticipate anything but a normal birth. On December fifteenth, Dr. Mintz's examination showed that I was dilated enough to expect the baby any day, and he and I discussed my wish to attend the premiere on the eighteenth. He told me that, if I remained in bed, I could perhaps slow up the process long enough to attend the opening before going into labor.

I had read books about "natural childbirth" and had practiced the breathing and exercises, but I had not had any special instructions. Maybe a natural-birth center existed in those days, but I wasn't aware of it. Dr. Mintz and I discussed the fact that he had never assisted a woman during a natural birth, and that the maternity section of Mt. Sinai could not remember a woman's having given birth without anesthesia—so mine was to be a daring experiment for all concerned. Nevertheless I was determined not to take drugs because I wanted to fully experience the moment of birth.

After three days in bed, I got up gingerly the evening of the eighteenth and slowly dressed myself in the evening attire which I had worn to the *Giant* premiere. Jack hired a car to stay with us, and my small hospital case was placed in the trunk. I didn't have to worry about getting in touch with my doctor in case my water broke while I was in the Victoria Theatre, because I took Dr. Mintz to the opening with me!

I didn't dare risk being jostled by the crowds at the main entrance, so it was arranged that Jack, Dr. Mintz and I would enter quietly by the side door of the theatre. We also sat on the side aisle, with a clear escape route to the exit in case it became necessary.

After the turn the publicity on the film had taken, Warner's wasn't interested in the fanfare of a typical Hollywood opening. Aside from Marilyn Monroe, I can't remember any other Hollywood personalities being there. As the first night was an Actors' Studio benefit, no tickets were sold to the general public, so the audience consisted of New York theatre people, patrons of the Actors' Studio, and the members themselves.

I don't know what I was most nervous about—the possibility of going into labor, or how the film would be accepted by my friends. As the lights went down, my heart was pounding and my baby was kicking me furiously.

It was impossible for me to judge my own performance, because I was far too concerned with the first audience reaction. Suddenly the laughs came, not in ripples, but in grand spontaneous bursts. The comedy was working even beyond my expectations. I could feel the audience's total absorption in the film. What I enjoyed most was *their* enjoyment.

The professionals dubbed the film an artistic triumph! How marvelous that they were not swayed in their judgment by the snide quips of the reporters who had been looking for sensationalism in order to sell newspapers. Everyone agreed that it was a great pity that we had run up against a controversy with the Legion of Decency, which was hurting our chances for proper recognition.

The compliments and congratulations I received from my peers that night gave me enormous self-confidence. And I had learned my lesson. This time when Marilyn Monroe said she thought my performance was wonderful, I accepted her comments gracefully. I was glowing as Arthur Miller, Lee Strasberg and so many other respected theatre people heaped generous praise for my performance upon me. And I thanked baby for cooperating and letting me enjoy that special night.

The New York newspapers the next day carried rave reviews. The critics recognized the humor in the film and roundly gave the performance critical acclaim. As for me, while they said that a star was born, I still wished there had been a little less praise for my sultriness.

On the afternoon of the nineteenth I felt some stirring from the baby, but it turned out to be a false alarm, and I didn't check into the hospital until the morning of the twentieth.

Although it is one of the largest, most modern hospitals in the city, with an enormous maternity section, in 1956 Mt. Sinai had not yet made provisions for "natural childbirth."

In the 1940s, a British obstetrician by the name of Grantly Dick-Read had developed a technique of delivery which he called "natural childbirth." He believed that any young woman who was healthy and determined could do without anesthetic, participate actively during labor, and experience the moment of birth. His premise was that childbirth did not have to be excessively painful, that labor pains are the result of an unnatural physical tension which is caused by fear. He maintained that fear could be counteracted by understanding and being able to relax. Exercises to strengthen the musculature and proper breathing were what his method prescribed to attain this needed relaxation.

For the first couple of hours Jack sat beside my bed and counted the length of the contractions. It was all happening so slowly, and I got a bit bored with his overconcern. I asked him to go downstairs to the coffee shop and give us both a much-needed break. I had begun to wonder if this weren't another false alarm, but when Dr. Mintz popped in during his rounds he felt that everything was proceeding normally. He told me that first childbirths were often slow, to relax and have patience. He would stop in to see me in another hour, or if I needed him before then I was to have him paged.

I was fortunate enough never to have been in the hospital before, and I knew nothing about hospital procedure. It did seem odd to me that I was being given so much attention. Once Dr. Mintz and Jack were no longer with me, a succession of interns, one after another, began to examine me at four- or five-minute intervals. I wondered with some alarm just how many interns worked in maternity, if they were all going to examine me, and why my condition called for such extraordinary surveillance.

After I had been poked and prodded twenty-five or thirty times by just as many different pairs of hands, I became weary and would have paged my doctor had he not shown up. When I complained, Dr. Mintz looked amazed and admitted that it was totally uncalled-for behavior on the part of the staff. He summoned the head nurse and gave orders that only one intern was to look in on me and not more often than was absolutely necessary.

I was handling the pain without difficulty, but as the contractions grew closer together, one nurse after another began to badger me about having an anesthetic. Their nagging was tiring, but more exhausting still was having to explain over and over again that I didn't want the needle, why I didn't, and, yes, that my doctor was in complete agreement.

It was time to call Jack so that he could take over the job of defending me from injections and I could get on in peace with my breathing. I had asked for him to be paged, but I got the feeling that no one had bothered. When an intern came straight over to me holding a syringe without even announcing his intention, and I had to suffer the contraction without the benefit of the panting breaths, in order to fight off the determined young doctor, I decided to take matters in hand. Immediately after the intern—who still doubted my word—left my room, I got out of bed and went into the hall. I was dressed only in a short, open-down-the-back hospital gown, but I was nevertheless headed for the elevators and on my way to the main floor to find Jack. There was panic at the nurses' station when they saw me. No patients, especially those half-clad and already in labor, were permitted to leave the floor. With my hand on the elevator call button, I laid down my ultimatum: they were to page my husband and either page Dr. Mintz or see that his orders for natural birth were carried out without any more arguments.

They obviously hadn't bothered to call Jack before, because now he came up within seconds of the page. His protection against the hypodermic needles came just in time, for once I was back in bed, the contractions sped up and I had my work cut out for me. I got to the point at which I had to pant steadily. There was little time to rest between contractions, and then no time at all.

I was helped onto a movable bed and wheeled into an expansive operating room. Over my head was a bank of strong lights, and when I squinted I could make out the railing of the circular balcony of an open mezzanine. All around the railing was a moving, white, zigzag fringe. I could hear Dr. Mintz's voice encouraging me to push down during the contractions, and although my own sounds were close and continuous as I alternately panted and pressed my abdominal muscles, I thought I also heard a murmur circulating above me on that mezzanine.

Each time I squeezed my lower muscles, my face and eye muscles involuntarily pinched closed. When the overhead sound vibrated into a kind of sing-song chant, I intentionally relaxed my face and eyelids so that I could see properly. Good grief, the moving white zigzag was a body of observers, and I was the focus of their attention! Maybe a hundred or more white uniformed interns and nurses were leaning over the railing, or perhaps they were medical students.

I didn't feel that I could spare the breath to ask and anyway Dr. Mintz was too busy to have answered me. He kept urging me with precise regularity to push, and each time he said the word "push," the voices in the balcony echoed him like a chorus.

Grantly Dick-Read had been right about the lack of pain, because I was working so hard pressing my muscles and panting that I had no time to be tense. There was no pain once I understood it by its rightful name: fear. I knew that, if the full measure of the experience was to be mine, I had to fight fear with every ounce of my will.

My fear was not of the creaking noises of the stretching pelvis, or the feel of the straining, separating pelvic bones. My fear was not of the cold instrument that snipped twice through the taut external lip of the lower birth canal, nor of the pressure in the passage. My fear was far more terrible and awesome because it was of that great unknown space where I balanced between life and death and understood that I was helpless.

Once I had accepted this helplessness, fear lost its grip, and I experienced something extraordinary. I seemed to drift to a place where the limitations of conscious thinking had never before permitted me to enter, to a vast metaphysical exultation where I became light and sound and movement and they, me; we were pure energy, and energy was everything, and the source of the energy was God.

As the contractions grew ever more intense, Dr. Mintz's urgings grew ever more energetic and the chorus crescendoed in rousing, encouraging syncopation. The theatre pounded and resounded with the roar of "push, push, push."

A hot rush of life burst forth. A loud, prolonged cheer went up from the crowd. A mucous-covered little creature was held aloft, and wild applause accompanied the cheering.

There was a hush. I held my breath. Dr. Mintz was poised to slap, and then suddenly the baby whimpered all on its own.

"It's a girl!" Dr. Mintz said.

"It's a girl!" "It's a girl!" "It's a girl!" was repeated round and round the gallery.

The nurse took the baby from Dr. Mintz to wash and weigh her and pronounced, "Eight pounds and four ounces."

"Eight pounds and four ounces!" "Eight pounds and four ounces!" "Eight pounds and four ounces!" "That's a big baby!" came more excited voices from above.

The baby was wrapped in a small, white sheet, and I could see only a form out of the corner of my eye.

"Let me see her! Let me see her! Please, please!" I cried out.

Dr. Mintz took her from the nurse, unwrapped her, and held her close in front of me. She was clean and pink and white and chubby, with a full head of dark, curly hair.

My first instinct was to examine every inch of her. She had perfectly formed fingers and toes, a straight back, shapely arms and legs, her head?—yes, it felt fine. I looked intently at her ears and her nose and her red bow lips pouting to form tiny coos. When I looked into her eyes and saw that they were bright and trying to focus on me, I thanked God that she was all right, and tears welled in my eyes.

Then I took her from the doctor. Jack and I had decided on a girl's name long before. I nuzzled her and kissed her soft, plump little cheek, and whispered, "Hello, Little Blanche!"

There was a silence in the balcony and now I again heard murmurs chorused, "What's her name?" "What's her name?"

I got on one elbow, and resting the baby on my shoulder, I turned her gently on her back. Then with my best stage projection I called to the balcony, "Hello, there, cheering section. Meet Blanche Joy Garfein."

"Hello, Blanche!" "Hi, Little Blanche!" "Welcome, Blanche Joy!"

And a wonderful and theatrical welcome to the world it was, for we were applauded and cheered all through our exit from the room.

Blanche and I were temporarily separated at this point; she was taken to the nursery, and I was wheeled into the recovery room.

The other women around me were still unconscious from the anesthetics they had been given. I was the only one awake, and I was full of energy. Also, it had been over twelve hours since I had eaten last, and, with the hours of exertion I had just put in, I was famished. Still, they made me wait in the recovery room for another hour.

It was five o'clock when I got back to my private room, only to discover that of the trays of food being served, none was intended for me. I begged and pleaded for food. "I haven't had a sedative. I haven't had any medication at all. I'm not sick to my stomach. I haven't eaten in twelve hours and I'm starving. If I'm not listed for a meal then, please, just give me something. Give me some cheese and crackers and a glass of milk!"

Well, I couldn't make anyone see the logic of what I was saying. It was up to Jack to smuggle food in, and I gave him my order with great relish: a cheeseburger, French fries, and a chocolate milkshake!

The next morning I was tired. A good tired, but I was sleepy and physically exhausted when they awakened me at 6:30 A.M. If I had been bright and full of pep the afternoon before, while the other new mothers had been knocked out, it was now quite the reverse. I could hear the women on the floor laughing and talking and asking for visitors, while I could hardly raise my head. Nonetheless, I forced myself out of bed and straight down the hall to the shower room before the inevitable crush of women got there. It then seemed to take forever to have the breakfast tray removed, the linen changed, and the room cleaned so that I could go back to bed. It was nearly 9:00 before I closed the Venetian blinds and crawled under the covers, aching for some undisturbed sleep.

But before my head hit the pillow, everybody and his brother began tramping into my room in an unending parade: new mothers, friends, and perfect strangers. I had requested that a "Do Not Disturb" sign be hung on my door, but it deterred absolutely no one. Worst of all were the staff, who never stopped pummeling my sore abdomen, taking my temperature and my blood pressure, asking me the same questions, and pummeling me once again.

It seemed that everyone was overcome by curiosity to see and talk to the "Baby Doll" girl. My audience in the delivery room had been medical students as well as all the off-duty staff. I found it difficult to believe that people would take such an interest in me. Fame was so new to me that not only could I not relate to the sudden attention, but I kept forgetting why I was the object of their curiosity.

Apparently, new mothers are edgy and their emotions are close to the surface. What happened to me on my third night in the hospital would have been traumatic at the best of times. It was ten o'clock at night, visiting hours had been over at nine, and the entire floor was now quiet. I was getting ready to go to sleep. I had taken off my nightdress and slipped into a clean hospital gown. The gown was short, and it was open down the back save for two string fastenings, and I had nothing on underneath it. I turned off everything but the night light and entered the toilet cabinet. When I stepped out of the cabinet and into my dimly lit room, there was an enormous black man, dressed in rough street clothes, hiding something behind his back, leaning against my closed door and blocking my escape to the hallway. He was grinning and peering at my bare legs. I was sure that he had a knife concealed behind his back and that he had come to rape and murder me. My only hope was to reach the intercom switch and alert the nurses' station. I took mental aim on the position of the switch, flung myself the width of the room from the cabinet to the head of the bed, landed with a crash, flipped the switch to open and let out a long, blood-curdling scream.

The black man vanished. Pandemonium broke out on the floor. Patients and staff came flying from all directions. For a long time, I was hysterical.

The hospital security cops were jolted into action, but the man was never caught. In the emergency stairwell, they found a bouquet of flowers which had been scattered in flight, and a trampled card which read: "To the Beautiful Baby Doll from your fan."

The press were tying up the hospital switchboard and making a general nuisance of themselves in their quest for information. The woman in charge of Mt. Sinai's public relations suggested that I permit one general press call and allow the newspapers to take pictures of the baby and me while we were protected behind the glass enclosure of the nursery. Photos of Blanche and me appeared in newspapers across the country and even around the world. The photos differed slightly, but the captions were all the same: "Baby Doll gives birth to a Baby Doll!"

Chapter Nineteen

MY SON HERSCHEL

Blanche Joy was truly the joy of my life. I'd never known such happiness and contentment. I wanted to sit in the rocking chair and cradle her in my arms forever, just letting the rest of the world go by.

Warner Brothers, on the other hand, wanted to promote my child-woman sex image. As a contract player, I had no say in the kind of films they put me in, and my only defense was simply not to show up for work. Warners' answer for that was to put me on suspension without pay. I had the right to appear in one outside film a year, but only after I had completed my two films for Warners or with their special permission.

As I did not have script approval, they refused to consult me before purchasing a series of books as starring vehicles for me. The first of these was the Diana Barrymore autobiography *Too Much Too Soon*. The opening line was: "I know that I'm a nymphomaniac." No way was I going to play a nymphomaniac!

Of course, I was the bigger loser because when I refused to do that film, Warners refused to give their permission for me to appear with Sir Laurence Olivier, Burt Lancaster, and Kirk Douglas in *The Devil's Disciple*. Not only could I not do this prestigious film for an outside company, but since I had just been nominated for an Academy Award as "Best Actress" for *Baby Doll*, the production company had raised its offer from $100,000 to $150,000!

Giant received ten nominations that year. Among them, both

Jimmy Dean and Rock Hudson were nominated as Best Actor; Mercedes McCambridge as Best Supporting Actress; George Stevens as Best Director; and *Giant* as Best Picture.

Aside from my own nomination, *Baby Doll* won three others: Tennessee Williams for his screenplay; Boris Kaufman for black-and-white photography; and Mildred Dunnock for Best Supporting Actress.

We were less fortunate when it came to the actual awards. Out of a possible fourteen awards for both films, only George Stevens was a winner for Best Director. Dean and Hudson lost to Yul Brynner for *The King and I;* and Dunnock and McCambridge lost to Dorothy Malone for *Written on the Wind.* Tennessee's screenplay lost out to *Around the World in 80 Days,* which also won Best Picture. I lost to Ingrid Bergman, who had made her comeback in *Anastasia.*

The awards presentation was filmed in both Los Angeles and New York in those days. Jerry Lewis was the L.A. master of ceremonies, and Celeste Holm was the New York mistress of ceremonies—with Anna Magnani and me as presenters. Boy, was I glad I wasn't sitting in that Hollywood audience, because they couldn't focus the camera on me as the winners' names were called out, and I didn't have to make that superhuman effort to hide my feelings of disappointment.

Warners bought three Erskine Caldwell books. I liked Caldwell's writing, but I knew that the characters were "hot" little Southern numbers—white trash who were often obliged to exchange their sexual favors for the necessities of life.

Saying "no" to these three films meant that I was punished by not being allowed to do *Three Faces of Eve* for Fox, and missing out on a two-picture deal at MGM to star in *The Brothers Karamazov* and *Cat on a Hot Tin Roof.*

I had completed *Baby Doll* in December of 1955, so it had now been fifteen months since my last paycheck, and the cupboard was nearly bare. Jack's theatre earnings wouldn't stretch to cover our new family and our larger apartment. I simply had to go back to work.

William Wyler (*Mrs. Miniver, The Heiress, The Best Years of Our Lives, Roman Holiday*), wrote to me, proposing a film that he and Gregory Peck were coproducing for United Artists. It was to be a Western with an all-star cast: *The Big Country.* My character would be a complete departure from *Baby Doll*. It was the role of a spoiled rich girl, a wealthy ranch owner's daughter, who is engaged to marry the man she fell in love with (Gregory Peck) while at school in the East.

Warners just had to let me do that film! After weeks of negotiation between Warners and Wyler and my agents, Warners finally agreed to let me do it, providing half of my salary remained with them in escrow until such time as I fulfilled my contractual commitments to them.

I was thrilled to have the opportunity to star with Gregory Peck in a film directed by William Wyler, and very relieved to know that money would be coming in shortly. My plan was to take the contract to the bank and borrow against my future salary.

However, when the contract arrived, I couldn't sign it in good faith: I'd discovered that I was pregnant again. Of course I wanted another baby, but the timing couldn't have been worse: two babies, only thirteen months apart, when I'd been out of work so long, we needed the money so desperately, and I had finally won Warners' agreement to let me appear in a quality film!

I couldn't be underhanded and conceal my pregnancy. I had too high a regard for Peck, Wyler—and the movie industry—not to be truthful about my condition. I flew to the West Coast to have a private meeting with Peck and Wyler, because I felt it was too delicate a matter to handle on the telephone. If they agreed to let me work while pregnant, it would be wonderful; if not, well, Jack and I would just have to somehow find a way to make ends meet. If I could have my baby and do the film, it would make life a lot easier; if not, the baby came first.

At the meeting, impressed as I was with Wyler and his films, it was Peck who got most of my attention. I couldn't keep my eyes off him. He was so tall, handsome and immaculately dressed, so charming and funny and such a perfect gentleman —he would have turned any girl's head.

I explained to them that my pregnancy would not be at all evident for the next four months, that in rereading the script I had found nothing physical I wouldn't be able to do, and that if they would accept me in my condition, I would love to play the part.

186

Both men were very kind, and I could tell by the way they reacted that they both really wanted me in the film.

Wyler said, "Thank you for being honest with us."

Peck said, "Thank you for letting us know. I want you to be in the film and as far as I'm concerned I'll say 'Yes' right now. How about you, Willy?"

Willy Wyler said, "Yes, I agree with Greg. As you know, you're my first choice for the part. I think it is only fair, however, that I discuss your pregnancy with United Artists. They are, after all, putting up the money and we should give them the opportunity of voicing their opinion."

Oh, how relieved and delighted I was when Willy called me in the morning with a positive response from UA. Except for Willy and Greg and the men who had been informed at UA, we decided that my pregnancy should remain a secret for the duration of the filming.

Jean Simmons had been able to accept the other female lead before my ability to participate had been confirmed, so she got second billing after Peck. Charlton Heston was a little slow in answering, so he got billing after me in fourth position. Burl Ives, Chuck Connors, Charles Bickford, and the comic Mexican actor Alfonso Bedoya rounded off the top acting roles.

We filmed for two weeks near Stockton, California, but most of the picture was shot somewhere in California's Mojave Desert. We were lodged in the only motel for miles around. I can't imagine why this comfortable, modern motel had been built so far away from a town, because few cars ever stopped and we were nowhere near the chic resorts of Big Bear or Lake Arrowhead. Perhaps it was intended to capture the business of the many film units who used this barren, rolling countryside for Western movies.

The motel suites were spacious, and the restaurant served tasty food—a good thing because there was nowhere else to go. We were without many conveniences—like a post office, a dry-cleaner or laundry, even a newsstand.

Blanche was five months old and proved to be no trouble at all when I took her and a nanny with me on location. She took at once to the strange surroundings, and loved sitting in the restaurant for meals, trying new grown-up foods, and watching the people come and go. The nanny was a bit more difficult to entertain. We worked Saturdays until 5:00 P.M., so I could only give her Saturday evenings and Sundays off. If I hadn't found something to amuse her during that day-and-a-half respite, she was hell to live with the rest of the week. I have always found trying to keep nurses happy to be the working mother's most grating chore.

Gregory Peck flew back to L.A. every weekend to be with his stunning French wife, Veronique. The other stars also flew home most Saturday nights, as did my star nanny. It cost me quite a bit of money, but I found that it was worth the added expense, because I relished those hours when I could be completely alone with my little girl. There were so many things I missed during the working week, such as having her all to myself during meals, playing with her, and giving her her bath.

After those long working days in the hot desert sun, I'd spend those precious moments with Blanche, and that left me very little time to socialize with the other actors. Also, being pregnant made me exceptionally sleepy and I went to bed early most nights. Everyone flew home for the weekend or had their families visit them except Jean Simmons—she was the only one who was always alone. She had the suite next to mine, and although I knew how lonely she was, I couldn't have more than an occasional drink with her. Jean knew that she was welcome to have dinner with Blanche and me and Nanny, but she seldom wanted to eat that early. Also, seeing Blanche only made her miss her own little girl, Tracy, all the more.

Stewart Granger apparently wouldn't allow Tracy to visit Jean on location, since he thought Tracy was better off with an undisturbed home routine. I don't believe that Stewart ever came to visit Jean, and I can't remember her ever flying home.

From snatches of conversation, I gathered that Stewart was rather stern, and that Jean bowed to his every wish—even if doing so made her suffer. I never met the man, so my view could certainly be one-sided, but I was flabbergasted that a young, beautiful, and very sweet girl like Jean smoked and drank so much and seemed so desperately unhappy.

Jean Simmons and I are what is considered the average height for a woman, about five-feet-five-inches, but the guys made us look like midgets. The top of my head reached Gregory Peck's chest, Charlton Heston's stomach, and Chuck Connors's belt buckle. When Peck kissed me he had to double over from the waist, and I had to lean my head back in order for our lips to meet. Heston had to straddle me and then place me in a back-bend just to reach my mouth. Thank heavens the script didn't call for me to kiss Connors—I hate to think what contortions that would have called for.

Chuck Connors was a cut-up and a big tease. I didn't have any scenes with him, but offscreen he would pick me up at the waist or stand me on a box to talk to me. Chuck was the first one to suspect that I was pregnant. "Why are you always having soda crackers and milk instead of coffee and doughnuts? I'll bet you're pregnant!" I evaded the truth, but I always had to answer or he wouldn't have let me off the box.

A stunt director should have been consulted during my "kissing-fight" scene with Heston. The scene was a passionate one in which he forced his attentions upon me. I was supposed to break out of the kiss and hit him with my riding crop, and then he was to grab my wrist and subdue me.

It should have been a good scene, but I did not have the height, weight, or physical strength to fight him properly. The truth was that he could have done anything he pleased with me, and I would have been helpless to defend myself.

Willy said, "Cut! Carroll, it doesn't look as if you're struggling enough."

"Willy, I am trying but I'm completely overpowered. Chuck is just too big and too strong for me." I simply could not do it. It was like a pussycat attempting to break the hug of a grizzly bear.

After the next take, Willy again urged, "Carroll, you must fight your way out of Chuck's arms and then hit him as hard as you can with the riding crop."

We did it again, but although I struggled until I was breathless and red in the face, I remained buried in Heston's gargantuan arms and chest. Finally I dissolved into laughter, and peering from behind a huge bicep, I giggled, "Willy, there is no way I can get out of Chuck's grip. In fact, with just a little more pressure, he could pulverize the crop and crush me to death!"

We transposed the scene so that I first became angry and beat

Heston with the riding crop; then he grabbed my wrist, twisted it behind my back, and enveloped me in the long embrace and kiss.

After the first take of doing the scene this way, Heston was unhappy. He said, "Carroll, could you put some muscle into hitting me with that riding crop? I'm supposed to give a reaction here."

We did a second take, and this time I really slashed him. Ordinarily I would never have dreamed of hitting another actor that brutally but I felt he wanted me to, and I would do it only once.

But Chuck still said, "Carroll, I can't feel anything. Could you really hit me with that riding crop?"

"What?" I gasped in disbelief. "I am striking you with all my might! Surely you felt it?"

"Not really. It would help me to motivate the scene and to react if you really hit me hard."

"Halt!" Willy gritted angrily, "I am the director here!" Then Heston and I stood like bad children while Willy paused to think about the scene. "Carroll," Willy said caustically, "what you're doing looks convincing. It would be fine on the stage. But for the movie camera you're screwing your face too much. And I don't want you to fake it. I want you to really hit Chuck. Now let's go again."

I lashed at Heston's chest with every ounce of my strength until the riding crop was burning hot in my hand, but Chuck was still unsatisfied. "Sorry, Willy, could we go again? I have no motivation. I'm just not having any reaction." Then he said to me, "Don't be afraid to hit me, Carroll. You can't hurt me."

"Of course I can't hurt you, you big thick lummox. A normal man, an ordinary human being, would be writhing in pain by now!"

"All right," Willy intervened sharply, "let's try it one more time."

"Wait a minute, Willy, please," I screeched in frustration. "I know that's the end of my strength. Here, Willy, you try it. You hit Chuck." I offered him the crop.

So Willy took it and whacked Heston a few times, really very hard. I winced. Willy asked, "Well, how was that, Chuck?"

Chuck hesitated and then haltingly and without enthusiasm replied, "Yeah, I sorta felt that."

In his sternest Germanic voice, Willy said, "Well, Chuck, that's impossible." He handed the crop back to me and said, "One more time. Carroll, do the best you can. And Chuck, you will just have to find a motivation other than pain! Try *acting* the scene!"

The biggest scare came the night I thought I was going to have a miscarriage. Greg and I were riding in a buckboard (a light four-wheeled wooden carriage in which a long board is used in place of a body and springs). Sitting on that board makes it one of the hardest of rides, because nothing cushions the vibrations. In the middle of the scene something spooked our horses. They reared and began to run away with us. Greg braced his feet, pulling on the reins with the full weight of his body. But they ignored the bits in their mouths and tore into an uncontrolled gallop. I was jostled mercilessly, and bounced up and down on that rigid board until I began to hemorrhage.

The stunt boys were at last able to cut off our horses and bring them to a halt, but not before I was pouring blood and frantic. I was rushed to my motel bed, and the local doctor was with me within seconds. He gave me a sedative to calm me down and make me sleep. My water hadn't broken and the bleeding had stopped, so it was a question of waiting forty-eight hours to see if my condition would stabilize. Two days later, I thanked God that my baby was safe.

There was one more buckboard scene left, but both Greg and Willy insisted upon doing it in long shot with my double. I was very grateful for that decision even though the doctor had assured me, "You see, Miss Baker, you can't shake good fruit loose."

The film ran over schedule. I was five months pregnant and my belly was beginning to show. In the party sequence I had to be filmed full-figure walking down the staircase into the ballroom, and later waltzing with both Peck and Heston. My ball gown was too tight and revealed too much of a bulge. Another one had to be designed for me. The new gown was of black satin, with valances on the sides so that it minimized my middle; the eye drawn to the width of the hips.

The Big Country was an excellent movie with one fatal flaw: they had begun the filming without knowing the end of the story. We were over schedule and over budget, my guaranteed contract was about to expire, and we still had no finale. We stopped production for two days while Greg and Willy and the scriptwriters tried to knock out some conclusion for the story, but when at the end of those two days they couldn't come up with a satisfactory ending, I was released. It was my sixth month, and I could have just about gotten away with concealing my form for the concluding scenes, if only they had been written.

The finished film never succeeded in tying up all the loose ends of the story, and it was most peculiar the way my character dropped out of sight without explanation.

Jerome Moross's music was probably the best score ever written for a Western. Even if you haven't seen the film, you are bound to have heard that fabulous music or countless imitations of its catchy theme.

I went back to New York, and on January seventeenth again checked into Mt. Sinai to give birth, this time to my son, Herschel David Garfein. Herschel is a Biblical name, and it had been Jack's father's name. Remembering how Jack had lost his parents during the war, I felt it only fitting that they be remembered in the naming of their grandchildren. So Blanche was named after her grandmother, Blanka, and not, as I have been asked so many times, after Tennessee's Blanche du Bois.

My son and I had a very difficult time at his birth. Dr. Mintz had to pull him out with forceps and I was terrified that he would be permanently maimed. (We later discovered that Herschel had been born with the largest head of any baby on record at Mt. Sinai Hospital. I'm happy to report that there turned out to be a lot in that head, as Herschel has an exceptionally high IQ.)

At first his head was conical and he had very nasty bruises on his temples. He weighed seven pounds and eleven ounces, but he was very long, which made him look thin. Also his feedings had to be every two hours, instead of four, because his appetite was poor and he could consume only small amounts at a time. Nor was he aggressive like Blanche had been. Herschel seemed to sleep more. And although I had been told that the second child is often more quiet and less demanding, I was concerned by his calmness. When we went home from the hospital after a week, his bruises had faded somewhat and his appetite had picked up a bit, but I still worried about him.

We no sooner got home from the hospital than I was forced to stop fretting over Herschel, because I became gravely ill. I had developed an internal infection, and my fever shot up to 104 degrees. When I began to pass blood, the consensus of two specialists was that a tiny piece of the placenta had broken off and was still inside my womb.

The doctors felt that the move to the hospital would be very dangerous, and, anyway they didn't dare operate as long as I had such a high temperature. I was covered high with blankets and administered the largest doses of penicillin permissible. That night my fever went to 106 and my pulse grew very weak, but it was just a matter of waiting and praying; nothing more could be done for me medically.

About 5:00 A.M. I passed the piece of placenta, the infection began to drain, and my fever slowly subsided. It was, I'm told, a very close call, but I was unaware of being so close to death. I was far too occupied in the fight for survival. I knew that I was very ill, but not for a moment did I entertain the idea of its being fatal.

My little Herschel, too, in his own calm way, was determined to survive. At three months he was a round, robust boy with a healthy appetite and a remarkably intelligent curiosity.

$\mathscr{C}hapter$

Twenty

A QUARTER MILLION DOLLARS IN DEBT

It was now time to pay those Brothers Warner their dues. Jack and I took the two babies and rented a house in L.A. I couldn't very well refuse to do Warner's film, and I agreed to come to work knowing only that I would be playing a nun.

Well, weren't they obviously making an effort not to typecast me? How much further away from a sexy role can you get, than playing a nun? Ah, but I should never have underestimated the prurient persistence that lurks in the minds of movie moguls!

The film was entitled *The Miracle*, and it was loosely based on a famous Max Rheinhardt stage production. The story was a Spanish legend about a statue of the Virgin Mary that comes to life to take the place of a nun who has lost her faith and has run away from the convent. Once the Madonna exchanges places with the nun, natural disasters follow as if in warning to those who would desert the work of God. The people of the Spanish village mourn until the day that the wayward nun realizes the errors of her ways, regains her faith, and returns to the convent to repent her sins. At that point the Virgin Mary steps back onto her pedestal, which puts an end to the disasters and restores peace and happiness to the village.

Well, now, that's the legend. This is what we filmed: First of all, we did not film the story of a nun but rather of a postulate who had not yet taken her final vows. No doubt this was less of a bone of contention to the Catholic Legion of Decency than a full-fledged nun breaking her vows would have been. Also, my postulate had not yet cut her long, luxurious mass of black hair, which meant that sans veil, she was still a very dishy dish.

Within the first five minutes of screen time, the nunnery and church are only briefly and hurriedly introduced before Roger Moore, the divinely handsome young cavalry officer, comes riding up to the convent gate on his white charger. My postulate sees the twenty-five-year-old Roger Moore dressed in his red-and-gold uniform, prancing about on his white stallion and ogling her, and she swoons with excitement. An enormous close-up of my eyes and then Roger's eyes, and then my eyes and then Roger's eyes, unquestionably establishing love at first sight. With hardly a word or at least without wasting a moment of screen time before getting down to the "naughties," Roger sweeps me onto his horse and we gallop off into the forest.

Meanwhile back at the church, an eerie green light illuminates the face of the Madonna (who looks amazingly like Carroll Baker's postulate); the Madonna, who has now turned to flesh, steps down from her pedestal!

Back in the forest, Roger and I have dismounted. He takes me in his arms and kisses me and we fall passionately to the ground. The camera pans up to reveal birch trees bending in the wind, that well-worn movie technique of filming an analogy for fornication.

Roger Moore must join his unit and go to war. My postulate knows that she is a sinner, a lost soul, and she has a premonition that she is on the way to even greater sin.

Now we are told that my postulate, Theresa, has, in fact, scalding gypsy blood surging through the veins of her milky-white and irresistible skin. Theresa meets up with a wandering gypsy thief (Walter Slezak, would you believe?), and they go together to live at a gypsy camp where Vittorio Gassman is cock of the roost. That night, as Theresa and her fierce gypsy lover, Vittorio Gassman, are unable to contain their lust, the camera cuts to the flames licking and searing the campfire logs.

But don't forget the disasters of the legend. We now witness war, pestilence, storms, and drought.

There are also human weaknesses and transgressions. When another gypsy lasciviously advances toward the now sexily dressed, raven-haired Theresa, Vittorio Gassman must challenge this other stud to a duel.

Both men die. This gives Theresa a rather substantial hint that she brings bad luck.

Theresa must continue to roam.

Theresa is dancing the flamenco in a tavern when Spain's most famous bullfighter (played by that dashing Spanish actor, Gustavo Rojo) enters, sees her, and is instantly smitten by her beauty. During the dance there are many shots of Theresa's legs, shoulders, bosom, and smoldering expression. It is too much for the man in this matador to resist. He must have her. "No, no," she pleads, "I bring bad luck." But he is too inflamed to place his safety above the desires of his heart, and the desires of other parts of his anatomy clearly outlined in his skin-tight matador trousers. Predictably, the very next bull Gustavo Rojo encounters makes mincemeat out of him.

Theresa must continue to roam.

Theresa meets the wealthiest duke in all of Spain, and he must possess her. He must also own her radiance forever in a portrait painted by none other than Goya himself. We never see the painter, but we do see an atrocious portrait painted by the prop department which must have made the great Spanish artist spin in his grave. At that moment, we are treated to the worst line of dialogue in this script rife with zingeroos: "Isn't the portrait lovely? It was painted by my friend, Goya."

As mistress of the wealthy duke, Theresa becomes the most celebrated courtesan of Europe. Dressed in her plumed picture hat, her silk brocade dress, and her garland of precious jewels, riding through the streets of Brussels in her golden, horse-drawn carriage, she is suddenly confronted by a military parade. Riding at the front is Roger Moore, the young officer who first took her heart, not to mention her virginity.

Well, just as she is sorely tempted to chance her run of misfortune, throw caution to the wind, and flout her happiness in the face of fate by marrying her true love, the handsome twenty-five-year-old Roger Moore—lo and behold, at the mere possibility of losing her, the old duke is seized by a heart attack. Theresa is convinced once and for all that she is a jinx. She must not endanger her true love by allowing him to partake further of her tantalizingly lovely, but lamentably lethal, flesh.

Driven to despair, she flees through the countryside, there to witness the death and destruction inflicted upon her people as God's punishment for her hanky-panky.

Day and night she travels, without sleep, until she reaches her convent and her church with its missing Madonna. She prostrates herself on the stone floor and cries out for the Virgin Mary to forgive her and permit her to spend the rest of her life as a faithful servant of the church.

Lightning strikes over Theresa's outstretched form.

The Madonna, who is now disguised as a nun with an eerie green-lit face (who looks remarkably like Carroll Baker and the Theresa of our story), leaves the procession of nuns and steps back on her pedestal where she again turns to stone. Theresa looks up in tears of gratitude, the camera cranes to a high shot of the church interior, and a heavenly host composed of the Warner Brothers' choir and orchestra rings out as "The End" appears on the screen.

There are psychological disadvantages to straddling the East and West coasts. I should have been close to the motion picture industry, my industry, and acquired a firsthand knowledge of its inner workings, instead of running back to New York and judging movies by some unrealistic theatre standard. I should have been close enough to meet in person with the men who were in charge of making movies, instead of trying to deal with them through intermediaries from a distance of 3,000 miles. I might have saved myself countless heartaches born of misunderstandings. Also, living near my place of work would have forced me to concentrate on the importance of my career, instead of periodically treating it with such off-hand flippancy.

The Miracle was not my cup of tea, but since it made money at the box office, Warners felt they had been justified in its production. I should have tried to reach a compromise with the studio; maybe I could have accepted their stories while getting them to agree to better scripts and better directors. That might have failed, too, but I should have tried. I didn't. I saw a sneak preview of the film while I was in New York, got into a huff, and asked my agents to negotiate for me to buy my contract back from Warners. That decision, reached in a moment of pique, proved to be very costly. It began a period in which I found myself always short of money, and money worries are the Achilles' heel of a Depression baby.

Buying out my contract from Warners was the first link in a chain of events which lead to a spiraling, ever-deepening, disastrous deficit. Hiring a series of slick, fast-talking, percentage-gobbling leeches added nothing to my career, while it sliced deeply into my paychecks. But the worst mistake of all was losing control of the purse strings.

In the meetings with my advisors they always agreed with one another, and I always came away feeling lost, confused, and pressured into working nonstop:

"One film won't get you out of debt!" "Nor will two."

"Maybe by the third picture you can break even." "But you'll have to go back to work immediately afterwards!"

"Why am I always broke?"

"Because you earn a lot of money."

"But that doesn't make sense to me."

"It's the system. The American system. Everything is done on credit."

"But I don't own anything. I just live from week to week while you own your own car, and so do you!"

"Yes, but for you, Carroll, car hire is tax deductible."

"You all live in your own houses!"

"True, but rental is a tax deduction for you."

"I can't read these financial statements!"

"Of course not. But neither can the tax people!"

"I was hoping to do a play."

"You can't!" "Absolutely not!" "There isn't enough money in a play." "Maybe you can squeeze in some summer stock." "This is what you have to do, *But Not for Me* with Clark Gable. It goes right away."

"The Gable picture is a nice little comedy, but it isn't anything special. Maybe I should wait for a better part?"

"You can't afford to wait!" "So what if the script is so-so? You'll be starring with Clark Gable." "Paramount will pay you a lot of money." "The picture goes right away." "You owe Warners money right now!" "And then there is this to be paid, and this, and this." "You have to do the film, so just sign here." "Oh, yes, while you're at it also sign here and here and here and here and here. . . ."

I had spent most of the last two and a half years working in California. It hadn't made sense to pick up the children and move them from coast to coast. Nor had it been wise to pay double rents and all those airfares. What I should have done was settle in L.A. and just let Jack do the commuting. That was the problem. Not only Jack's work but his life seemed to revolve around being in New York. And I had been instilled so strongly with the concept that a woman always obeys her husband, follows him, and sacrifices her own needs to his, that at the time I hadn't been able to bring myself to admit that as I was the breadwinner, my comfort and the children's should take precedence over Jack's.

During the filming of *The Miracle,* I had rented the ideal house. It was small, easy to take care of, and all on one floor. Its greatest feature was that all the back rooms opened onto a beautiful, spacious patio, surrounded by a lovely garden and enclosed by a tree-lined wall. When I got home from the studio in the evenings, there was still sun on the patio, and the children and I ate our meals outside as often as possible.

I have always regretted not buying that house. I never found another one in L.A. that was as comfortable or that appealed to me quite so much. It represented the best of California living and the children and I were extremely happy there.

I had just the opposite experience during *But Not for Me.* Once I'd signed the contract, I had to report immediately to Paramount Pictures, and that meant renting the first house that became available. It was a cliff dwelling in the Hollywood Hills, a house of horrors which made our entire four months' stay a continuous nightmare.

Fortunately, I had a patient, energetic Swiss nanny who just about managed to cope with caring for Blanche and Herschel in that impractical, isolated, and exhausting location.

The front of the house was a square fortress, a straight, sheer drop, embedded in the mountainous road below. The back of the property had six steep stone terraces leading only to a small patch of grass and one avocado tree. The inside of the house was also on six levels, which meant five flights of stairs.

There were foxes and wild cats living in those hills around us. We heard things creeping near the house all night long and occasionally saw eyes reflected in the windows. Some animal or other always overturned the garbage cans, even after I had secured the lids with heavy stone slabs. Every morning the garbage would be scattered all over the road in front of the house.

I hired an exterminating service which came every Monday, but by Wednesday or Thursday the basement was teeming with rats again. The rats ate every avocado the second it ripened, and in four months I never managed to outsmart them and get even a single pear.

It was only after we had moved in that I discovered that the previous tenants had been Elizabeth Taylor and Mike Todd. They had been occupying the house at the time of his tragic air crash. (I'd been in New York when I heard the horrifying news of Mike's death. My heart had gone out to Elizabeth, but since I didn't have her address, I sent her a telegram expressing my sympathy, in care of the Screen Actors' Guild in Hollywood.)

My living room was on the fortress side, a stone's throw from the living room across the road where every evening my neighbor sat at his piano and played the theme song from Mike's film: "Around the World."

My bedroom was the powder-blue-and-gold room with a balcony overlooking the stone terraces at the back. I was always sad when I sat in that giant rococo, powder-blue-and-gold bed, because I couldn't help thinking of how Elizabeth must have sat there, shocked and grief-stricken.

I never opened the glass doors to the balcony after that first night when a huge owl had flown in, landed on the foot of my bed, and frightened me half out of my wits. Once he had gotten the upper hand, he came nightly to the balcony to hoot at me, sealed in my airless room.

Near the end of the filming, a house on Maple Drive in the flats of Beverly Hills became available, and I moved the family out of those spooky hills. I'd decided to stay around after the movie was completed, but by this time my career was in the pits! With *But Not for Me* I'd reverted back to a dull ingenue role— one that would have been suitable only at the beginning of my career while I was waiting for a better opportunity to come along.

As a movie, *But Not for Me* wasn't damned or praised, it was one of those run-of-the-mill little comedies turned out regularly in those days to keep the studios active. After his long years in the business, Gable could afford now and then to slip in one of these "bread and butter" flicks. But I was in no such position. I'd taken a gigantic step backwards, committed a type of professional suicide, and suddenly I was stricken by the horror of what it means to be no longer in demand. No offers came my way: three months, four months, six months.

And I had signed myself into debt to the tune of some totally unreal number, a quarter of a million dollars. A quarter of a million dollars? That can't be a deficit. It must be the title of a popular song:

> Come on, swing, don't fret
> You're only a quarter million dollars in debt.
> Let's laugh—no sweat,
> What's a quarter million dollars in debt?

Dear Mother,

Do you remember my first nervous breakdown? You and I have never talked about that. Maybe you'd be shocked if I brought it up now after all these years.

I'm writing about that portion of my life now and I realize that there are so many blank spaces. So many puzzling things about that first break-down which I've never bothered to find out. Like how did you find me when I ran away and locked myself in that hotel room? Did you ever know how I got there? Where was I?

Chapter

Twenty-One

A SUNDAY IN APRIL 1983:
TWO YEARS AFTER I BEGAN THIS
BOOK

Today, I made my usual Sunday telephone call to my mother, only this time we didn't talk about the tornado warnings in Florida, or her grandchildren, or whether or not I was taking my vitamins. This time, finally, I asked the most difficult of all questions: the one I had avoided asking for half my lifetime.

ME: Mother, there is something I can't remember—I have amnesia. It was around the year 1959, sometime after I'd made *But Not for Me*, I think. I only remember feeling helpless, lost. Was I—was I locked in a strange hotel room somewhere?

MOTHER: Pittsburgh.

ME: Pittsburgh! What was I doing in Pittsburgh? How did you find me there?

MOTHER: A Pittsburgh psychiatrist telephoned me. You had locked yourself in your hotel room, and you refused to open the door. You were screaming, "Mother! Mother! Mother!" He kept talking to you through the closed door and finally you gave him my phone number.

I didn't even pack a suitcase, I grabbed my handbag and coat and took the first plane out, whatever time it was. . . .

When I got there, I was the only person you let in the

room. You fell into my arms crying and sobbed your heart out for four or five hours. Then you fell asleep with me sitting on the bed holding your hand. And you slept for a long, long time. You were exhausted.

You'd started out on a personal-appearance tour about six weeks before from California, all across the country, one-night stands. You hadn't had any rest at all, no decent meals, no sleep.

You'd work from early in the morning, all day long, appearance after appearance, then rush back to the hotel, pack your suitcase and travel to the next city, staying up half the night. Your nerves were shattered. When you got to Pittsburgh you just couldn't go on any longer.

After I got there, it only took about four days—you recovered. But until you were steady enough to see people, I wouldn't let anyone in that room, not even the psychiatrist. I only arranged for you to talk to him when you said you were ready.

Those one-track-minded publicity people were trying to get me to coax you to continue the tour. I told them you were going home—the hell with this—she's a sick girl and she needs a long rest. Well, they too had been damned scared. They agreed to cancel the rest of the tour.

ME: What about Jack?

MOTHER: Oh, he wanted you to continue the tour. He kept calling and telling me that your career was in trouble and that you needed to make those appearances. Well, you can imagine what I told him!

ME: No, Mother, I mean didn't he come to Pittsburgh. Didn't he at least come to take me home?

MOTHER: Well, he wouldn't have, if the psychiatrist hadn't asked him to. Jack just pooh-poohed the whole thing.

ME: What do you mean?

MOTHER: The psychiatrist felt it was important that he speak with Jack. But Jack told me that he didn't believe in those doctors and had no intention of telling him anything, that it was none of the psychiatrist's business.

I told Jack he couldn't ignore the fact that you had broken down—he couldn't pretend it was just business as usual.

And I said he'd better get to Pittsburgh and take his wife home. That was the least he could do.

So I waited until Jack got there. Then I left and he took you home, back to New York.

You were all right by then, Carroll, you were yourself again. If you hadn't been, I never would have left you.

I didn't know you had amnesia about that part of your life. Why have you never told me before? Why have you never asked me about it before now?

Me: I don't really know, Mother. Now that I have, it seems so simple. I guess that's one of my problems.

So now I know. But it rings no bells. It hasn't triggered even one more fragment of remembrance for me. And I wanted so to remember! I want those lost days back—and not as a second-hand account. I want to find them and replace them in my head. But I guess I'll have to be patient a little longer. . . .

My memory is shaky even concerning the year or so after I recovered from that first nervous breakdown, because 1960 and '61 I remember only as a kaleidoscope of rotating images: some events clear, others diffuse; some slow-moving, others rushing by. The long locations in foreign countries seemed non-ending, whereas the children's development happened speedily and mostly without me.

I had been studying French, and I entered Blanche in a French kindergarten and Herschel in the same school's nursery class. I found a sweet and loving French-speaking German nanny to look after them, then I packed my suitcases for *Bridge to the Sun,* with James Shigeta—off to Washington, D.C., Paris, Tokyo and Kyoto, Japan. It's exciting, it's hard work, it's constant adjustment to other cultures, but above all, it's lonely. I call home— Herschel fell and cut his head open, forty-eight stitches—he's fine, now, but I wasn't there. Blanche recites for me over the telephone in French, "The Three Bears," a story lasting twenty minutes with the yen ticking away. Jack's had a falling-out with his producer and has been fired from his first TV show.

I return home laden with presents, anxious to make up in

every way for my absence. Blanche and Herschel greet me casually as if I've been to the corner store. They have been well looked after by the German nanny. What a wonderful woman!

Jack fought with the maid while I was away and she quit. An office-building service now cleans the apartment at a cost of $50 a day. Jack has been sending his socks and undershorts to be dry cleaned!

Jack needs directing work. We do a short summer tour of *Arms and the Man.* I have to admit that Jack has become impossible to work with, wants everything his own way, and expects his actors to be puppets. Blanche has to have her tonsils and adenoids removed. My mother comes from Florida to be with her. I fly in from Chicago during the day to take Blanche to the hospital. She is such a lovely big girl now. It is a struggle to carry her, but I want her to see the hospital in the security of my arms. I have to fly back to Chicago for the performance of *Arms and the Man,* so Mother stays with Blanche during the night.

The French school that the children attend needs money. Vera Stern, Isaac Stern's wife, and I launch a fund-raising campaign. I give two dozen speeches at fund-raising parties before packing my suitcases for *Station Six Sahara*—London and North Africa. First, a quick trip to Paris for a gown MGM is buying me; then, four days in Venice, Italy, because *Bridge to the Sun* has been nominated in the festival as best film and I as best actress. Neither the film nor I win, but it has been a glorious whirlwind of attention and glamour, and MGM has let me keep the Givenchy gown of heavy white satin with a sheer overlay of blue net and sparkling diamond- and sapphire-like beads which Rene Claire's wife helped me choose. From Venice to London for pre-production.

The producers of *Station Six Sahara* allow me to go to Paris for my wardrobe. Since I know I need guidance in the selection of that wardrobe, I telephone Marlene Dietrich. My lawyer, Arnold Weissberger, has given me a letter of introduction to Marlene. Marlene, who also has received a letter from our dear mutual friend, Arnold, invites me for tea. There is an instant sympatica reaction between us.

Marlene takes me to her favorite designer, Pierre Balmain. Monsieur Balmain accompanies Marlene and me to dinner at

Maxim's on Friday night. As we enter, the orchestra plays the theme from *The Blue Angel* for Marlene, and the *Baby Doll* theme for me. I tell Marlene that at any age it is beautiful to be called a Blue Angel but that I would hate, in years to come, to be referred to as a Baby Doll.

From Paris back to London and on to North Africa.

Tripoli is no place for a woman! At noon in the bazaar, the Arab men roughly push me out of their way. The beaches are white and inviting, but no woman dares be seen in a bathing costume. It isn't safe for me to be on the streets after dark, so I watch the night life of the city from my balcony.

The days in the Libyan Desert are an endurance test, with sand storms and burning sun and temperatures of 120 degrees in the shade. Walking across the sand during the scenes, my feet are badly burnt through the soles of my delicate Parisian sandals.

Station Six Sahara is a German-British coproduction. I am the only American and the only woman in the all-male cast; Peter Van Eyck and two other German actors, with Denholm Elliott and Ian Bannen making up the British side. At the end of the day, the fellows and I pile into jeeps for the long drive back to Tripoli and the hotel patio where steins of cold beer will finally quench the maddening thirst of the day. Dinner in the hotel dining room is whatever they serve us, because we don't speak Arabic and the staff doesn't understand any other language. The boys are invited to parties at the homes of wealthy Arab sheiks. They can go to nightclubs or the cinema or a bowling alley, but because I'm a woman I'm confined to the hotel.

We are there during the sandstorm season. My skin and hair are caked with sand at the end of each day, and it doesn't seem to wash away. The sand filters into my hotel room, where it is gritty and crunches under my feet and clings to my bed linen.

I can't make the telephone receptionist understand that I want a cup of tea, and I can't make the local telephone operator understand that I want to call New York.

Jack never writes. I receive charming drawings and notes from my children and reassuring letters from their German nanny. The children are healthy and delighted with their school and their playmates. Jack, she tells me, is seldom home and has been fired again. When he does come home he complains about everything and has made her life unhappy. She wants to quit but, of course, not until I get back to the States.

I come back home to wonderful news—the offer of a Broadway play! Garson Kanin has written a comedy, *Come On Strong*, for Van Johnson and me. What a thrill to be back on the stage! There is a long newspaper strike which takes its toll on the Broadway theatre. We open during the strike, and the future of *Come On Strong* appears doubtful. Van and I manage to keep it running day by day for five months—no advance in the morning and then at 6:00 P.M. people begin buying tickets as they would for a movie.

The children are thriving. It is so good to be able to work and live at home where I can be with Blanche and Herschel. Oh, God, I must do everything to save my marriage for their sake!

Chapter
Twenty-Two

THE FORTUNE COOKIE

After *Baby Doll* I'd missed my chance to solidify my position as a top star. Could I ever make a comeback? Certainly not without the right parts and in large-grossing films. The films I had chosen to do since my independence from Warner Brothers all showed promise, but none had turned out to be particularly exciting or rewarding. I came to the conclusion that either I wasn't a very good judge of material or that the picture business was more a question of luck than "smarts."

The Shanghai Cafe was an inexpensive Chinese restaurant on Broadway and 125th Street, a favorite of Jack's and mine for years. We knew the owner and the food was so superb that it was worth the long trip uptown to the dicey neighborhood.

One evening, we sat in the Shanghai Cafe while I deliberated about an important career decision. My California agent had been vague and had given me very little information with which to judge an offer for a picture that was supposedly a big-budget film planned by MGM—but there was no title, and I would have to accept the part without reading a script or knowing anything about the character I was expected to play. It was to be an all-star cast with alphabetical billing, but so far no one had been signed. MGM was asking me to commit myself on blind trust, and insisting upon an answer by morning.

At the end of the meal, while sipping my tea, I reached for the fortune cookie nearest me. When I broke the cookie and looked at the fortune, I couldn't believe what it said: "Go to Hollywood!"

I went straight to the pay phone in the foyer and made a collect call to my agent in Hollywood.

"Hello, Mort," I said. "The answer is yes. Tell MGM I agree to do the film. And don't worry, Mort. I won't blame you. If the film doesn't work out, I'll put the blame squarely on a fortune cookie!"

It turned out to be one of the best career decisions I ever made. The movie was the Cinerama production of *How the West Was Won.* It had one of the most inclusive all-star casts ever assembled; it received marvelous reviews; and it drew gold at the box office.

The story traced the journey west of the Prescott family, with Karl Malden and Agnes Moorehead as the parents of Debbie Reynolds and myself and our two younger brothers. Leaving by way of the Erie Canal the family begins its trek in search of fertile farmland on which to build their new home. Our parents and our brothers do not survive the journey. I marry a mountain man, Jimmy Stewart, and we settle down in Kentucky to farm and raise a family. Debbie goes in search of the glamorous saloon life and marries a gambling man, Gregory Peck. The story then takes up with the next generation by following the fate of my grown son, George Peppard. At the end, the only members of the family left are Debbie, as an old woman; my son, George Peppard with his wife, Carolyn Jones; and a promise for the future in their two small children. In the meantime there has been the difficult and dangerous journey west, complete with Indians and gunfights and buffalo stampedes. We see the flowering of towns during the gold rush, the Civil War in the West, and the new and united country that is connected by railroads and stretches from sea to shining sea. It is a story that will forever be exciting and moving and worth retelling. Cinerama gave it added scope and the thrill of immediacy.

As How the West Was Won encompassed so much of early American history, its running time was estimated at three hours or more, and our producer, Bernard Smith, hired three great Western directors to share in its making: Henry Hathaway, John Ford, and George Marshall. Other acting parts, large and small, were played by such illustrious names as John Wayne, Henry

Fonda, Eli Wallach, Richard Widmark, and Robert Preston, among others; Spencer Tracy narrated.

After costume fittings, makeup and hair tests at the MGM studios in Hollywood, we began at our first location—Paducah, Kentucky. Paducah was selected not only because it was sparsely populated and situated in a vast open countryside, but also because it marks the spot where the Kentucky River, having converged into the Tennessee River, meets in a triangular fork with the Clark and Ohio rivers. In the midst of this watery triangle lay a deserted island, perfect for our filming. The island had assorted wildlife, overgrown vegetation, thick groves of centennial trees, and no trace of civilization there or on the surrounding river banks. Such a spot was ideal—the Cinerama camera, with its 190 degrees, was in no danger of registering highways or distant buildings or that bane of all period films, electric and telephone wires and poles.

In the early summer of 1962 Jack and the children and I arrived to check into the motel in Paducah. Blanche was six and had just completed first grade, and Herschel, who had gotten his chocolate-smeared and dog-eared diploma from kindergarten, was five years old. I was so grateful to be able to have my family with me. Too often I had been forced to leave the children at home in New York for months at a time when I had gone off to distant locations.

Debbie Reynolds had had her children at almost exactly the same time as I had. Her daughter Carrie was Blanche's age, and her son Todd, like Herschel, was five. I was hoping that she would bring Carrie and Todd with her. It wasn't only the thought of our children playing together that appealed to me, but the possibility of our nannies keeping each other company.

I arrived some hours before Debbie and went to meet the director of the opening sequences, Harry Hathaway, as well as the crew and actors who had thus far assembled. I knew some of the crew from having worked with them on other films. My old pal, Karl Malden, had checked in, but I had never before been introduced to the wonderful Agnes Moorehead, or any of the featured players. Jimmy Stewart, whom I was trembling to meet, was not due for another ten days. When all our members would be accounted for, we would practically outnumber the local population.

Rumors were circulating that Stewart was a regular guy, and that Reynolds was spoiled and a snob. The rumors about Jimmy being a super person were true, but those nasty ones about Debbie were totally untrue. She was neither difficult nor stuck-up; in fact, nothing could have been further from the truth. It's odd how unflattering tales get started. Perhaps because Debbie had begun in films as a young girl and had been a star now for so many years, people who didn't know her automatically expected her to behave like a grande dame.

There were whispers that she would bring a large entourage, that she would always be late, and that she would be unreasonably demanding. I was therefore totally unprepared for the real Debbie Reynolds—a delightfully down-to-earth actress, woman, mother—and friend.

Late evening of the first day, while we were still unpacking, I heard a knock at the door. A perky five-foot-two-inch elfin sprite, dressed in blue jeans and a T-shirt with a bandana covering her hair, was prancing on my doorstep. She had a little boy in her arms and a little girl by the hand. From the moment I answered the door, she took over with bubbling enthusiasm.

"Hi. You're Carroll. I'm Debbie. This is Carrie and Todd. I told them that your kids are the same age. So we've come to get acquainted."

In my surprise and delight, I must have hesitated in replying because she went on to say, "Look, I know that you're a serious method thespian and you probably think that I'm a corny musical comedy actress, but we are going to be movie sisters and it will be great for our kids to play together. Anyway, I'm a pushy broad and I'm determined to be your friend. So why don't you invite me in?"

That was how our friendship began. Our fondness for one another has grown and lasted, and is one of those rare and cherished friendships where we can begin a conversation one year and take it up again after any length of time without missing a beat.

I didn't have the opportunity to meet Jimmy Stewart the night he arrived. My call sheet said he and I would be sharing a car in the morning; we were to be picked up at the motel and driven to the dock where a boat would then take us to the island. Out of respect to Stewart, I got to the car early so as not to keep this venerable actor waiting. I was terribly nervous because I just knew that I would be tongue-tied at my first sight of him.

My goodness, he was such a daunting sight as he approached the car, dressed in his buckskin suit and coonskin cap, that I had difficulty saying hello. Imagine the feeling of suddenly sharing a long car ride with Jimmy Stewart! He was warm and friendly, but shy, like me. After the hellos and nice-to-be-working-with-you, we were both at a loss for words. I racked my brain for something to say, but absolutely nothing entered my head. It was ridiculous how awkward the ride was becoming, and I forced myself to say something totally banal about the weather.

After another interminable silence, while both of us were self-consciously looking out our respective windows and pretending interest in the monotonous landscape, Jimmy, without looking at me, said in his famous drawl, "Aw . . . Carroll . . . have you ever played a game called . . . count the cows?"

"No," was all I managed to reply.

"Wall-l, would you . . . like to play . . . count the . . . cows?"

We were both so serious during this exchange that anyone listening to us and not understanding the language might have thought we were about to discuss Einstein's theory of relativity.

"I don't know how to play," I offered apologetically.

"Wal-l, now . . . this is what you do . . . [and he paused here for what seemed like a full ten minutes] You count all the cows on your side of the road, and I count all the cows on my side of the road. Then when we reach the location—whoever has the most cows wins."

I know it sounds asinine, but I have never played a game that was more fun. We were passing through grazing country and there were so many cows that often the car had zipped by a herd faster than I could count them. We played the game for over an hour and we arrived on location breathless, giggling, slightly hoarse, and instant good friends.

The filming had been two days late in getting started because the advance team had discovered that our island was infested with rattlers. Twelve men with shotguns were sent in on a hunting expedition to kill off the poisonous snakes and make it safe for us. When we did begin filming, Debbie and I walked gingerly when entering the underbrush, and for the first days kept looking over our shoulders at the slightest sound, but we never saw a snake.

This kind of large-scale action film was fraught with danger. We were gathered near the shore one day filming a scene; and as background atmosphere, a long rowboat of extras, dressed in pioneer garb, were slowly making their way across the river. Henry Hathaway was a gruff, no-nonsense director, and everyone, especially the extras and bit players, was terrified of incurring his wrath.

I had my back to the scene, moodily looking out to the river. I noticed with surprise that the extras had all stopped rowing and were standing up in the boat. Then it dawned on me that the pioneers were slowly descending into the water and that the boat must be sinking. They stood immobilized as the river covered their ankles and then their homespun trousers and long skirts. Not one of them called out or made any effort to save themselves for fear of spoiling the "take." It was, at the same time, horrifying, fascinating, and hysterically funny. Pointing to the river, I screamed half in terror and half in laughter. Everyone on shore froze at the sight, it took minutes before a rescue boat was launched, and in the meantime Henry had forgotten to yell "Cut" over the bullhorn, so that the extras stood motionlessly sinking into the river until it reached their shoulders.

The motor boat had been slow in starting out, but the rescue itself was accomplished swiftly and without incident; but by that time I had wet my pants laughing.

The Cinerama camera had three lenses and cost more than the price of twelve ordinary movie cameras. Our camera was very precious indeed, and the crew treated it with the utmost care. In one scene our movie family was required to witness a trading post burn to the ground. Karl and Agnes were in the background, Debbie and I were in the foreground nearest the fire, and in between were our two brothers, one of whom was stretched out on the ground with his leg in a splint in order to match an earlier sequence. A *Life* magazine photographer was up a tree ready to capture the action in stills.

Henry found the first four attempted fires both unspectacular and unsatisfactory. He lost his temper and began to heckle the special effects men into giving him a fire worthy of Cinerama.

With Eli Wallach in *Baby Doll*

Baby Doll

With Eli Wallach in *Baby Doll*

Charlton Heston tries out his charms on me in *The Big Country*

With Gregory Peck in *The Big Country*

With Roger Moore in *The Miracle*

A change of habit in *The Miracle*

With Clark Gable and Barry Coe in *But Not for Me*

With James Shigeta in *Bridge to the Sun*

Filming *Station Six Sahara*: It was hot in the Libyan Desert!

Something Wild

Too much oil was used on the fifth take. The fire instantly became a roaring blaze which swept rapidly over the rest of the set and all the nearby trees. Debbie and I instinctively grabbed hands, turned, ran, and jumped straight into the river. Then Karl and Agnes and the one brother followed suit. The other boy couldn't move because of the splint, and he was screaming to be rescued. The *Life* photographer was yelling "Help!" as he was caught in the middle branches of a tree which was rapidly burning toward him from the top and the bottom. But Henry was yelling, "Save the camera! Save the camera!" All eventually were saved, but needless to say the camera was the first out.

We ran up against a week of stormy weather which, because we believed that turbulence always appears more menacing in the wild, we tended to underestimate. It became increasingly dangerous as the rains came down day after day, and it became more and more difficult to move our equipment and keep it dry and protected. Also, thick gumbo mud formed, and as the days passed, our trucks and cars had to grind to a halt farther and farther from the docking area.

On the fifth morning torrential rains and winds bombarded us nonstop, and we were unable to film a single shot. Film units always try to wait out a storm, so we stood around for several hours with rubber raincoats shielding our costumes. Considering the hazardous conditions and hard-to-reach location, we should have abandoned the shooting much earlier than we did.

By the time Henry dismissed us, the winds had reached gale force; the afternoon sky was black as night, the island was submerging, and the river, with its high waves, looked like an ocean. It had become an emergency that demanded lifesaving strategy. Our equipment was left to be retrieved only if the most able-bodied of the crew felt they could go back for it, and that only after the women and children and old people had been escorted off the island, away from the shores, and inland to the safety of the town.

Jimmy Stewart, Debbie, and I—we are all above-average swimmers—volunteered to remain and take the last boat off the island. I don't believe it was so much a question of bravery as it was that we all three seem to have been born with a love of adventure. (Stewart even goes big-game hunting in Africa every year!) Despite the way we were pitched and thrown, we managed to cross the river without falling in or overturning, but I felt as if I had left my stomach behind.

With such a large troupe, a certain amount of accidents and sickness is to be expected. I had been up all night with what I thought was an intestinal virus, and the next morning I was too ill to go to work. The local doctor was called in to examine me. His diagnosis was acute appendicitis, and he wanted me rushed immediately to the hospital for surgery. Jack was visiting at the time, and he didn't trust the opinion of the country doctor. He was also reluctant to let me be operated on at the small local clinic. He telephoned our family doctor, Dr. Louis Finger, and requested that Louie take the next flight out of New York with connections into Paducah.

In the meantime I had been admitted into the clinic so that in case my appendix burst—as the local doctor predicted it might—I would be on the spot for an emergency operation. I was stretched out on one of those hospital tables with wheels, in a room adjacent to the operating room. I spent the next six hours awaiting either emergency surgery or Louis Finger. The local doctor kept passing by my door, peering in at me, and then shaking his head.

The waiting was torture, and knowing that Dr. Finger might also recommend surgery, I think I would have preferred to get it over with. But Jack was adamant that nothing be done until Louis gave us his opinion.

At four in the afternoon Louis Finger finally arrived. He pressed my stomach three or four times and then leaned over so that the local man could not see him and winked. As diplomatically as possible, Louie told the local doctor that he realized how difficult it was to make a diagnosis when the symptoms were identical, but that I had nothing more than an intestinal virus. However, they made him sign a statement that I was being released at risk and upon his cognizance.

Louie went straight back to New York, and I went back to work the following morning. Forty-eight hours after my appendix scare, the local doctor was called in to examine an ailing Karl Malden—and his diagnosis was that Karl had to be rushed to the hospital to have *his* appendix removed!

Karl asked to see Jack and me at once, before the ambulance arrived. When we got to his room Karl was doubled over in pain.

Jack placed a call to Louie Finger in New York, and Karl questioned me about my symptoms. I told him that we had all the same symptoms with the exception of the pain. The moment Dr. Finger heard from Karl that his cramps were so severe that he couldn't walk, Louie told him to go straight to the hospital for the operation. So it was Karl who left his appendix behind in Paducah.

Oddly enough, after all the trials, hardships and dramas of Paducah, it was a scene we did back in the comfort of the MGM studios that turned out to be the most dangerous and terrifying for the Prescott family: Agnes, Karl, Debbie, the two boys, and myself. We had not been asked to do the raft scene on location because of the obvious perils of going over the river rapids. Stuntmen dressed in our costumes were filmed on the actual spot. Personally I would rather have chanced the real rapids of the wild than that simulated scene of horrors they prepared for us at MGM.

At the studio, the setting for our additional shots of the raft scene was that famous large swimming pool which had been used in *Mutiny on the Bounty* and a hundred Esther Williams extravaganzas. The Kentucky scenery was projected onto the white walls surrounding the pool, gigantic high-powered fans were employed to manufacture wind, wave machines churned the water of the swimming pool, and the raft was anchored underneath on a sort of motorized gimbal which enabled the technicians to rock it back and forth and tip it sideways by remote control.

The logs of the raft were slippery, there was nothing to brace your feet against, and very little to hang on to for support. Physically, it was hardest for Karl, who had not yet fully recovered from his operation. He still moved slowly in a stooped position, and found the exertion of hanging on for dear life extremely painful. Falling off meant possibly being struck by that raft, which must have weighed several tons. Debbie, Agnes, and I were most frightened of being dragged under and getting our long skirts caught up in the mechanism, where we might have been trapped and possibly drowned before we could have been released. Once the camera rolled, they began making the raft leap, blasting us with forty-mph winds, and hitting us with walls of freezing cold water. No acting was necessary. They simply filmed what were our real struggles and our expressions of genuine terror.

The middle portion of *How the West Was Won* was directed by John "Pappy" Ford. I admired and adored Pappy, and I shall forever be grateful that I was able to work with him twice (*Cheyenne Autumn* was the other film) and call him my friend. Kazan was unquestionably the best "actor's" director, but Ford stressed the "motion" in motion picture and he taught me more about the visual side than I could ever have learned from Gadge. It was a unique experience in the way that working with Clark Gable in *But Not For Me* had been; Gable had also shared secrets about being in front of the movie camera that no amount of time at the Actors' Studio could have provided.

It was also in this middle section of *How the West Was Won* that I first worked with George Peppard. Today, George is a super guy, a gentleman whom anyone would find it a pleasure to know and work with. Sorry, George, but in the '60s I couldn't help thinking that you were a pretentious, egotistical brat and that was just for starters!

George had been introduced in the film version of *End as a Man* (later entitled *The Strange One*) which Jack had directed in 1956. So I knew George and was aware of his background. He arrived on the set of *How the West Was Won* trying to pass himself off with a phony identity. Although I had met his wife and children, even in front of me he denied their existence. He claimed to be a bachelor, and he had conveniently dropped seven years off his age.

A few months later, George and I worked together again in *The Carpetbaggers*. When George won the plum role of Jonas Cord (Howard Hughes?), it seemed to go to his head. He acquired delusions of being far more than just a talented young actor who was working his way up the ladder of success. I got the impression he felt he was God's gift to women and the cinema.

From the moment I walked on the set of *Carpetbaggers* to play Rina Marlow (Jean Harlow?), George's attitude toward me seemed bizarre, as though he had never met me or had any awareness of the existence of my husband. George asked me not *if* he could see me in an intimate setting, but *when*. He showed up uninvited at my house late one night and gave me a stern warning: "If you don't have a love affair with me, I'll make love to Elizabeth Ashley."

I did a nude scene in *The Carpetbaggers,* which caused the press to keep following me around, perhaps in the hope of an encore. George was jealous of the attention I was getting and one day snapped, "I don't know what all the fuss is about. She isn't the first—I did a nude scene in my last film!"

Alan Ladd played Nevada Smith. Alan had recently been through horrendous times in his life and his work. The poor man was making a superhuman effort to steady himself and make a comeback in his career. I remember how his hands used to shake. One day during a scene with me his drink spilled over the sides of his glass because of the trembling. Out of sheer frustration, he punched the door of the set with his hand still holding the glass and cut himself quite badly.

Paramount employed a tattletale system whereby the assistant director kept a record of every spoiled take and who was to blame. Alan was desperate that his name not appear too many times on that list. Our director, Eddie Dmytryk, when he saw Alan begin to flounder, would jump in with, "Cut! It's my fault. I'd like to go again."

Most of the actors did the same thing, tried to take some of the blame in order to ease Alan's pain and anxiety. As I remember, everyone showed tolerance, except George. Perhaps he was too insecure about his own position to be compassionate toward Alan?

George arranged the "end of filming" party, and he wouldn't allow Bob Cummings, Martha Hyer, the director, or me to contribute toward the cost of the closing-day celebrations. We agreed to let him be the "big cheese" only if he held the party jointly with Alan Ladd. It was to be remembered that Alan Ladd, although he had fallen on hard times, was still the biggest star and had done more important films than all the rest of us put together.

The party was to be held on the last remaining set, the ballroom set where I would be drinking champagne while dancing on a twelve-foot-high chandelier before it came crashing down thirty-six feet to the floor below. The producers had assured me that at the moment of release, after I had dropped out of sight of the viewfinder, the chandelier would be pulled clear by wires, and that if I jumped away from it and onto the prepared mattresses, I couldn't possibly get hurt. If they were so sure, why had they scheduled that fall as the very last shot of the film?

The moment had, indeed, been well planned. I dropped to my feet and rolled unhurt onto the mattresses. When the crystal smashed I was a safe distance from the shattering spears of glass. But I have found that in most stunts it is always the unexpected that catches you. My hairy moment had come at the very beginning before the cameras turned. I was lifted by crane up to the chandelier, but before grasping it I paused to apply resin to my sweaty hands. As I moved to apply the resin, the crane platform swayed slightly, touching its metal bar to the metal bar of the chandelier—and a deadly spray of electric sparks flew. The wiring was faulty and had to be redone and grounded more securely. That moment's hesitation had saved me from being electrocuted!

The Carpetbaggers was, like *How the West Was Won,* another enormous success which I had accepted purely on chance. I had been at a charity ball in New York before leaving to film *How the West Was Won,* and met Joe Levine for the first time. He said, upon meeting me, "You're just the girl I want for my next film. It is the best part you've had since *Baby Doll,* but you have to take my word for that. Without any question, you must accept the part and shake my hand to bind the deal."

So that is exactly what I did. I shook Joe Levine's hand. It wasn't until months later that I discovered I had agreed to play Rina Marlow in *The Carpetbaggers.* And it was that part in that film which shot me back up to the top of my profession. In showbiz circles it was to be hailed as a remarkable comeback.

Chapter
Twenty-Three

FRIGID: BUT I WAS ONE OF JOHN FORD'S SOLDIERS

In the late summer of 1963, before beginning work on *The Carpetbaggers*, Jack, I and the children moved permanently to Beverly Hills. I had given in to the purchase of a house I loathed. It had belonged to a recently divorced movie producer, whose wife had been awarded the house as part of their divorce settlement. She wanted to get away from California quickly and was willing to sell at a sacrificial price. Jack was convinced that it was a rare opportunity for us to own a piece of choice Beverly Hills real estate, but if I had been on my own, I wouldn't have accepted it as a gift.

The house seemed as if it had been sucked dry of any warmth or happiness. It was sterile and cold and lifeless. The walls, ceiling, woodwork, furniture, and carpeting were all white on white. Unrelieved room of white opening onto rooms of white culminating in a colorless glass wall. It reminded me of an exclusive insane asylum or a posh morgue.

The house nevertheless met all the requirements of a typical "Hollywood" home. It had some token grass and shrubbery, a kidney-shaped swimming pool, an indoor and an outdoor barbecue, a professional soda fountain, a projection room equipped with a stereophonic sound system, and a motorized Cinemascope movie screen which descended by the push of a button into one of the three identical living rooms. Among all this opulence I also found in the kitchen a narrow clothes closet with a floor drain for the purpose of hanging wet drip-dry shirts out of sight.

The down payment for this Beverly Hills corner lot with its "movie star" home was only ten thousand dollars! But we didn't have nearly that much cash, so Jack, who was never shy about borrowing money, went ahead and borrowed it from Debbie Reynolds's husband, Harry Karl, without consulting me. I was so embarrassed that he would take advantage of my new friendship with Debbie. But Debbie apparently didn't mind, and she assured me that it was no hardship for Harry, who was the wealthy owner of the Karl Shoe Store chain. Harry was also kind enough to co-sign the mortgage.

We moved to the West Coast in time for the new school year. It wasn't much of an adjustment for Herschel, who was beginning first grade, but Blanche was entering second grade and she was very disturbed by the change from French school to the Beverly Hills public school system. She had done so well in her French studies, and I wanted to enroll her in a private école, but Jack felt that we couldn't afford the tuition.

God, I was such a coward when it came to lengthy discussions! Most days my work, my children, maintaining a household and a demanding career left me drained of energy. I ached for a few minutes of peace and quiet. Jack seemed determined to have his own way in everything. It seemed to me that while he never tired of arguing, I tired far too quickly. Little by little I forfeited my own needs and my own judgment just to avoid prolonging the battles. Maybe I was also afraid of crushing Jack's already badly bruised ego—sadly, he had no work of his own any longer. He had gotten into difficulties with too many people and producers now considered him a risk.

Being out of work was terrible for Jack because he had little if anything to occupy his thoughts or to consume his energy. He hadn't developed any interests or hobbies. He didn't play games or take part in sports or even, for that matter, get enough exercise. He would never stoop over to pick up his clothes. In fact, he left everything strewn about the house where he'd last used it. Someone was always picking up after him—during the day it was the maid or the nanny, and at night it was me, time after weary time. How could I resent the fact that he had become slovenly and inconsiderate when I had overlooked it for so many years, had actually stood by and allowed it to develop? Once I realized that I had spoiled my man rotten, it was too late to try and change him.

Jack's concentration shifted to my career. He was becoming so obsessed with this self-appointed role as my Svengali that I couldn't convince him to ease off. He was even failing to recognize the limitations of my endurance. He wasn't tired sitting on the sidelines, so how could I be? He spent hour after hour on the telephone setting up meetings, interviews, photo sessions, and public appearances in endless succession. He arranged a herculean schedule of appointments which I was supposed to honor and be properly grateful for.

At the beginning of our marriage, Jack and I had shared a vibrant, exciting sex life. Now I no longer either responded or much cared. The sexual act, which had once brought me such pleasure, had become a joyless duty, a hateful obligation which I forced myself to tolerate. Of course, my loss of interest in sex had developed gradually, but I associate the start of my frigidity with my move to California and to that frigid house.

Ironically, my condition also coincided with the making and release of *The Carpetbaggers,* and the subsequent resurgence of my sex-symbol identity. Little did anyone know that the actress who had played Rina Marlow was herself desperately in need of some sexual stimulation. This, however, is in retrospect; then I had no leisure in which to contemplate my frigidity, or any of my other problems. Time, you might say, was stuck in the fast-forward position.

I had eight films released in 1963–64—it's hard for me to believe. Those 703 days of frantic nonstop activities don't seem real, much less humanly possible. I must have raced at an incredible speed, and that's why my impression is of time stuck in the fast-forward position. The one thing I do understand now is how and why I ultimately ground to a halt, burned out.

In order to tell of those two years, I'll have to slow the picture down and sometimes even "freeze-frame," otherwise the telling itself is in danger of becoming exhausting. Just remember, please, that from here on in, while it was happening, there were no pauses.

Joe Levine certainly played a big part. Joe thought of himself as a great showman and he was hyped up by his success as the producer of *The Carpetbaggers*. Joe recognized in me the perfect puppet to execute his extravagant publicity campaigns. And he was shrewd. He quickly learned that no amount of publicity, no matter how taxing, would be refused as long as Jack Garfein was consulted first.

Together, Joe and Jack scheduled for me a tight series of rushed personal appearances to launch *The Carpetbaggers*. The first week I covered the middle of the country from north to south—Duluth, Minneapolis-St. Paul, St. Louis, Memphis, and Birmingham. Those were the only play dates which coincided, and the rest of that month I hopscotched on airplanes from distant points like San Francisco to Chicago, Detroit to Seattle, and Kansas City to Pittsburgh. I was continuously on and off airplanes, working from early morning until late at night doing interviews. I didn't have a break or even one day off to fly home to see my children.

When I thought I was free to go home, Levine arranged for me to fly immediately to New York to pose for a life-size sculpture. In two weeks' time, when Joe was due to throw a gala *Carpetbaggers* party, the artist was to have duplicated the sculpture in ice. The ice statue was to be dressed in a sheer black negligee and placed in the center of the pool at the Four Seasons restaurant.

While I was in New York, Jack telephoned with the news that he had persuaded Joe to send me to Paris to have a gown designed for the Hollywood premiere. I couldn't come home. I had to leave immediately for Europe.

When I arrived in Paris the first person I tried to contact was Marlene Dietrich, but Marlene was in Switzerland. It was just as well that I didn't see her in person because Marlene was so warm and sympathetic and cared so much for her friends that I surely would have cried on her shoulder about my unhappiness, making a complete bore of myself. As it was, when I reached her by phone in Geneva we had great fun by discussing nothing but clothes.

Marlene said, "You're in Paris for only one gown! But, my darling, you are a silly little fool! With all the promotion work you are doing for this producer, he must at least buy for you a new wardrobe. That is certainly what Mike Todd would have done. You will give me now his name and phone number, and I shall make him feel ashamed for being so stingy."

Levine must have fallen off his chair when he received a phone call from Marlene Dietrich, but he never said a word about it to me. Pierre Balmain received a letter of credit to make me a wardrobe and Levine announced to me his generous offering as if it had been his own idea.

Marlene advised me to get a classic suit which would always be chic and would, with the French hand-stitching, last for years. She thought I should get a beige or neutral-colored wool-jersey daytime dress with a matching cloth coat and hat, one black cocktail dress, and one other evening outfit aside from the gown for the *Carpetbaggers* appearance. The evening outfit she suggested was the newest craze in French *haute couture*—an evening slack suit. As for the *Carpetbaggers* dress, I asked her if she would mind if I copied one of her costume ideas: a slinky, jeweled, net-and-chiffon transparent gown, which I had seen her wear in her Las Vegas nightclub act.

"No darling, I don't mind," she said. "That would be perfect for you. One must have a firm, trim figure like yours to wear such a gown. It would look vulgar on a plump woman." She proceeded to detail the secret mechanics in the design of such a garment and then finished with a warning, "You must, however, remember the importance of standing on your feet in the sheath and supervising the placement of every single jewel. Your body will be shown to the best advantage if you carefully select what you show and what you don't show. So don't be a lazy girl."

That dress caused a sensation when I wore it to the Hollywood premiere of *The Carpetbaggers*! It looked gorgeous—sparkling and devastatingly daring. I wore nothing underneath, and the skin-colored net and chiffon blended under the bright lights with my own flesh just as Marlene had predicted it would. I believe every newspaper in the world printed a photograph of me in that transparent dress, with claims that I had appeared virtually nude.

Peculiar as it may seem now, it was not the transparent gown, but the Balmain sequined evening slack suit, covering me from neck to ankle, which caused the bigger controversy. I wore it the night I accepted my statuette at the Foreign Press Awards dinner. When I rose from my table to walk up to the microphone,

I was stunned by whispers of shocked disapproval from the audience. Although they were the latest fashion in France, pants had never before been worn in Hollywood for a formal occasion, and I was instantly labelled outrageous for my daring unconventionality. My acceptance speech could not be heard because the audience "Tish-tished" all throughout it. Both Louella Parsons and Hedda Hopper rushed from the room, either in indignation or to get the scandalous story on the wires first.

It is customary for all the winners in a category to be photographed together. When I went backstage where the photographers were waiting, the other recipients in my category scattered and fled so as not to be seen with me. Jimmy Stewart had already posed for his photographs and was on his way back to the ballroom when he noticed me abandoned on the platform. He walked the length of the room, climbed back on the platform, put his arm around me and said, "Carroll, I think you look beautiful. Now just let's you and I pose for these press boys."

Jack was in the habit of rushing to the publicity office every day to study and count my clippings. The office placed the latest clippings on a long conference table. Usually one half of the table was filled with photographs and articles about me and the other half consisted of all the other Hollywood publicity. Jack got to the point where he expected that ratio, becoming quite disappointed if my clippings on any given day receded by even an inch.

Jack was fired with excitement by the dozens of daily requests for me to make personal appearances: I flew for one day to Paris for the European premiere of *How the West Was Won,* one evening to Las Vegas for the American premiere of *Station Six Sahara,* one day to New York for the opening of *The Carpetbaggers,* one day to Denver for the motion picture exhibitors' convention. I even ended up going to Montreal for a fur breeders' convention!

Jack and Joe Levine were in the midst of arranging an Australian tour to promote *The Carpetbaggers,* when I frustrated their plans by telephoning George Stevens and asking him if there was a part for me in *The Greatest Story Ever Told.* I had read in the trade papers that George planned to have stars playing cameo roles in the closing sequences. He offered me a brief appearance as Saint Theresa, and I was thrilled at the opportunity to work again in a George Stevens film. John Wayne, Sidney Poitier, and I had trailers next to one another, and I had a great time between takes getting acquainted with those remarkable men. What a bonus! All three of us had the time to sit around, gab, and now and then even get into more serious discussions. The only subject Sidney and I learned to steer clear of was politics. Wayne's views tended to be altogether too far right for either of us, and neither Sidney nor I felt like taking on the big "Duke"!

I was only on the set for five days, but they were five days of bliss, away from my otherwise relentless publicity schedule. That week was just enough to make the Australian tour impossible. However, the tour itself was not cancelled; instead of sending me, Joe Levine sent my transparent dress! There was a Carroll Baker look-alike contest in each city and the lucky winner got to model that gown in her local cinema.

One day I managed to sneak away and visit my old buddy Steve McQueen and his adorable wife, Neile. I think I must have pretended that Steve and I wanted to discuss a movie idea, but, in fact, he and Neile wanted to show me their new house. Neile told me to wear jeans because they couldn't afford furniture and we would be sitting on the floor for lunch.

What a monstrous, great, spooky-looking estate it was! I parked my car outside the large, forbidding iron gates, and Steve took me on his motorcycle through the vast grounds and the winding, tree-lined dirt road that led up to the mansion. It would have made the perfect location for the filming of *The Haunting of Hill House!*

"Steve, this is a nightmare," I told him. "How can you and Neile and the children possibly live here?"

Steve laughed. "Well, this is Hollywood. You got to put up a front. I'm going to begin demanding a king's ransom for my next films and these bastards will pay it—if they think I don't need the money."

"Steve, I loathe my house because it's just a showplace. It's impossible for everyday living. I hate to tell you, but I think your house is worse than mine."

"Just wait, Carroll. Wait until you see the party I'm going to throw. Instead of buying furniture, I'm putting all my money into a bash. A bash that will stand this town on its ear."

Sure enough, in a few weeks' time Steve and Neile threw the party of the year. Those acres of ground were festooned with colored lanterns and the outside of the mansion was lit by kleig lights. An entire dance floor was constructed on the front lawn, and we danced to the music of a live orchestra. Waiters in red and gold uniforms poured champagne like water, and a sumptuous buffet was served in an enormous, specially constructed candy-striped tent fit for "The Arabian Nights."

No one entered the mansion or was aware of the corridors of empty rooms. The message of the evening was luxury and wealth. Nor had Steve miscalculated the effect, because his next picture salary indeed did double!

John Ford wanted me for his new film, *Cheyenne Autumn,* and I again had a much-needed reprieve from my Garfein-Levine duties. I also really needed to get away from that sex-goddess image. The more I exposed myself and played available, the more I turned off personally. That flagrant, unnatural whorishness I was pretending seemed to harden my own state of frigidity.

Cheyenne Autumn was a touching story about the Cheyenne Indians. Forced by the government to resettle on an arid reservation in the Southwest, the tribe longed for their rich Montana homeland. Finally, in defiance of the United States Cavalry, they set out on the long trek back to their beloved territory in the north.

I was to play a Quaker schoolteacher, a devoted woman who decides to make the journey with them in order to care for the Indian children. Richard Widmark was to play the officer in charge of the cavalry, and Jimmy Stewart was to portray Wyatt Earp in the Kansas City sequence.

Pappy Ford wanted me to become an expert in the handling of horses because during the filming I would be responsible for the safety of the Indian children riding in my buckboard. After that scare in *The Big Country,* when the horses ran away with Greg and me in the buckboard, I was anxious to learn.

Pappy arranged for me to go every day to a ranch in Bakersfield to take lessons from the famous wrangler, Monty Montana.

In the weeks of training that followed, Monty let me drive a buckboard until it became second nature and then he put me through every conceivable obstacle course. I learned that in any type of runaway situation, if I forced the horses to circle and then made the circles ever and ever smaller, the horses would eventually slow down. By the end of the month Monty even had me driving a stagecoach! There was little chance that I'd ever be cast as a stagecoach driver, but once I had the security of knowing that I could control with the reins those six strapping horses and balance the considerable weight of that coach, I no longer had any fear about my ability to handle two horses and a buckboard.

Saturdays were the most fun because Herschel had no school and I could take him with me to Monty's. He looked darling in the miniature red-and-blue cowboy outfit I bought him, and he was so thrilled to be on a real ranch with real cowboys, that in remembering him as he looked and reacted then, I find myself laughing and crying.

During the filming on the Utah and Colorado locations, the trek was so slow and the driving so effortless that I began to wonder if I would ever be called upon to use any of my expertise. Then the unexpected happened!

My Indian children ranged in age from three to five and none of them had learned to swim. We began a long shot of a river crossing. The Indians in front of me were on horseback, and I was the first wagon in the lineup. I had crossed rivers and streams before in the filming without incident, but this time, the moment the front wheels of my buckboard were submerged, I realized that the outwardly calm appearance of the river camouflaged a tremendously strong undercurrent. The buckboard swayed dangerously, and I knew instantly that I had to abandon the "take." Monty had taught me never to fight a current but go with it at an angle. I steered very wide toward the opposite bank of the river in order to maintain equilibrium. The buckboard behind me, which attempted to cross in a straight line, immediately overturned.

Two stuntmen dressed as Indians, seeing that I was veering out of the shot, rode to the front of my horses and grabbed their harnesses. I tried to shout to them, to make them let go and stop attempting to straighten me out, but with all the thundering noise in the river they couldn't hear me. When they pulled my horses in the opposite direction from the one my wagon was being pushed in by the current, I knew the children and I were near to capsizing. I just couldn't let that happen! I stood up and beat the stuntmen with my long horsewhip until they were forced to let go. In the nick of time I tugged the horses back in line with the buckboard, regaining control.

The take had been a panoramic view from the mountain top encompassing the entire Indian tribe plus the regiment of cavalry following us. The preparations for that shot had taken all of the previous day to set up and now this ruined take wiped out the entire morning's work. Once the children were safely on dry ground, I began to wonder if Pappy had understood that I had taken the only possible course of action.

It seemed to take forever for Pappy's car to bring him down to us from the mountaintop. When he arrived he ignored everyone else and walked directly toward me. From the distance, with his low-slung soft-brimmed hat and his black eye patch, it was hard for me to read his expression. He approached me very slowly and deliberately, all the while chomping on his unlit cigar stub. Finally, he stood silently over me, looking at me with his one piercing eye and continuing to gnaw his cigar. After an agonizing wait, he curled back the brim of his hat, took the cigar from his mouth and with cutting sarcasm he said, "Well, that's wonderful! So in keeping with this film. I have a marvelous shot of two Indians being horsewhipped by a Quaker girl."

He flipped the cigar back in his mouth and continued to glare at me with his good eye. And I decided to say nothing.

Pappy was half-deaf and half-blind, but I was convinced that there was nothing that he couldn't hear or see. Despite his gruff attitude, my instincts told me that he must have known I was right. I couldn't defend myself without blaming the stuntmen, and Pappy would have considered me a bad soldier. He believed in honor. If someone else were to blame, they had to come forward. Otherwise, I had to accept the punishment.

Without turning his head or taking his eye off me, Pappy called out to his assistant, "Wayne, anybody hurt when that second buckboard in line overturned?"

"No, Mr. Ford," Wayne called back, loud, clear, and succinct, the way Pappy always wanted to be answered.

"Didn't think so," Pappy said, directing his words at me. "Not a bad touch . . . that buckboard overturning . . . could have used the shot . . . the reason the scene had to be cut was because I was filming a violent Quaker . . . or maybe you didn't know that the Quakers preach love, peace, and nonviolence?"

Chuck, one of the stuntmen "Indians" who had interfered with my horses, stepped up beside Pappy, took off his hat in respect, and asked, "Mr. Ford, can I say something?"

"Can you?" Pappy munched without removing his cigar. "You mean now that you're dressed up like an Indian, can you still say something in English?"

Chuck looked puzzled and shook his pigtailed wig, "No, sir, I mean can I tell you that me and Harry talked over what we did with Carroll's horses and decided we was wrong."

Pappy's expression didn't appear to change but his mood turned jubilant. He plucked the cigar out of his mouth with a sucking movement and, pursing his lips, said, "You mean that if Carroll hadn't beaten you away and continued to angle the wagon, that those little Indian children might have ended up in the river?"

Chuck said hesitantly, "Yes, sir."

"Well, then," Pappy continued, "I guess we have a heroine on our hands. Wouldn't you say so?"

Chuck, still looking puzzled, replied, "Yes, sir."

I loved being treated as an equal with the guys! It couldn't have been easy for Pappy when he had to be stern with me. I felt that he thought of me as a daughter and I knew that I was his pet on the film unit. While we were on location, I always ate lunch and dinner by his side. He used to watch my plate and never allow me dessert or bread and butter or potatoes. I was a slim 118 pounds, but Pappy didn't want me to gain even an ounce in my face. He was continually amazed and alarmed by the huge quantities of food I consumed. The day I saved the Indian children, my reward was a hug and the permission to eat mashed potatoes and a piece of apple pie—but just that once.

Chapter

Twenty-Four

MY SEX SAGA WITH ROBERT MITCHUM

After *Cheyenne Autumn,* United Artists felt it was high time they collected on my IOU for the postproduction costs of *Something Wild* (which Jack and I had produced and had run out of completion money on). They put forth a proposition: they would star me in a comedy film with Robert Mitchum, pay me my going rate, deduct my debt to them, and give me the meager amount which remained. I liked the story, and it wasn't an offer I could very well refuse.

With only a weekend between jobs, I packed my cases for Kenya, East Africa, and flew there to begin the filming of *Mister Moses.*

I can now only think of that movie as my sex saga with Robert Mitchum. Although he never overtly made a pass or invited me to his room, never has a man tormented me so much with his sexual availability. At least it made me realize that I was still capable of being aroused.

Every aspect of that three-and-a-half month location reeked with unadulterated, unrelieved sensuality. The winds, the dust, and the sun—combined with the sounds and the smells and the colors of Africa—are titillating enough to the senses. When you add the feel of being in close proximity to a primitive, half-naked tribe, and a gorgeous hunk of a man who parades his manliness twenty-four hours a day outside your lonely hut—well, who could possibly retain her cool, even if that irresistible force didn't happen to be the terrific Robert Mitchum?

Nor do film companies ever consider safeguarding their leading lady's chastity. No, they place you right next door to temptation by housing you beside your leading man. If our company had wanted to settle Mitchum and me into an undisturbed romantic site, they couldn't have planned it better. We lived for the duration of the movie at an isolated English inn, twenty miles into the bush country. My bungalow and Mitchum's were within whispering distance of each other. We were separated from the main building, which was also on the level ground, by two city blocks of thick vegetation. The other bungalows were scattered in the hills above.

Countless times each day, Mitchum did the mating dance of the proud male of the species. Barefooted and bare chested, he would strut on his front porch, the railing of which nearly touched mine.

His physique was nothing less than a marvel of nature, with his long iron-hard legs, slim hips, trim waist, mammoth back, broad shoulders, and, oh, those enormous muscular arms and that magnificent full-blown chest sheening with sweat! I was driven to distraction, while peeking out of my shuttered window, by just a glimpse of him. But Bob had no mercy on me and he continuously slunk up and down, up and down on that porch like a tiger in heat. He stretched, yawned, mewed, twisted, hummed, and scratched his back on the wall. He caressed the porch steps; slithered into a chair; and proffered his luscious, prostrate, half-naked body in a low-slung hammock, hypnotically swaying toward me and away from me and toward me again, as a perpetual prurient invitation.

On the set, although other people surrounded us, there was no escape from Mitchum's allure. Even when he drank coffee, I began to ache deep down inside because of the way he licked the rim, and sucked the fluid, and gurgled with smacking sounds of satisfaction.

I wanted so much to be faithful to Jack and our marriage vows, but where was I to find the strength? I was lonely, in a seductive atmosphere, and tempted day and night by one of the world's most attractive, desirable, and clearly hot men. What girl, forced to live for three-and-a-half months, alone and secluded in

Africa, could possibly resist falling into the arms of her next-door neighbor, especially when that neighbor is Robert Mitchum?

I took cold showers and drank gallons of herbal tea, a tea for which I had traded my best necklace; one the witch doctor had guaranteed was a tranquilizer. I hung heavy clothing over the windows to cut out the sight, and I played classical music to drown out the sound. I even placed the juju charms of "discouragement" on my bed and in my underwear. But nothing kept my desire under control. My attempt to sublimate the call of the flesh was a losing battle.

It was at the very moment when I considered giving in to all that promised pleasure, that chance intervened. Fate, as they say, knocked on my door. The knocking was brisk and loud. Who could it be? Nobody ever came to my door at that time of night. It had to be him. My heart pounded, and my mouth went dry, and I began to shake in anticipation. Had he been reading my thoughts?

I opened the door with shaky hands and then gasped in surprise—standing before me was Shirley MacLaine!—in the middle of the night, in the middle of Africa!

"Hi, Carroll," she squealed. "Are you surprised to see me? [Surprised? I thought I was having a hallucination!] I just got in. I surprised Bob, too. He didn't know I was coming to visit him."

"Gee, Shirley, that's wonderful," I choked, and wondered if I had turned green to match the way I was feeling.

"Come on over and have a drink with us," Shirley insisted.

So for the first time I went into Mitchum's bungalow, but not the way I had dreamed of going there. I had to look away when Shirley sat on his lap and kissed him. I tried to smile and laugh. I drank three Mitchum-made martinis which knocked me straight on my ear, and for that night, at least, I passed out when I hit my bed. As Shirley stayed at another inn, if they were more than friends, at least I never heard lovemaking sounds through those thin, close-by walls.

The latest issue of *Newsweek* magazine was passed around our set. It had an article with the worst kind of advance publicity any film can have: it made us seem like a bunch of tasteless idiots carelessly throwing together a ridiculous movie. When the *News-*

week reporter had been on our set some weeks before, Mitchum had ignored him, but I had been very nice to him and had even given him a guided tour. Now here was his article. It was not only snide and cutting, but it strongly insinuated that Mitchum and I were hitting the sack together! God, was I angry!

It took me eight hours to get a phone call through to Jack. Aside from my own assurances that I was not having a romance with Mitchum, I also put both our director, Ronny Neame, and our producer, Frank Ross, on the telephone. They each confirmed that Shirley was visiting on the q.t. and that if there were any romancing, she was the most likely candidate.

We had arrived in Kenya just after Uhuru (Independence) had been declared. Kenyatta had called for the ferocious Mau Mau to come out of the hills and surrender their weapons, but they were slow to acquiesce and there were still many bands of these terrorists maiming and slaughtering whites. The British Embassy had warned us to be extremely careful, especially at night, and the locals had advised us never to stop our cars for a road accident, in case it was a trap. Apparently a white man had stopped his car when he saw a bicycle and rider strewn in the middle of the road. As he got out to assist the seemingly lifeless figure, the black man jumped to his feet and three of his accomplices sprang from the bush. They robbed him and then hacked him to death with their machetes.

One night at three o'clock in the morning I was awakened by a pounding. Through the lacy curtain on my glass door, I could see the shadowy form of a tall dark man. I was paralyzed with fear. After a few minutes of pounding he called out to me, and I recognized the voice of the Kikuyu man who worked in the hotel office. It was a long-distance phone call. I slipped my coat on over my nightdress and followed the Kikuyu man and his flashlight beam through the foliage to the office and the telephone. My adrenaline was still pumping and now my fright turned to the prospect of bad news. It seemed it could only be an emergency at this time of the morning, and I was terrified that something might have happened to one of my children.

It was Earl Wilson, the gossip columnist of the *New York Post*, calling to ask me if the rumor about Mitchum and me was true!

After I had gone back to bed for perhaps five minutes, I was again called to the telephone. This time it was Radie Harris of the *Hollywood Reporter* asking me to confirm my romance with Mitchum!

Those were only the first of a series of annoying enquiries which, because of the time difference and long delays, normally came in the middle of the night. Mitchum refused to be summoned for early-morning phone calls, but because of the children I always dragged myself out of bed to see who it was on the other end of the line.

The day I told Mitchum that the world press were accusing us of having an affair, he looked at me with those sleepy, half-closed bedroom eyes and said, "An affair with you? I'm sorry I missed that."

Two weeks after the story appeared in *Newsweek,* and while I was still being badgered by the gossip columnists, the same *Newsweek* reporter actually had the gall to show up again on our set! He was a personal friend of the man whose land we were renting for our film location. The reporter and his wife, in the company of the landlord, marched straight into our luncheon tent and brazenly helped themselves to our catered buffet! These three behaved as though they were nobility and we were lowly peasants, powerless to object to their blatant effrontery. The crew were steaming mad and so were the producer and the director. At the actors' table Alex Knox and I were dreaming up ways of getting even, and the other actors were offering their suggestions.

We came up with a deliciously evil plan. Everyone agreed that since I had suffered most from the man's mendacious gossip, I should be the one to execute his punishment and taste the sweetness of revenge.

I went up to the buffet table and heaped a plate high with oodles of sloppy fruit salad, gobs of sticky marshmallow sauce, and mountains of slippery whipped cream. I walked past the unsuspecting reporter's table, faked a trip, and planted the gooey mess directly on his head.

The crew broke into loud spontaneous laughter and the entire tent rocked with cheers and applause. The wife looked straight ahead as if nothing had happened, while the reporter sat in shocked stillness as the fruit and marshmallow and whipped cream slid slowly down his face and neck and shirt.

In a delayed reaction the landlord jumped to his feet and screamed with indignation, "That's not funny. He is my guest. When you insult him, you insult me. At the end of the week, you are to clear off my land." Then the three stormed out.

Frank Ross came up to me and said, "Carroll, you were perfectly justified in what you did. If you refuse to apologize, I understand. But I'm in a real pickle with this film if I have to tear down the set and move somewhere else."

"Don't worry, Frank," I said, "I wouldn't let that happen. As far as I'm concerned the reporter and I are even now. I'll be happy to go and see the man and shake his hand."

Frank drove me to the landlord's estate. The reporter had cleaned up and changed his shirt, and he, his wife, and the landlord were seated on the veranda. All three scowled at me as I got out of the car and approached them.

I went up to the reporter, held out my hand, and said, "Will you accept my apology? You wrote a rotten article and I hit you with a fruit salad. I think that makes us even. Will you be a good sport, shake hands, and let bygones be bygones? I am truly sorry for the messiness and any humiliation I might have caused you."

Do you know what happened? That bad sport, that humorless dud, that sourpuss actually refused to shake my hand or accept my apology. The landlord sneered at me and reaffirmed his vindictiveness: our company would be penalized and made to vacate his property by the end of the week.

When I got back in the car, Frank went to talk with the landlord but he remained adamant. Poor Frank was distraught. He wasn't sure United Artists would come up with the extra money, a considerable amount, to move location and reconstruct the set. It also meant the loss of a few weeks' filming, which could be disastrous because we had to finish before the torrential rains came at the end of March or the beginning of April.

I felt rotten. It was all my fault. All through dinner that evening I kept moaning to the other actors about the terrible repercussions of my actions. "What can I do? The man refused to accept my apology. What can I possibly do now to right the hopeless situation I've gotten our film into?"

Orlando Martins, the famous Nigerian actor, spoke up, "Why don't you ask Kenyatta for help?"

"Kenyatta?" I gasped. "You mean go to the president of the country, Kenyatta, and ask him to intervene?"

"Yes," Orlando assured me, "I know him quite well. He adores actors. He used to do some stage acting himself. I'll call and get him to invite us."

Sure enough, the next evening we were invited to dinner at the presidential residence, a large English colonial mansion, spacious but yet informal. The meal was more like a relaxed family dinner than an audience with the leader of a country.

Mitchum, Orlando Martins, Alex Knox, Ian Bannen, Raymond St. Jacques, and I attended. Kenyatta had also invited half a dozen military officers who now held important posts in his government. Nobody brought their wives, however, and I was the only woman at the festivities. We knew that Kenyatta had many wives and hundreds of children, but upon arrival we had been introduced only to his newest wife, a plump, lovely native child of fifteen who was very pregnant. She spoke no English, smiling shyly when the president introduced her, and then she slipped silently away.

Kenyatta was a thoroughly jolly and charming host, with a disarming earthiness and the most infectious of laughs. He took me completely by surprise: I saw no trace of Kenyatta, the fierce commander of a hideous, bloodthirsty uprising, the victor over the imperialists, and supreme ruler of his people.

Orlando was right: Kenyatta did, indeed, adore actors. He kept encouraging us to tell more and more acting stories. He was particularly delighted to meet Mitchum and wanted to know all about his films. Mitchum was seated at Kenyatta's right, and I sat at the opposite end of the table with a black officer on either side of me. Mitchum's stories, delivered in his wisecracking and wry humor, sent Kenyatta into gales of laughter, and his officers parroted him.

I waited for a cue from Orlando to begin my story of our about-to-be evicted movie company. Kenyatta shook with hearty laughter as I described how the fruit salad, marshmallow, and whipped cream had slowly dripped off the nasty reporter's head. When I got to the part about my apology not having been accepted and the landlord's ultimatum, Kenyatta, who was wearing a fully decorated general's uniform, all at once stiffened and his eyes blazed. His uniform ceased to be decorative and took

With Jimmy Stewart in *How the West Was Won*

With Karl Malden, Agnes Moorehead and Debbie Reynolds in *How the West Was Won*

An artfully concealed me in
The Carpetbaggers

With George Peppard in
The Carpetbaggers

The famous chandelier scene from *The Carpetbaggers*

With Richard Widmark in *Cheyenne Autumn*

I take the reins in *Cheyenne Autumn*

George Maharis seems to like my satin slip in *Sylvia*

With Robert Mitchum in *Mister Moses*

As Jean Harlow

The Harlow look

With Peter Lawford in *Harlow*

on its true meaning. I suddenly recognized the ferocious warrior Kenyatta, leader of the cruel Mau Mau.

He roared instructions in his native tongue.

His six officers instantly shed their previously adopted soft, cultivated appearance for a demeanor that made my blood run cold. It was savagery personified.

Oh, God, what terrible violence had I unleashed?

Through a wall of fear, I heard Kenyatta say in English, "This man will be dealt with forthwith," and I froze.

"The officer beside you on your right, Miss Baker," Kenyatta said tightly, "is my Chief of Security [secret police!]. He will silence this landlord! We do not like these white men who still call themselves lords of our land!"

I glanced briefly at the officer on my right, the man who had been so polite and genial during dinner. His eyes now had a gleaming, impersonal stare.

"Oh, no," I cried out, "you mustn't kill him!"

Kenyatta roared again. My breath caught in my throat until I understood that he was roaring with laughter, slapping his thighs as if to punctuate his pleasure. Then all the uniforms around the table laughed and resumed their amiable, civilized guises. I realized that I had been panting. I swallowed to calm my breathing. There was a look of undisguised relief on Mitchum's face, and Alex Knox rolled his eyes upwards to heaven in thankfulness that the danger seemed over. Orlando grinned from ear to ear over our accomplishment and then wiped the sweat from his palms with his napkin.

Kenyatta couldn't stop laughing. "That is a very good joke. A very good joke. You are a woman. You are truly a woman for you wish me to stop this man, not with a machete but with a feather."

The Chief of Security repeated, "With a feather!" and everybody laughed again.

Kenyatta was smiling broadly and displaying rows of white teeth. "We will, as the British say, reach an understanding with this land—" he paused to spit out the second half of the word "—lord."

"My Chief of Security will talk," he continued, "and this land-lord will understand." And this remark also brought fresh bouts of laughter. But I was still feeling very uneasy.

To this day I do not know what was said or done, but about

mid-morning of the following day, Frank Ross received a note from the landlord. The note stated that, in his anger, he had been too hasty in his judgment, and that we were welcome to the continued use of his land.

One of my most prized possessions is a silver dinner plate presented to me by the cast. The engraved emblem is the cartoon of a man reacting to a plate of food dumped on his head. The inscription reads:

FOR GALLANTRY IN THE FACE OF THE ENEMY

PRESENTED TO

MISS CARROLL BAKER

BY

Ian Bannen	Robert Mitchum
Alexander Knox	Ronald Neame
Orlando Martins	Raymond St. Jacques

Frank Ross

Chapter
Twenty-Five

ANOTHER SLAVE CONTRACT

I thought I had coped rather well with my African experience. When confronted with sexual temptation, I had struggled long and hard with myself and had in the end exercised control. Although I had been exposed to any number of health hazards, I had been cautious and had taken the proper preventive measures so that I had not contracted any serious illness. Yet, I had a dormant disease still lying in wait to be revived, a disease peculiar to civilization called—what?—stress, tension, frustration, disillusionment? And is it caused by running away from the truth? Put to the test of nature, although I had battled continuously, I had survived, feeling fit and sound; and most importantly I had found myself for once liking and approving of *me*. But this sense of confidence and well-being deserted me within days of my arrival in Los Angeles, and my old insecurities and confusion returned to eat away at me.

I had no desire for food, and I began to lose weight at an alarming rate. I had to force myself to swallow powdered protein dissolved in milk, and then fight to keep it down. Was it physical in origin? Or was it a lapse in my will to live in what seemed like a hopelessly trapped and joyless existence?

Perhaps the men who controlled my life sensed that I was ready to make a move beyond their reach, because they became more demanding than ever, almost as if they instinctively banded together to bring me under control. I never want to think that they deliberately set out to demolish my spirit. But

241

Jack Garfein, Joe Levine, the agent, business manager, and publicity agent joined forces with the Paramount Pictures executives to attach a lien on my future. They presented me with a seven-year contract and a united front of pressure for me to sign. Naturally, their argument was always "It is for your own good."

Actors no longer had to sign slave contracts. We had arrived at the day of the independent production. Artists were now enjoying the freedom of being freelance and having control of the material they worked on. Why were they all urging me to chain myself to a system that for the most part had become obsolete? I suppose it had to do with money and promises, but I have never really understood.

From morning to night I was coaxed and cajoled and badgered to sign that contract. Forced into a corner, I turned everything inward and became quite ill. I went for lengthy medical tests. The doctors looked for an amoeba, but none was ever found. I couldn't keep food down, but I suspect now that it was actually that bitter pill of a contract which I couldn't swallow.

I no sooner signed that dreaded contract than the disadvantages of being limited to a studio came rushing in on me. Gene Kelly telephoned me. Gene Kelly! Any dancer or ex-dancer will understand the thrill and excitement and almost disbelief of receiving a proposal to dance with Gene Kelly.

We arranged to meet at a rehearsal hall where Gene put me through a number of routines. I was rusty after so many years without practice, but Gene was looking foremost for style. Of course, when I danced with him, I wasn't even aware of what I was doing—I was dancing on a cloud with Gene Kelly! It was as if I had never stopped dancing. My muscles complied easily with every signal from my brain during that strenuous hour. (The next morning, when I attempted to get out of bed, however, my legs crumpled under me. I had to crawl to the bathroom.)

"You've got style, and it can easily be developed," he said.

As usual, I wore my most stupid and blank expression.

"As for your ability," he continued, "there isn't anything that you can't do."

At that instant I imagined myself dancing "Slaughter on Tenth Avenue." It had always been one of my favorite modern ballet pieces, and I had dreamed hundreds of times that I replaced Cyd Charisse.

When I came out of my reverie, Gene was explaining that he wanted to do a dance extravaganza as a television special starring the two of us.

Whenever I'm overwhelmed, I just stand there looking dumbfounded. But now, in my mind's eye, I could already see the entire show. I could visualize myself in beautiful costumes gliding across the stage with Gene Kelly . . . just as Gene said, there was no dance step I couldn't do.

Suddenly, the rude awakening came when I heard him say, "Of course, you will need to practice every day for the next year."

Practice every day! Where would I find the time? And, of course, I didn't belong to myself any more: I was obligated by contract to Paramount and Joe Levine.

It was heartbreaking not to be able to say to Gene Kelly, "It's a dream come true. I'll do it. Yes, yes, yes." Instead I told him that I would have to ask for permission.

When I discussed Gene's project with Levine, he promised to let me do it, perhaps even to produce the show himself. That was only the first of many broken promises.

The dressing room assigned to me at Paramount was number one, the first in that charming, one-story building which housed all the stars' dressing rooms. The entrance porch had been graced on either side of its columns by twin white urns of beautiful, sweet-smelling camellia bushes. The front door had been enameled white and decorated with a flowered porcelain knob. In spite of myself, tears came to my eyes when I saw that they had also engraved my name in script in silver metal and centered it on the door above a newly placed silver star, the only one of its kind on the entire lot.

The inside too had been completely repainted and redecorated for me. In the sitting room the woodwork was white; the walls were papered in shiny, glamorous silver; the couches and chairs were Louis XIV, covered in luxurious heavy white satin, the wall-to-wall carpeting was of the deepest white-wool pile;

and in the middle of the room hung a crystal chandelier made up of a thousand glistening pendants that looked like diamonds.

The room beyond was decorated in the same style, with the addition of a dressing table and a concealed refrigerator stacked high with champagne. To one side was a newly installed bathroom.

There were bouquets of flowers everywhere. Every department had sent one and attached a note of welcome. I was completely overcome, and once I had stopped oohing and aahing, I realized that I was ravenously hungry—for the first time in weeks!

An introductory party was laid on for me on one of the sound stages. I met every member of every department, and they were all genuinely and sincerely warm in welcoming me. I felt like hugging and kissing them all.

Burt Lancaster was making a film on the lot at the time, and I was floored when he stopped by between set-ups to wish me well, because we didn't even know each other. By the time the dancing began, both Kirk Douglas and David Janssen had finished filming for the day and had joined the party. I was treated to a whirl around the floor by each of those attractive men. Kirk, who was gregarious and full of wit, was always easy to talk to. David, on the other hand, was reticent and shy. We had often run into one another at various functions but had never managed to say more than hi. Now we were dancing in silence, and we both realized that we were being very awkward. Suddenly, David rasped with dry good humor, "You and I could make beautiful music together," and we both collapsed in laughter.

The biggest surprise of the party was played on us by the "king" of the lot, Jerry Lewis. We all stopped talking when we heard this repeated screech and anemic-sounding Tarzan call. It was unmistakably Jerry but we couldn't see him anywhere. Suddenly he came swinging on a long rope from the highest part of the rafters. His legs were bicycling wildly and he was giving a running comic patter of distress. He swung back and forth, barely missing our heads, and then dangled precariously over the center of the main table, giving a brilliant performance of farcical panic, before falling spread-eagled into the hors d'oeuvres. From then on Jerry filled my every day at Paramount with anticipation, trying to guess what his next kooky antic might be.

I say that Jerry was the "king" of Paramount because he was the only other actor attached exclusively to the studio. He had the run of the place. Jerry's production offices were two dressing-room suites in the middle of the star block, and I used to marvel at the constant activity going on just a few doors down from me. I've never known a man to work with such manic concentration. He involved himself in every aspect of his films: writing, producing, directing, editing, even composing and scoring the music. But when he felt the need for some relaxation, all hell broke loose! At those moments Jerry could be found in the commissary in a ridiculous waiter's uniform wreaking havoc with everyone's food order, or hanging upside down in the guard's booth attempting to direct the incoming traffic to go out and the outgoing traffic to come in, or suddenly being discovered in the executive offices wearing a frilly bonnet and seated in a baby carriage.

Jerry had a bright banana-yellow panel truck with caricatures of himself outlined in black on the sides. Often he would bound out of his offices, fling himself into his truck, and drive wildly around the lot, seemingly in circles.

When I moved into Paramount as a regular, Jerry was beside himself at the thought of having, in close proximity, a pretty girl to tease. And not just one. I had a beautiful blonde secretary named Bonnie. Bonnie was a godsend to me because she was sweet and gentle and a mistress of diplomacy, while at the same time being a highly efficient secretary. She was loyal, devoted, and extremely protective. Bonnie had no difficulty dealing with the executives of Paramount, including the president, but she was constantly being thrown off balance by Jerry Lewis. I sometimes worried that she might resign on account of his behavior.

The first time Jerry saw Bonnie and me walking together in deep conversation past his offices, he barked and howled like a wolf. We smiled but more or less ignored him. That was obviously a mistake. The next instant, Jerry bounced out the door. He raced up behind us, crouched over like a chimp, and began sniffing and biting our ankles. At first we tried shaking him off while tucking our skirts between our legs, but he was so persistent that we ended up running down the block to the protection of my dressing room.

When Paramount decided that I shouldn't be made to walk from place to place in the hot sun, they provided me with a motorized golf cart; the prop department quickly requisitioned it for its proper ornamentation. I knew that the fellows in the prop department, Sam and Harry and "Fat Joe," must be having a ball dreaming up the decoration for my buggy. They were very proud of my beautiful dressing room decor, and had been so pleased when I stopped by the workshop to thank them personally. Now they wanted to surprise me with an unusual cart. "Fat Joe," who had a crush on Bonnie, kept phoning to tease her. Once he asked how green with purple polka dots sounded to her, and another time if she thought it would be nice to make the whole thing into a giant mushroom. All three came to present the finished product. What they returned to my front door was a hot-pink cart, with artificial flowers on the fenders, covered by a striped canopy with dangling red fringe. I'll never forget how they stood around it grinning like Cheshire cats, as Bonnie and I clapped with delight.

When he saw the two blondes putt-putting down the street in that flashy pink buggy with its provocative swinging fringe, Jerry went totally mad!

Chasing our little four-wheeler with his big banana-yellow truck became Jerry's main source of amusement. He used to lie in wait on a side street or inside a soundstage and roar out at us, frightening us half to death. Bonnie drove and trembled every time she got behind the wheel. On the other hand, the people who worked on the lot thought it was great sport and used to rush out or hang out the windows to cheer on the race.

One day on our way to the commissary, after Jerry had chased us in circles around the whole of Paramount, Bonnie and I were overheated and exhausted. We decided to return to the dressing room and order our lunch to be sent in. Bonnie was on the phone in the sitting room giving the order and trying to ignore Jerry, who by that time was scratching at the front door. I ignored him, too, and told Bonnie that I was going into the other room to have a quick shower before the food arrived. Once I was naked and under the water jets, I heard muffled screams coming from the outer room. The connecting door burst open, and before I could wipe the water from my eyes, Jerry, with all his clothes on, was standing in the shower beside me!

We managed to get him out, but not until he'd mimed a whole shower routine, complete with shampooing, soap in the eyes, losing the soap, sliding on it, and strangling himself with an imaginary washcloth.

Chapter
Twenty-Six

CREATING THE IMAGE

Most of the time I felt more like a beauty-contest winner on a goodwill tour than I did an actress. I wondered if we were ever going to get around to filmmaking again. Definite orders had come from somewhere high up, probably from Levine, that my image was all-important. That image seemed to be an extension of Rina Marlow from *The Carpetbaggers.* Edith Head designed and the wardrobe department executed dozens of slinky dresses and gowns, and I was expected to wear nothing else. It was unbearable to think that the days of a comfortable pair of jeans and a sweatshirt, or one of those simple dresses that Jimmy Dean had so admired, might be gone forever.

At parties someone from the publicity department was always snatching my glass of whiskey away and replacing it with champagne. It didn't matter that I preferred whiskey; a glass of bubbly was more glamorous. My neurotic loss of appetite had subsided and I had regained my normal weight. But now I could never seem to get at the food. There didn't seem to be time between interviews and photo sessions; and at the cocktail parties and dinners, any plates of food I had were whisked away along with the whiskey lest some sneaky photographer should snap me with my mouth full.

During this period I had no home life, no sex life, and no family life. I went home only to sleep; and tired as I always was, I never fell into a deep slumber. I tossed and turned half the night.

There was a stiff pain in the back of my neck which never left me. Never. But this was a common Hollywood ailment. Debbie Reynolds had tried massages to cure hers—but I couldn't find that quiet, uninterrupted half hour in which to have a massage. I dreaded the thought of mussing my hair and having to get it done again; Dean Martin said alcohol helped, but I couldn't keep enough down; Mervyn LeRoy suggested his treatment (the most popular method at the time), a neck brace attached to a pulley. Imagine people sitting down to dinner with their necks in traction! Only in Hollywood!

I never understood the adoration of total strangers; but I did appreciate the excitement and the vicarious thrill my image seemed to provide those who worked with me at Paramount. When Kate did my fittings or Mabel dressed me, they used to glow. Once when I did the final fitting for a particularly stunning pink evening gown embossed with delicate pink roses, both gals stood back silently to observe the picture. That vision and their contribution to it brought tears to their eyes.

Guy, the studio photographer, would have liked to have had me in the still gallery every day if possible. He made love with his camera to a vision of womanhood, and was so in love with his results that he hung huge color posters of me on every available inch of wall space at Paramount.

The fellows in publicity were overcome by the press attention they were able to generate. Bob, who was the head of the department, used to have to drag himself away from the demands for me to attend to his other promotional duties. And Joel, who was assigned to me personally, was so enraptured by all the hype that I sometimes imagined him spending his spare time rolling and playing like a puppy in a pile of my clippings.

Nellie Manley was always delighted when I came to the hairdressing department for my weekly color touch-up. She seemed to be so pleased to have an opportunity to mother me (as she had so many others over the past twenty years). She even fibbed to the head office about the length of time she required for the work so that I had a few minutes to gab with Shirley MacLaine or Martha Hyer (neither of whom was under contract any longer, but both of whom used to stop by weekly to visit).

When we finally got around to making a movie, one called *Silvia*, it seemed to be a commitment to film of the same glamour I lived out daily. *Silvia* showed a glamorous girl in glamorous surroundings, but with no clear situations. The script needed work, but when I suggested we hire another writer, the front office let me know that I was to have nothing to say about the story or dialogue. They insisted that I involve myself with only "girly" concerns, such as the correct handbag for each scene.

It was on the day when I had finally given up arguing, and lost even the slimmest hope of having some say in artistic matters, that I returned to my dressing room to find it stacked with dozens of handbags. Usually when I got overexcited, Bonnie was able to talk some sense into me. But on that occasion, out of sheer frustration, I opened the front door and slung every handbag, one by one, out onto the street.

Within minutes my telephone rang. It was New York. The president of Paramount, George Weltner, was calling me from three thousand miles away to ask me why I was in a temper over handbags.

I was delighted to have George's ear because I wanted to impress upon him the fact that I was interested in the quality of the film. I explained to him that the front office was asking me only to test handbags, and that they were dismissing my pleas for script revisions. George was very sympathetic, and he seemed genuinely interested when I outlined the weakness in the script. At the end of the conversation, he assured me that everything would be taken care of. The result was that our director, a perfectly competent man whom I liked, was replaced. The script was never rewritten or improved. But it was very noticeable that "Silvia" was one woman who never carried a handbag.

Because of the purse incident the word spread like wildfire around Paramount that I was throwing tantrums. The front office sent flowers but stayed clear of me. Jerry Lewis made a point of coming to see me and giving me a heart-to-heart. He told me that the only way for an artist to function was to have an independent company and control of the project.

Peter Lawford (my costar in *Silvia*, along with George Maharis) dropped by for a drink and gave me his philosophy. "Just do the best you can, Carroll, with what you're given. There is no sense in fighting the system because you'll only destroy your own peace of mind."

I telephoned Steve McQueen to find out what his words of wisdom and advice might be, but Neile told me that the tension pain in Steve's neck was so bad that he had been in a hot tub for the last two hours. She couldn't say when he might be getting out.

When I called Debbie, she was rushing out to a charity affair and didn't have time to talk. She said that Harry was going away for the weekend, and why didn't Blanche and Herschel and I join her and Carrie and Todd at their Malibu beach house for a mother-children weekend.

There is an old joke in Hollywood about servants. A maid who works for a non-show-business family says to a butler who works for a famous actor:

MAID: Gee, you work for that famous movie star.
BUTLER: Yes.
MAID: I bet you get to meet all the stars?
BUTLER: I do.
MAID: Well, when you wait table, you must get to overhear their conversations!
BUTLER: I certainly do.
MAID: Gosh, what in the world do those celebrities talk about?
BUTLER: Most of the time they discuss us.

"The help" was truly one of the big headaches facing a working actress, and what a difference there was in the homes where only the man went out to film. Veronique Peck made the most delicious French meals, and Greg took great pride in inviting guests to dinner. Ann Douglas ran a marvelously organized household for Kirk, and Lydia Heston made a home for Chuck which was always a pleasure to visit. Debbie, and I, and all the other ladies I knew who had a career never knew what type of chaos to expect when we got home, or even if the new cook was preparing to poison us at mealtime.

One notorious chef gave half the community gastroenteritis before his reputation caught up with him. He had been the

White House chef to a President and, also his meals were gorgeous and served with great style and flair.

I was a guest one evening at a Debbie and Harry Karl dinner party that included Edward G. Robinson. The first course was a delicious fish in white wine sauce which everyone lapped up. We were relaxing between courses when all at once everyone began to feel a bit queasy. Edward G. was most apologetic, but found it necessary to ask for an Alka Seltzer.

"I'm sorry," he said, "but my stomach hasn't acted up like this in months. Not since I fired that chef whose meals gave me heartburn."

Harry said, "You know, I've been having bad heartburn lately. I went to see my doctor because I was worried at first that it might be my heart."

"Yeah," said Edward G., "the same thing happened to me, and my doctor told me to take up golf."

"My broker was told to take up golf," Harry said, "and this chef used to work for my broker."

"My God, it's him!" said Edward G.

When Blanche and Herschel and I arrived at Debbie's house in Malibu on Friday evening about six o'clock, Debbie ran out to the driveway to meet us. After the greetings, she said, "I'm sorry, Carroll, but we are going to have to sit down to dinner immediately. Mrs. Y has announced that she wants an early evening."

"Who is Mrs. Y?" I asked.

"Well," Debbie said, "you know how Harry insists on good meals. So I hired this marvelous Chinese chef, and he wouldn't take the job unless I also hired his wife to serve the meals. Little by little they kept bringing relatives to live with them in the guest house. Now Mrs. Y sulks when I ask her and Mr. Y to come to Malibu. Mrs. Y rushes me through dinner so that she can get back to Beverly Hills and be with her family."

When we sat down to dinner, Mrs. Y wasn't just sour-faced and nasty—she was rude. At one point Debbie asked her to serve some butter for the rolls, and Mrs. Y went around the table literally throwing the patties of butter onto our bread plates. She grabbed our dishes away before any of us had finished, and she asked if we wanted dessert in such a threatening tone of voice that even the children passed up the chocolate cake.

Once she was out of earshot, I told Debbie, "Let her stay in Beverly Hills for the next two days. We don't need servants. You and I and the children can fend for ourselves. We can have fun making hamburgers and hot dogs."

"Well, if you really don't mind," Debbie said with some relief, "I'd love getting them out of my hair for a few days."

The maid only came in during the day, so without anyone else in the house, Debbie and I let the kids loose to scream and play and tear up the entire place, while we made several trips each to the bar and got well and truly plastered. I don't think we ever got around to having an intelligent discussion about my problems on *Silvia*.

In the morning, Blanche and Herschel, who always tried not to disturb me on a day when I could sleep in, tip-toed into my room and stood beside the bed looking at me.

"Hi," I said. "Are Carrie and Todd up yet?"

They both nodded yes.

"Is Debbie up?" I asked.

They both shook their heads no.

"Well, why don't you kids fix yourselves some cereal?"

"We tried to," they said in unison.

"Well?"

"There isn't any milk for the cereal," Blanche said.

"Oh, there must be milk in the refrigerator," I yawned. "Everybody keeps milk in a household where there are children."

Herschel said, "Probably there is milk, but the refrigerator is locked."

I started to laugh, "Okay, I'll come downstairs with you. The door is probably stuck. Nobody locks their refrigerator."

When I got to the kitchen, Debbie was already there pounding her fists on the counter. Before leaving, Mr. and Mrs. Y. had placed a chain with a padlock around the refrigerator. I decided that they must have been in too much of a hurry to take inventory. Anyway, we didn't let it spoil our weekend, we just went out for most meals.

Personally, I didn't even attempt to hire fancy servants. Somehow I was always fortunate in finding a conscientious nanny. Beyond a nanny, I looked for a cleaning woman to come in during the day; and a cook to prepare a simple, nutritional meal for the children to be served promptly at six o'clock.

It was out of the question, then, for me to reciprocate my friends' invitations by inviting them to intimate sit-down dinners. I used to wait and invite everybody at one time to a big party with a catered buffet. Anyway, my house, that glacial white elephant, was best suited for large gatherings. It fulfilled its one apparent reason for being when the sliding doors were opened to make the three living rooms into one vast reception area.

Probably the best party I ever gave was one in honor of John Ford. The theme was Western. I had collapsible dance floors put down over the carpeting, a chuck wagon of food on the patio, and a five-piece Western band complete with an old-time fiddler. John Wayne was on location and unable to attend, but he arranged for Chasen's restaurant to send over an enormous kettle of Pappy's favorite chili con carne. Pappy sat center at the head refectory table and directed the after-dinner entertainment, encouraging everyone to perform.

Debbie treated us to a swinging modern song, and then Pappy coaxed Andy Devine to give us his squeaky rendition of "My Darling Clementine." Gilbert Roland played the guitar and sang a haunting Mexican love song. Ricardo Montalban guided me through a sexy tango. Chuck Heston impressed us all by reciting some Shakespearean sonnets, looking so tall and dashing in his red-and-white satin rodeo costume, that it made the sad passages seem all the more poignant. Horst Buchholz, who was on one of his first trips to Hollywood and hadn't met many people yet, was nonetheless sport enough to recite some passages from Colette.

Shelley Winters rushed in from the kitchen waving a broom and challenged everyone to dance the "limbo." Shelley only managed to shimmy under the broom the first three times it was lowered, but the way she shook her bosom and hips made it her performance. It was slim, agile Sal Mineo who won because he was able to squirm under the broom, lying flat on his back, through a space not more than four inches high.

I can't recall everyone who was at that particular party, but Natalie Wood had the most beautiful outfit—a cowgirl skirt and matching shirt of aquamarine suede decorated with multicolored rhinestone flowers and birds.

Rory Calhoun, I remember, made the most spectacular entrance. It was always necessary to hire security guards because of the hordes of impostors just waiting to crash Hollywood parties. Three fellows had to be bounced out at the beginning of the evening, and when we heard a terrible ruckus at the front door, we all assumed that there must be some persistent gate-crashers making trouble. Jack went to have a look and then we heard him laughing and calling out, "Let him in. Let him come in like that." There was a clomping on the newly laid boards, then everyone gasped and applauded as Rory Calhoun rode into the living room on his horse.

My memory of the film *Silvia* is a montage of impressions: George Maharis was super to work with; our director, Gordon Douglas, never took off his baseball cap. (Gordon's trademark was twisting the brim of his cap sharply to the back of his head to indicate "roll camera.") I was "raped" by Aldo Ray in a flashback to Silvia's early life. Frank Sinatra visited the set to see Gordon and Peter Lawford, and I got to meet him! And a very important consideration in Hollywood: *Silvia* came in on schedule and on budget.

Paramount was extremely high on the film and felt it would be a big moneymaker. I thought it was a piece of fluff, but had to admit that it had commercial possibilities. Although he was tied into my contract and received a fee for every movie I did, Joe Levine was nonetheless sorry that he had not associated himself with *Silvia* as its executive producer. Then and there he made up his mind to take complete charge of all future Carroll Baker projects. Oh, woe is me . . . woe is me . . . !

A few years after my sagas with Joe Levine had ended, I had a most unusual introduction to Peter O'Toole. Peter and I were both at the Irish Embassy in Rome at a St. Patrick's Day celebration. I was surveying the buffet table when I was suddenly grabbed from behind and lowered over the food into a jokey backbend kiss by the handsome Mr. O'Toole.

"I love you," he said.

"Isn't this rather sudden?"

"No, I've loved you for years, ever since I learned that you too worked for and suffered under the producer of a thousand broken promises, Joe Levine!"

Chapter Twenty-Seven

THE EXECUTIVE PRODUCER

"I piss on you!"

From holding his breath, like children do to get attention, Joe's face had puffed and strained into a red-blue-violet about-to-explode balloon. When he at last permitted the trapped air to escape, those were the words he spewed at me: "I piss on you!"

My husband, my agent, and I stood in stunned silence at the entrance to Joe's suite in the Beverly Wilshire Hotel. We had arrived for what we thought was going to be an important production meeting with Levine concerning my new film, *Harlow.* Instead, we had entered to find him bouncing up and down in a self-induced frenzy of petulance, an amazing display of spasmodic convulsions and obscenities. His behavior was particularly bizarre in view of the fact that we had been summoned to the meeting to find a practical answer to a rather urgent problem.

The executives from Paramount and the top men from Joe's own company, Embassy, all of whom had arrived before us, were studying Levine in shocked fascination. They reminded me of men who had come to a screening room prepared to seriously view their own movie, but were confronted instead by the projection of some pornographic film

"I piss on this contract! I piss on her! I piss on this movie!"

He was waggling about the room so as to include everyone present in his gorge of expellants—panting, farting, and burping. It was genuinely alarming the way he kept circling the buffet table, grabbing sandwiches and stuffing them in at the same time as he tried to splutter his words out.

Harlow was due to go before the cameras in two weeks' time and our lengthy script had not yet gotten Jean Harlow past the age of twelve! How could we possibly make a movie about the life of the "Blonde Bombshell" without including her fabulous career, or her glamorous romances, or her untimely death?

We had all come to the meeting expecting Levine, as executive producer, to make a vital decision: a decision, no doubt, to postpone principal photography. That is certainly what he ought to have done.

We were approaching the deadline. Extra time was needed to get a story down on paper, to know what we intended to commit to film. Only Joe had the power to grant that extension, but he was not going to do it; instead, he treated us to his gross exhibition of mental collywobbles. So he pissed on the contract, he pissed on the movie, and he pissed on me.

Harlow had begun as an exciting and sought-after property. A recently published biography had generated a widespread curiosity about the sensational "Platinum Blonde" of the Thirties.

That wonderful British director, Sir Carol Reed, asked to meet with me to outline his ideas for a screen version to be produced for another company. Sir Carol's enthusiasm and his brilliant concepts of re-creating the mood of the 1930s, especially that gung-ho slapstick quality of Jean's early movies, convinced me that he was the ideal man for the project.

With the completion of *Silvia,* I had fulfilled the first of my two Paramount commitments for that year. Contractually, I had the right to appear in one outside picture before my second Paramount film. My agent announced my desire to claim that right, and Jack Karp, the head of the studio in Hollywood, instantly granted me the permission.

Then all hell broke loose in the internal affairs of the Paramount executive in New York. Apparently Levine felt that he had been stabbed in the back: hadn't he made it clear to Paramount that he was going to produce Carroll Baker's next film? Wasn't *Harlow* the perfect vehicle not only for Baker but for himself as well, with his powers of promotion and showmanship? (As far as I know, Levine hadn't even thought of the idea before discovering that I was planning to make Harlow's life story for someone else.)

Jack Karp was forced into an early retirement. Rumor had it that Levine was responsible for his ouster. I had no way of knowing for certain if Levine had been the culprit, but I was deeply saddened to see Karp go.

The permission for me to do an outside film had not been put in writing because that had never been necessary with Karp as the head of the studio. Now that Karp was out, my agent was asked to submit our request all over again, this time in writing. In the meantime, Paramount acquired the rights to the Harlow book, and sent me an official notice calling upon me to fulfill my second commitment for them. I felt double-crossed and miserable over losing the rare opportunity to work with Sir Carol Reed. I felt outraged by the injustice: had they shuffled out an honorable man like Karp, just to pull a fast one? Where was the sense of values in our profession if we permitted a man's life to be ruined over a single film project? I stormed around the house, but there seemed nothing I could do about it.

Things may have changed now, but in those days, a man would only deal seriously with another man—one's husband or some other male proxy. As I said earlier, by this time Jack had been out of work for a number of years; he still hoped he would one day get back into directing, and therefore was loath to become known officially as my manager. I'm afraid, though, that that's what he had become.

So it would have been Jack who tore into Levine for losing me the higher salary that the outside filming of *Harlow* would have provided. I wasn't permitted to be present, of course, but I suppose Jack would have opened the discussion with Levine by saying something like "Carroll is unhappy over the new turn in events. It's bad for the picture and the relationship." (Meaning, "We've got to appease the 'little woman.' As we all know, these women are emotional, irrational creatures. They are not of the same species as we strong, clear-headed, intelligent men.")

My peace offering from Joe Levine was a diamond necklace—an elegantly simple platinum chain studded with gorgeous blue-white diamonds. I am ashamed to admit that I did enjoy holding it to the light and marveling at the beauty of those brilliant, sparkling gems. I also hated myself for being so dazzled by it; for trading my self-esteem for a bauble; and, ultimately, for propagating the myth that a woman could indeed be bought.

My discomfort at accepting the bribe was heightened when rumors spread that I had been given the diamond necklace by Levine because I was his mistress. I never had sexual relations with Joe Levine. Ugh! Nonetheless, I felt like a well-worn mistress who served not only Levine but all the men around me. And they appeared in my eyes to be little more than pimps who were using my ability and exploiting me as a sex object for their own profit.

As my part of the bargain for the necklace, I smiled vacantly, kept my mouth shut, and bottled up my true feelings.

The Carpetbaggers was about to premiere in Europe. To promote those openings as well as the forthcoming *Harlow*, Levine took over the entire first class section of the *Queen Mary*. I sailed from New York to England with Jack, Levine and his wife, publicity, hair, and makeup people, and executives representing Paramount and Embassy Pictures. Every other cabin on the first-class deck was reserved for journalists and photographers. There must have been hundreds!

Working hour after hour without a break, I still wasn't able to be interviewed or photographed by everyone on board. It might have been the first time in the Cunard Line's history that a passenger went down the ramp more exhausted than when she had embarked. I wasn't able to use the swimming pool, walk on deck, or even eat a single uninterrupted meal. On the third day out, Levine and the publicity coordinator urged me to work faster in order to take advantage of all the press coverage. I burst into hysterical tears. Naturally, that was thought to be feminine and unreasonable.

The morning we docked at Southampton, the main deck was packed with British photographers, and on the four-hour train ride to London I conducted a marathon of interviews with British journalists.

Then I rushed to my hotel suite. Without a chance to spend ten minutes relaxing in a warm tub or being able to sip a cup of coffee, I rapidly showered and changed clothes so that I could be taken off to radio and TV interviews.

I arrived back at my hotel with no time for dinner and just twenty minutes to change into my gown before I was due to leave for the premiere of *The Carpetbaggers*.

Lunch had been dry sandwiches in the limo en route from one appointment to the next. I hadn't been able to take a bite because my nervous system had been racing. The conditions under which I had been forced to face food since my employment by Paramount and Levine had put me off eating. I went to the premiere without having had any nourishment all day and perhaps little or nothing for the last several days.

It was a typically damp, cool evening in London and with my resistance so low, the moment I stepped outside my hotel and into the waiting limo, I began to shiver uncontrollably. Once inside the limo, my shivering increased and my teeth actually began to chatter. My English chauffeur offered me a hot water bottle, apologizing for the fact that the heating in the car was not working. Considering the amount of my anatomy which was exposed, I speculated on where I might place that hot water bottle, and with too much pent-up emotion my laughter exploded unnaturally. My eye makeup ran down both cheeks and I had a terrible time trying to repair it in the dim light of the moving car.

Paramount had engineered a new transparent dress for me. It was a skin-colored net foundation embroidered with strategically placed pink rhinestones in the form of roses. The stole was a mass of fluffy pink tulle roses. Needless to say, my outfit was not much of a covering and it provided almost no warmth. I alternated the hot-water bottle from my feet to my stomach to my back, and even from one nearly bare tit to the other.

The publicity department did not want my husband to be present in any of the photographs, so Jack had gone ahead to the theatre. As the car approached Piccadilly Circus, I could see the searchlights above the theatre and enormous crowds of people for blocks around in every direction. The traffic to the theatre was hardly moving. Once I had been recognized, a huge cheer went up and people began gathering around the car to get a closer look. It was flattering but a little spooky, and I wished that Jack were there next to me. However, Joe Levine insisted on being the one to be photographed with me.

Joe was waiting at the curb for my car to pull up, and he was surrounded by more photographers than I had ever seen congregated before in one place. When the driver opened my door and helped me from the car, Levine attempted to step forward and take my arm for the pictures, but the photographers rushed to get in front of one another and Levine was pushed into the gutter. Since the photographers were swarming and shoving to position themselves, Levine couldn't get back on the sidewalk. I'm sure he'd had visions of the press captions reading: " 'Mr. Starmaker' and 'His Star' Arrive at the Premiere," but Joe couldn't retrieve his shattered dignity; nobody even tried to help him, and he was caught below the curb for ten minutes without ever having a flashbulb pointed in his direction.

The photographers were drowning out Joe's calls for assistance and shouting above the roar of the crowd as well. "One more Carroll"—"This way beautiful"—"Turn to me Baby Doll."

Once inside the theatre lobby, I sensed an imminent tragedy. The fans couldn't see me because of the photographers, and they were pushing up against the glass which enclosed the lobby on all sides. The theatre personnel were calling for the security guards to disperse the crowds, and I was pleading for them not to shove people away, people who might have been waiting all day just to get a glimpse of me. But when I tried to get closer to the spectators, the press always moved in front of me, blocking the view. Finally it was Vittorio de Sica, whom I hadn't even met before, who saved the day. Fearing riot, he stepped forward to take charge. In his best director's voice, but always exuding his great Italian charm, he ordered the press to move off and the security guards to stay put. Amazingly, everyone became silent. He then smiled, bowed, and offered me his arm. We strolled slowly by the windows as though we were playing a scene from one of his films. We promenaded, posed, and said hello to the crowds on the other side of the glass. They applauded and cheered and, I hope, felt rewarded for their long wait.

While we were out of the States ballyhooing the projected film, *Harlow* was being written into a first-draft screenplay. No production planning had begun, of course, because the filming was at least six or eight months away. However, while we were in England, a small company in Hollywood announced that they were also going to make a "Harlow" film, rapidly and cheaply. They were going to use a new process called "Electronavision" and make a Jean Harlow story in just six days of filming. They could have their film in the movie theatres (although it was not really a movie but a TV process, not yet fully developed and with many flaws) in a matter of weeks. It would cost a mere fraction of what our traditional movie-quality film would cost, and they would cash in on the publicity that we had been creating. They banked on the fact that large numbers of the public would be fooled into buying tickets believing it to be our show. To insure the confusion they even cast the title role with an actress named Carol.

Levine panicked and off the top of his head decided to enter a race for a release date with the tiny, unknown company. Everyone urged him not to attempt to compete on their level. They were an unproved TV process while we were a movie. My Jack urged Joe, as did some of the people at Paramount and Embassy, to buy out the smaller production. The total cost of buying them out wouldn't have added even another zero to our (of necessity) hefty production cost.

I begged Joe to provide all the artistic skill possible to make ours a brilliant entertainment, to outstrip them with our only possible weapon: quality. No matter how much pressure Joe applied, we could never bring our movie in faster than a TV show.

Levine would listen to nobody. He telephoned New York to the president of Paramount, George Weltner, and decreed that the filming was to begin in exactly one month.

The rest of the European tour was cancelled and we all were booked on the next flight home.

Chapter
Twenty-Eight

TOIL AND TROUBLE

The moment I stepped foot back on the Paramount lot I went into deep shock: Jerry Lewis was gone! I looked around for a reminder of him, but every trace of the king had been wiped out. His offices were shells undergoing reconstruction, his banana-yellow truck had vanished, and, although I wanted a souvenir, I couldn't find a photograph, a poster, or even a scrap of paper bearing his name.

Then I discovered that all of Paramount was in a state of turmoil. Many of my other friends were gone. People had been fired left and right.

I went to see Marty Rackin, the head of production, but when I got to his office I was told that Marty had been ousted shortly after Karp had been forced to retire. There was absolutely no one running the show! I called New York to try to speak with George Weltner, but it was his last day as president of the corporation!

The more people I spoke to, the more confused I became. I couldn't get a clear indication of where the orders were originating. Was Joe Levine responsible? If so, what did he hope to gain? Eventually Paramount was to be taken over by Gulf and Western, but did they actually cause the destruction of the old Paramount or did they just come in to pick up the pieces? I still don't know what happened, and I'm sure it's a very involved story. At the time I was too caught up in the chaos and about to go to pieces myself.

It was the afternoon of that first day when I read the screenplay for *Harlow*. The writer was a talented man, but he'd only been given the assignment two weeks before. What he had written so far only took Harlow up to the age of twelve. Now, given the new impossible deadline, he didn't want to go on with the project.

It was at that point when everyone directly involved in the production was summoned to a meeting with Joe Levine at his Beverly Wilshire Hotel suite at which we had expected him to discuss the hiring of another screenwriter and the postponement of the start date.

I left that "piss on everything" meeting completely distraught and sick at heart. I had only two choices, both of which terrified me: either to stay in the frying pan with *Harlow,* or jump into the fire by refusing to do the film. As was to be expected, my advisors urged me not to break my contract with Paramount and Levine. They warned me of the dire consequences of a court battle, both to my as-always shaky financial position and to my reputation in the business. Still, it took me three days of intensive soul-searching before I finally bent to their judgment by agreeing to stick with the movie. But I wanted John Michael Hayes to write the new draft. John had written *The Carpetbaggers* and the prize-winning screenplay of *The Country Girl,* and was very much in demand. I couldn't believe our incredible good fortune when he agreed to do our script. He also agreed to make every effort to complete it quickly or at least keep well ahead of us once the filming began. So, briefly, my hopes of salvaging the movie were restored. But once I reported to the studio to begin preproduction, I found myself embroiled in a series of events and conversations which made absolutely no sense. I simply couldn't believe what was happening. . . .

First my agent called in a panic to tell me that Joe Levine was not going to hire John Michael Hayes to write the screenplay. Apparently Joe had offered John only his minimum salary, and refused to pay anything extra for the extraordinary hours John would have to put in. Levine didn't care if we went ahead and filmed *Harlow* without a script!

I quickly telephoned John at his home in Connecticut and asked him not to take another assignment, to please give me a few hours to find a solution.

I needed Jack urgently so that we could discuss ways of persuading Levine to let John Michael Hayes begin the screenplay before we lost still another day. But Jack had gone out early that morning and hadn't left word of his whereabouts. I asked Bonnie to keep trying him on the phone.

Those few days leading up to the start of principal photography were like being trapped in a fun house, a hall of mirrors where all the images were distorted and there was no exit. A recording of insane laughter would have been appropriate as background noises to the proceedings in my dressing room.

Here is the way a scenario of those days might well have read:

(Peter Shaw, Angela Lansbury's husband and manager, telephones me.)

PETER: Angela is so hurt that you don't want her for the role of your mother in *Harlow*.

ME: Peter, what are you talking about? I'm not doing the casting. There's no script! There might not ever be a script! All of my efforts are going into trying to get a screenwriter.

PETER: Why don't you want Angela for the part?

ME: Peter, there is no part! There is no story! There is nothing on paper!

PETER: What will I tell Angela? She and I are both shocked because we both thought that you liked Angela.

ME: I adore Angela! She would be wonderful for the mother! But, Peter, there is no. . . .

PETER: Great! Can I quote you?

(Bonnie answers the door.)

BONNIE: Howard Koch, the new Head of Production at Paramount, is here to see you.

HOWARD: Hi, I'm Howard Koch. I'm looking forward to working with you.

(Bonnie slips quietly back into the other room to continue to try and reach Jack.)

ME: Oh, good, I'm glad to meet you. Will you be in charge now?

HOWARD: Well, I'm just feeling my way around. It will be difficult for me until I get my footing. There have been so many changes at Paramount. I know it will be difficult for you, too, to have confidence in someone new.

ME: No, I'm delighted to know who's taking over.

HOWARD: Well, I won't really be taking over for a while.

ME: But you'll be the one making decisions?

HOWARD: I doubt that I'll be making many decisions for a while.

ME: But if something comes up, you're the person I call. Aren't you?

HOWARD: Sure, call me any time. I don't know if I'll be able to help but. . . .

(Debbie Reynolds's brother, Billy, was my makeup man. I receive a telephone call from Debbie.)

DEBBIE: Hi, Carroll. Listen, didn't Billy do a good job on your makeup in the last film?

ME: Of course he did. Why?

DEBBIE: Well, he's too shy to ask you why you aren't using him again on *Harlow*.

ME: What? But I asked for Billy.

DEBBIE: Who did you ask?

ME (pause):   Probably somebody who doesn't work at Paramount anymore.

DEBBIE: You sound harassed. Do you want me to call Howard Koch?

ME: No. Howard doesn't seem to be sure yet if he's in charge or not.

(Jack comes rushing into the dressing room with a stack of papers.)

JACK: Here, sign these.

ME: What are they?

JACK: They're for the new company.

ME: What new company?

JACK: I haven't got time to explain right now. I have to get these back to the lawyer's office. We're coproducing *Harlow*.

ME: Jack, I don't want to coproduce *Harlow*. It's going to be a joke. A fiasco. A story and dialogue the actors make up as we go along.

JACK: Don't worry. I'll be getting a producing fee but my name won't appear on the screen.

ME: Since when are you getting a producing fee?

JACK: I think I told you about that. I worked it out with Levine.

ME: Jack, Joe won't pay John Michael Hayes.

JACK: I know. It's okay. I'll take care of it. You'll give John half of your percentage.

ME: What percentage?

JACK: I must have told you about that. It's part of this new company deal.

(Bonnie taps on the dividing door. She peeks in shyly.)

BONNIE: Hello, Jack. Excuse me, Carroll, Edith Head is on line two.

EDITH: Carroll, I'll have the wardrobe sketches to show you by this evening. Call me before you leave the lot.

ME: I'll call. Tell me, Edith, out of curiosity, what are you going by since there is no script?

EDITH: I'm guessing according to the book on her. I did want to ask you if you thought there would be as many evening clothes needed as daytime clothes?

ME: I have no idea. Maybe you should draw half and half.

(Red Buttons telephones.)

RED: Hi, sugar.

ME: Hi, Red. How are you?

RED: Me, I'm starving, my wife has me on a health-food diet. She only lets me have berries and nuts. Listen, sugar, Paramount has offered me the part of Jean's agent.

ME: That's a great idea, Red. Are you going to accept?

RED: Well, there is some big mystery about the script. They don't want me to see it. If I drop by, can I sneak a look at your copy?

(Howard Koch telephones.)

HOWARD: Carroll, I understand you're insisting upon Angela Lansbury to play your mother?

(Joel from publicity calls.)

JOEL: Carroll, Levine has set a press luncheon for Friday. He's flying in for it.

ME: A press luncheon for what?

JOEL: To announce *Harlow.*

ME: Announce *Harlow!* Surely, he's already announced it a dozen times!

JOEL: This will be to announce the official start date.

ME: And when is the official start date?

JOEL: The same. In a few days' time. We are going to re-open the Golden Gates of Paramount on the other side of the lot. It will be the first time they've been opened in twenty years. We'll have an antique convertible car and two white wolfhounds. You'll ride through the Golden Gates—you, Joe Levine and the wolfhounds.

ME: Won't it be crowded?

(My agent telephones.)

AGENT: Okay, the deal is set. John Michael Hayes is arriving in the morning. He wants to see you as soon as he gets off the plane before he checks into the hotel and begins writing.

ME: Great! What a relief!

AGENT: By the way, be careful not to give orders, Carroll. You know how touchy Levine is.

ME: What are you talking about?

AGENT: Well, orders about the casting and don't order evening gown sketches. Levine says he won't pay for any night shooting.

(I hang up. My neck is suddenly so stiff that I can't turn my head to look for Bonnie.)

ME (shouting):   Bonnie!

(Bonnie enters.)

ME: Bonnie, let's call it a day. I can't cope with any more of this lunacy.

BONNIE: I don't mind staying if you want to return some of these phone calls. Here are the messages.

ME: Read them to me, would you? And don't answer the phone any more tonight. Just let it ring.

BONNIE: A press woman from Chicago who wants to talk to you about how you're going to portray Jean Harlow. She sounded nasty.

ME: That can wait until tomorrow.

BONNIE: Three more calls from the publicity department and

Sidney Guileroff about your white wigs.

ME: It's too late to get Sidney. He goes home early. Oh, that reminds me—call Edith Head and ask her if I can see the costume sketches tomorrow around midmorning. The publicity department can wait. Anything else?

BONNIE: A girl called who worked with you on *The Miracle.* She had a small part and wondered if you remembered her. Her name is Georgina. Anyway, she's got a problem and wondered if she could come to the studio to see you. I told her you had a very full schedule. . . .

ME: Yeah, I remember Georgina. She's a pretty girl. I thought she was talented. I wonder why she hasn't worked more? Maybe I can find a few minutes tomorrow. . . . Oh, God, I don't know. . . .

BONNIE: You're too nice to people, Carroll. You should think more about taking care of yourself. You're tired. I can tell.

ME: Okay, okay, Bonnie, I appreciate it but don't try to mother me. By the way, have you been talking to my mother again?

BONNIE: Well, yes, she called today to see how you were. And she wanted me to remind you to take your vitamin pills.

ME: She shouldn't make so many long distance calls. Why didn't she ask to speak to me?

BONNIE: She knows how busy you are and she didn't want to disturb you. Anyway, she's fine and sends love. Then, Sammy Davis, Jr., wants you to make a personal appearance on a charity show on the. . . .

ME: No, I can't—I just can't take on anything else. Call him and give my apologies. No, wait, I better speak to him personally—remind me. Oh, damn, I forgot to call Peter Lawford back.

BONNIE: It's okay. I talked to him. He said he'd drop by some evening with a bottle of cold champagne and the latest hot gossip. He asked me if Gordon Douglas was directing *Harlow,* and I told him I wasn't sure. Is he?

ME: I guess so.

BONNIE: I thought the idea was to get one of the great "woman's directors," like George Cukor?

ME: Yes, well, Levine made lots of promises in the beginning. Now he doesn't want to pay full price for a screenplay, and he just sent me a nutty message about no night shooting—therefore, no evening gowns. Ouch! My neck! What were we talking about?

BONNIE: Gordon Douglas directing.

ME: Yeah, Gordie is okay. He's the only director I know of who will be able to keep his sanity through all this. When there's a problem, Gordie will solve it by twisting his baseball cap the other way around. How are the kids? Any problems?

BONNIE: The kids are fine. If you leave now you'll get home in time to tuck them in bed. But Jack left a message for you to meet him at La Scala for dinner as soon as possible. He's working on a deal and he wants you to meet some backers. But maybe you should stop at home first because there might be a slight problem.

ME: What?

BONNIE: Well, when I spoke to the nurse, she sounded very unhappy. She's had another run-in with Jack and. . . .

ME: Oh, God, why doesn't he leave her alone? She's wonderful with the kids. As far as I know, he's never around. The least he could do is stop interfering. I can't—I just can't start looking for a new nanny! Edith is wonderful and the children are happy with her. Bonnie, what am I going to do? I can't deal with this picture now—I won't be able to deal with it at all if Edith leaves me. . . .

BONNIE: Don't cry. I'm sure if you go home and talk to her, she'll understand. She has before. She adores you and you're very good to her. I'm sure she won't leave you—

(Telephone rings.)

BONNIE: That's your private line. Do you want me to answer it?

ME: No, I'll get it. Make the calls we talked about and then go home.

(Ring.)

ME: Oh, and Bonnie, come in two hours later tomorrow. I want to have a private meeting with John Michael Hayes when he gets here in the morning.

BONNIE: Okay.

(Ring.)

ME: Hello.

JACK: Carroll, it's Jack. How soon can you get here?

ME (pause):   Jack, you bastard, you stop bossing around my nannies.

JACK: Edith has to be put in her place and it's good for the children to know that I'm the man, and the father, and the boss, and that my word is law!

ME: Screw you, Jack! I'm going home now to hold Edith's hand and coax her to stay. I won't be coming to La Scala. You can stick your new scheme up your ass! Do me a favor, you and your so-called backers, order a big fat fish at my expense—then with any luck maybe you'll all choke on the bones!

JACK: Now, now Carroll, I was only doing what I thought was right. Edith isn't that sensitive. Who loves you? (Pause.) Huh? Who got you John Michael Hayes? (Pause.) Huh?

ME: You did, I guess.

JACK: No guessing about it. I arranged for his percentage. Do what you have to do at home and stop by the restaurant later. This meeting could be very important.

ME: I don't know—I'm beat. And I've got a big day tomorrow.

JACK: Just stop by for a few minutes. You have to eat, anyway.

ME: I'll try.

JACK: No, I want you to promise me. You'll feel better after a glass of wine and some pasta. Promise me!

ME: All right, all right, I'll drag myself there, but I don't know what time it will be.

(The next morning. I get to the dressing room at 8:00 A.M. and have just put the coffee on. A knock at the door. I think it must be John Michael Hayes arriving earlier than expected. I open the door. A beautiful brunette with outsized sunglasses and a tight silk cocktail dress is standing there looking as if she hasn't been to bed yet.)

GEORGINA: Gee, Carroll, I'm sorry to just drop by like this. I'm Georgina. Do you remember me? We worked together on. . . .

ME: Sure, I remember you, Georgina. Come on in. I've just made some coffee. What can I do for you?

GEORGINA: I hate to bother you but, well, I don't know how to put this. . . .

ME (Looking for cups): Well, darling, just spit it out. I can only spare a few minutes. I'm waiting to have a very important conference.

GEORGINA: Oh, God, I really feel bad about bothering you, but—I don't know which way to turn—my life is such a mess!

ME (pouring coffee): Join the club. Please, Georgina, get to the point.

GEORGINA: All right, here goes. Do you think I have to fuck the second assistant director to get a part in *Harlow?*

ME: Cream and sugar?

GEORGINA: Just black. I mean, Gordon Douglas wouldn't see me. He sent me to the first assistant director and—you know what happened—but it's a great part and I really need the money.

ME: Who told you it was a great part?

GEORGINA: The first assistant director told me it was a small part but a flashy part that could really do things for my career. You must know which role he was talking about.

ME: I can't imagine.

GEORGINA: Oh, well, whatever the part is, I don't care, I really need the work.

ME: And?

GEORGINA: Well, I hope you don't think I'm awful —but—I've been sleeping with the first assistant for the last two weeks. Now that dirty bastard won't show me the script or tell me if I have the part. He sent me yesterday to see the second assistant.

ME: And?

GEORGINA: Well, you know, once they think you're an easy lay, they think they can pass you around.

ME: So?

GEORGINA: Well, do you think I also have to also fuck the second assistant to get the part?

(*Pause.*)

GEORGINA: You're not answering me.

ME: That's not usually the first question I get asked in the mornings.

GEORGINA: Okay, forget it. See you around. (She starts to leave.) Thanks for nothing.

ME (low): This picture might have a third and fourth assistant.

GEORGINA (turning): Huh?

ME: Nothing. If there's a part I'll mention your name to Gordon Douglas.

GEORGINA: What do you mean, if there's a part?

ME: Make sure Bonnie has your phone number.

GEORGINA: Oh, gosh, thanks a million. Listen, if there's ever. . . .

ME: Goodbye, Georgina. No promises but I'll see what I can do.

(*Georgina exits.*)
(*John Michael Hayes arrives.*)

JOHN: There is one thing I have to decide, Carroll, before I can begin to write.

ME: What's that?

JOHN: The point of view. I can either write the story about a girl who slept with everybody to get to the top, or an innocent girl who fought off the wolves, kept her integrity intact, and made it to the top on her own merits. Which do you think?

ME: I'd vote for the second character. The first one makes it a tacky story. Maybe I'm wrong but somehow I don't really believe many girls get ahead that way.

JOHN: I'm inclined to agree with you, and I'm glad you like the idea of the innocent girl. I was tending more in that direction myself, and we'll be able to sympathize more with the character. Well, I better get to the hotel and straight to work. I'll have the first few pages for you by tomorrow night. I'd like you to see them before I hand them in.

ME: Listen, John, feel free to call me day or night. The script is my main concern.

JOHN: Thanks. I might need someone to talk to. Levine only sent me instructions not to write any night scenes. Do you know what he means by that?

ME: He doesn't want to pay for outdoor night shooting. I'll ask Howard Koch or someone to explain to him that we can film night scenes indoors during daylight hours.

(John exits.)
(The head of the makeup department, Wally Westmore, telephones.)

WALLY: Oh, Carroll, you're in early, good! Listen, I hate to ask you this dumb question, but what size are your nipples?

ME: My bust measurement is 35 1/4.

WALLY: No, I told you it was a dumb question. What is your actual nipple measurement?

ME: Forgive me for laughing but this is really my morning for dumb questions. So let me ask you one: why do you want to know?

WALLY: Well, in our *Harlow* production meeting someone brought up the point that Jean Harlow always rubbed ice on her nipples so that they stood straight out in her slinky dresses. Do you think you ought to have big hard nipples?

ME: Not if it means rubbing ice on myself before every take!

WALLY: Exactly. Well, we could do what I used to do for Mae West. I used to take a mold of her breasts and then make to conform, some hard plastic nipples about three inches long.

ME: You're joking?

WALLY: No I'm not. Mae used to sit and file them into the pointed shape she wanted.

ME: You mean she actually wore them?

WALLY: Sure. We used to paste them on over her own nipples. It would mean I'd need you for about two hours to sit for the mold.

274

ME: O.K., I'll try it. When do you want to do it?

WALLY: Well, any morning about this time after the actors have been made up and left for the sets.

ME: I put two hours aside this morning for a meeting that only lasted ten minutes. Want to do it now?

WALLY: That's fine. Come on up.

ME: Okay, just let me tell the studio switchboard to transfer my calls to your room.

(Scene changes to Wally Westmore's room. I am seated in his makeup chair naked to the waist, with a board behind me to hold me straight while his brother, Frank Westmore, mixes the plaster and Wally applies the cold gooey globs, smearing them from my shoulders to the base of my rib cage.) (Although friendly, the atmosphere is as impersonal as a doctor's office.)

WALLY: Now, Carroll, you mustn't move, not even your arms. Any calls and one of us will hold the phone for you.

(The lady newspaper critic/reporter calls from Chicago.)

LADY REPORTER: Miss Baker, this isn't for an article. For personal reasons I want to know how you intend to portray Jean Harlow.

ME: What do you mean?

LADY REPORTER: Well, I'm old enough to have known Jean and I loved her. She was a wonderful girl in every way. If you dare to present her as a bitch or an alcoholic, I want you to know that I'll go on a crusade to destroy you.

ME: Let me ask you something. Do you think the story should be about a girl who slept with everybody to get to the top?

LADY REPORTER: Certainly not. Look here. . . .

ME: Well, then, should the story be about an innocent girl who fought off the wolves, kept her integrity intact, and made it to the top on her own merits?

LADY REPORTER: That's exactly right.

ME: Okay, then that's the way we'll write the story. Thank you very much for the idea. By the way, did Jean Harlow have big hard three-inch long nipples?

LADY REPORTER: Well, I was just about to congratulate you on being an intelligent young woman. Now I see that you are just as shallow and vulgar as I have always thought you were. Good day.

Too many years must have passed since Wally Westmore had made those nipples for Mae West. He must have forgotten some ingredient or vital step in the process because two minutes after my mold was removed, both the breasts on it collapsed.

After rummaging around in his old makeup trunk among the rubber masks, severed fingers, and wax eyeballs, he discovered a pair of Mae West's plaster nipples. However, we couldn't find a way to make them stick on my flesh. None of the various glues or tapes would hold them on; the least little movement from me and they hung down or dropped off.

Later at Wardrobe, when I tried on the antique beaded dress for the "Opening of the Golden Gates" ceremony, we made one more attempt at nipples by sewing two cigar-shaped buttons into the bodice. But they looked like deadly projectiles! So all departments abandoned the idea and the secret of those three-inch nipples remained forever with Mae West.

It was during this crazy period the press decided that they had written too much about me and needed a new slant. One national magazine published an ugly, vindictive article, heralding an onslaught of vicious attacks. I was no longer described as witty, daring, sensuous, or beautiful. Overnight I was redefined as dull, coarse, unsexy, too skinny and unattractive to play Jean Harlow. It became the "in" thing to take swipes at the "Baby Doll."

Although I must have realized that it happens at one time or another to most famous people, it caught me quite off guard. It cut very deeply at a moment when I had many other difficulties to cope with and was especially vulnerable. I was bombarded nonstop by reams and reams of hurtful publicity. The new attacks seemed pointedly directed at the physical and spiritual me. The fifth estate poured out hate and targeted it my way in deadly doses. It had the effect on me of some collective voodoo death-wishing ritual.

The pain in the back of my neck stiffened as though my head were being squeezed in a vise, and my delicate digestive system went on a total rampage. I decided to escape to New York for a day or two and there to consult my family doctor, Louie Finger. When Louie saw me, he was concerned about the general state of my health and insisted that I check into the hospital for a series of tests.

Louie diagnosed that I was in the midst of nervous exhaustion and ordered me to stay for a few days rest. The filming was delayed while I was in the hospital, and naturally Joe Levine accused me of deliberately sabotaging the movie.

Still furious over the fact that I had taken time off to be in the hospital, Levine attended the delayed "Opening of the Golden Gates" ceremony with a sizable chip on his shoulder. Then our overstrained relationship was shattered beyond repair by those energetic, determined white wolfhounds! The moment I was seated, they sprang into the antique convertible and spread their rumps on either side of me, leaving no more space on the small seat. Joe had wobbled to the running board. When he saw the dogs and me already posing for the photographers without him, he became livid. He never forgave me for not having wrestled with and ejected those gigantic hounds, despite my heavy silver bugle-beaded dress.

The master of ceremonies was at the microphone asking the crowd of press and spectators, "Ladies and gentlemen, can you think of anyone else as perfect for the role of Jean Harlow as Carroll Baker?"

Otto Preminger spoke up very loudly, "Of course not!" he shouted. "All the others are dead!"

I thought to myself, "Isn't that remark tasteless," and yet I shrieked with laughter.

It was in this spirit of abrasive ribaldry—akin to madness—that I began filming *Harlow*.

With John Michael Hayes at times handing in pages of script only three or four days in advance of filming, we somehow managed not only to get her onto celluloid but also to bring the movie in well within that skimpy, squeezed, impossible shooting schedule Levine had dictated in his race with the Electronavision version.

Probably for the first time in motion-picture history, the actors and director had not been given rehearsal time. We were permitted only one walk-through and that was for the camera, to establish the moves for the technicians. In order not to look like total incompetents when playing scenes in front of the camera, we rehearsed on our own time. It's amazing how good actors are so thoroughly devoted to their craft . . . Angela Lansbury got up at three to arrive for rehearsal at five before going into makeup at seven; Red Buttons gave up every lunch hour and break; and Peter Lawford was willing to work till all hours of the night. This schedule I had arranged was a real killer, especially for me, since I appeared in every scene! The camera set-ups were the shortest, quickest ones any of us had ever experienced. It was a race even to get a drink of water or to make a brief phone call while they readied the next shot.

Will I ever forget that young, pimply-faced fourth assistant they hired to follow at my heels? I was never a second late, so why had they ordered him to hang over me every moment of the day? When I changed costumes, I could hear his walkie-talkie outside my dressing-room door. "We're about fifteen minutes away, what's she doing now?"

("Oh, go get stuffed! For your information, I'm hurriedly wiping the sweat away with this towel so that I can wiggle into another sheath.")

"We're five away. Where is she now?"

("Hell, I don't believe it, he's followed me to the ladies' room!")

Unless something happened during the take, something as obvious as the walls of the set crashing down on the actors' heads, we were obliged to print the first and only take:

"Take one."

"Cut!"

"Print it!"

("Shit!")

There was no time for rushes. A team of editors stood by to cut the film the second it was hot out of the developing room.

The movie must have been dubbed and scored and titled within days of the final wrap. It was certainly thrown overnight into whatever movie theatres happened to be available. Little wonder that the first box-office indications had looked bleak.

The Electronavision version had been poor: a grainy, un-refined process, the finished product of which had been un-worthy of its fine cast. Electronavision had beaten us into the movie houses, but only just. We had been very close behind, just close enough to add to the public's confusion and to damage our own potential.

Joe Levine had been the first to call our movie a bomb, and he had blamed the rival version. However, it soon became and has since remained Carroll Baker's *Harlow.* Just as I had shouldered the burdens during the production, afterwards I was to shoulder any blame.

I had never seen the finished version of *Harlow.* I had never even seen any footage of that film, and had not in any way wanted to be reminded of her. Four years after the first release of the movie, I was on a plane from Rome to Buenos Aires and well tucked into my third scotch on the rocks when they announced that the in-flight movie was to be *Harlow,* and I was trapped. Actually, as I watched it, I was pleasantly surprised. John's script was dramatically valid and the performances were uniformly good. There was certainly nothing to be ashamed of; in fact, it was a remarkable achievement, considering the inhuman pressures and hardships.

Well, *Harlow,* poor old thing, I should have been the last person in the world to have shied away from you. After all, whatever blood you had, had come directly from my veins.

Chapter Twenty-Nine

THIS VERY MOMENT—

After the completion of principal photography on *Harlow* in 1965, I felt as though I were beaten to a pulp and couldn't drag myself forward even one more step. But it was May and time for the Cannes Film Festival. Joe Levine called and urged me to attend, saying it would be valuable promotion for our film. As an added incentive, he and Paramount offered me round trip air tickets for Jack and the children to accompany me, plus three months' vacation time. Renting a villa for the summer on the Riviera was an extravagance I could ill afford, but once our transportation had been paid for, the idea became increasingly irresistible. To truly relax, I felt I needed to get as far away from L.A. as possible, and what more heavenly location than the Côte d'Azur?

I assumed that Jack would understand how nervously exhausted I was and just how desperately I needed every second of free time. But he spoiled the first three weeks of the vacation by agreeing with Joe Levine that a *Paris Match* cover and story just couldn't be passed up. A photographer, reporter, and countless assistants practically lived with us for the first twenty-one days, waiting mostly for the weather to brighten. When *Paris Match* had finally cleared out, Jack shocked me with the announcement that he wanted me to initiate a strong demanding action against Paramount. He drafted a threatening telegram to the studio demanding to know what my next film would be, and outlining a list of demands for future projects.

The timing was completely cockeyed. I had just finished asking for a three-month vacation, and Jack wanted me in the next breath to ask them to come up with a project. And as for his demands—we had just finished agreeing upon a newly revised contract only weeks before. The time to have made demands or to have broken the contract would have been before suffering through the trials of *Harlow*. But now—with the ordeal behind me, totally drained of energy, and probably with a box office flop to live down—now was the worst possible moment to begin quibbling.

I have racked my brains but I cannot remember a single argument Jack put forth in defense of that telegram. It made absolutely no sense to me then, and it makes no sense to me now. Why did I, against the strongest possible protests of my lawyers, permit that inflammatory telegram to be sent? Well, I suppose it's difficult to believe that a person can be so exhausted that they lack the will to fight on home ground, even while knowing that by not standing firm they might be letting themselves in for war with a powerful corporation. But that's what happened. I did not have the strength to go against Jack's wishes. He badgered me day and night, which in my weakened state became a kind of psychological torture. He was so adamant that to defy him would have endangered our already failing relationship. I was clinging to the dream of that emotionally restorative vacation, that quiet time just to be with my children and my husband, to try to resolve the domestic problems I'd been forced to neglect for too many years. I simply hadn't the time to fully look into my personal feelings, and I wasn't prepared to destroy my marriage without first having tried everything within my power to put things right.

But as a result of that telegram, Paramount fired me! And they froze the paychecks from *Harlow* which had just begun to come in. We were stranded in the South of France without any money. We had to return to the States to petition the Screen Actors' Guild to collect my salary, and now Jack was talking about a lawsuit against Paramount. The summer's plans were shattered. From the moment I was told that I'd been fired, I began sinking into a depression.

Once I was at home, I slowly began losing my ability to function. I knew I might be heading for an emotional collapse, but

I couldn't prevent it. I could see nothing but blackness before me. I felt so badly about having been fired, and I knew I was in the wrong by sending that telegram. Now everyone was advising me that I had no alternative but to sue, even though Paramount had the resources to fight a prolonged court battle and I didn't. The old contract was no longer valid, and the revised contract had not yet been signed. I didn't see how I could possibly hope to win any lawsuit, but there seemed to be little choice.

When four months went by without another film company making an offer, I began to suspect that I might also be black-balled throughout the whole industry. Run down, without a reserve of emotional or physical strength to fall back on, without money, or work, or peace of mind, everything looked not only bleak but hopeless and I began slipping deeper every day into the recesses of my mind.

At Christmastime Bob Hope asked me to go with him on his USO tour to entertain the troops in Vietnam, and I jumped at the chance to get out of myself, to entertain, to do something very special for someone else. I know those ten days were very rough going, dangerous, but to me they were a tonic. In the hospitals I held the hands of damaged young men, and I realized that my pain was not exclusive: that in this world there was suffering much more terrible than mine. Everyone in our troupe, as they disembarked in L.A. after those ten grueling days in Southeast Asia, made the same remark: "It's unbelievable! We all look and feel like death warmed over. Carroll is the only one who looks better now than when she left!" I'm reasonably sure that none of them was aware of the deep depression I'd been in *before* going to Vietnam.

Warners was now very excited about a project for me which Jack had suggested to them. Then overnight the deal fell through and for no apparent reason. I asked William Morris, one of the biggest theatrical agencies in the world, to find out for me once and for all if my suspicions of being blackballed in the industry were true. They represented me for the next three months, worked on deals, saw them dissolve, and finally came to the conclusion that the word was out not to hire me. My career in Hollywood seemed over.

The thing to do was get out and look for work somewhere else, but how and where? By the Sixties the entire television industry had moved to the West Coast and now television, too, was controlled for the most part by those same movie studios that were banning me. A play was never easy to find, nor could I afford to make trips to the East Coast on speculation. I was smothering under a blanket of debts, and whatever money could be scraped up or borrowed had to go for the immediate household needs.

There was certainly nothing left for me in Hollywood, but I was trapped. There seemed to be no way out, not even suicide because that would have been the worst of all crimes against my children and my God.

Los Angeles: 1966
The Second Breakdown

What year is this? Oh, yes, it's 1966. Remember you glanced at the top of the newspaper? Was that this week or last? Well, it really doesn't matter. I'll probably just sit here under the shade of the jacaranda tree and stare at that fucking kidney-shaped swimming pool.

Jack might come home soon! I'll have to take some tranquilizers now, so that he'll sound like he's a long way off. He'll be all fired up about his next move against Paramount. He seems to get a perverse pleasure out of catastrophe. Why must he always keep at me until I've said, "Yes, Jack, you were right to send that telegram which led to this lawsuit." But I don't believe that! It was crazy! Everything is in ruins!

Oh, I hope he doesn't want me to sign another bank loan. I'm thousands and thousands of dollars in debt—I'll never be able to repay any of it—I'm blackballed in the industry—I won't ever be able to work again.

I feel so bad. I'm going to have to take more tranquilizers.

I wish I had the strength to divorce Jack. But how can I? How can I divorce a man who suffered as a child in the Nazi concentration camps? All right, I was a child myself, far away in America —but doesn't everyone share in the guilt? Wasn't I raised on anti-Semitic slogans?

I have tried to make amends. I named Blanche and Herschel after their slain grandparents. I've worked hard for organizations which help Israel and world Jewry. I took instructions in the Jewish faith because I was seriously thinking of conversion. Until my rabbi, Rabbi Charles Schulman, talked me out of it. Charles said, "Don't convert for the wrong reasons. Don't do it out of guilt or to take up the burdens. Convert for all the joy there is to be found in Judaism."

The Holocaust must have taught Jack some valuable things about life. But maybe it's left him suspicious of everyone—everyone's motives. Maybe a suggestion sounds like a compromise, a compromise like a threat.

Remember when Sam Spiegel said, "I can't believe your behavior. You! Jack Garfein! My Jewish director! Instead of understanding us, you give orders."

Wasn't that too harsh a condemnation? Wasn't Jack just scared to take orders, so he gave them instead? He must have deep emotional scars. . . .

Oh, but they're too complex, and too deep for me.

I have asked him to see a therapist.

But he won't.

Of course not. Jack refuses even to acknowledge that he has any problems.

I hear footsteps! Please don't let it be Jack. Not yet, not until the pills have taken effect. I can't cope with him, I just can't. . . .

What year is this? 1966 or 1967? Oh, yes, it's 1967. Remember, you glanced at the top of the newspaper? Was that this week or last? Well, it really doesn't matter.

In September of 1967 I received an invitation to be the guest of honor at the Venice Film Festival, and somehow I managed to get up out of that poolside chair, pull myself together, and get to Venice. Yes, after more than two years of being paralyzed by despair, I finally found the strength and the courage. And, by Christ, I did it! Because it all mattered again. Suddenly, in one miraculous instant, it all once again mattered very much. I had a premonition that this was my way out, my light at the end of the tunnel. Not that there weren't many struggles that still lay ahead of me, but it was a beginning, a chance to start out again on the road of the living, and I managed to take that first step.

The day I left for Venice it was mother, and mother alone, I wanted to take me to the airport. I'd come to lean exclusively upon her for my support. I still had a beautiful wardrobe, and Mother helped me make a list of the appropriate garments, and then to brush and press them, and to pack everything carefully folded in tissue paper. When we were in the car she asked me to check again the contents of my handbag. I had my passport and my complimentary air tickets, but I had not asked Jack for any pocket money. Before putting me on the plane, Mother pressed some bills into my hand, otherwise I would have traveled six thousand miles without a dollar in my wallet.

In Paris I had to change planes for my flight to Venice. I got off the plane like a lady with a purpose and began striding through that expansive terminal, through a maze of passages, tunnels, and walkways. After a lengthy walk, I wondered if I was going to get to my plane on time. Suddenly I stopped in midstride, confused and overcome by anxiety. I realized that my racing had been aimless, that I had no idea whatsoever where to go or how to make my connection.

I hadn't been alone in an airport for years. It was my habit to step into waiting limousines, to be ushered in and out of airports by an entourage of studio representatives. Other people had held my tickets, helped me on and off planes, and I had merely followed them, never having to rely upon myself or even to pay the slightest attention to where I was or how I'd gotten there. Now I couldn't even think of what to do next. I approached a gendarme and told him that I was lost. He asked me where I was going and I said Venice. He asked me which flight I was on and I had to admit that I didn't know. "Where is your ticket?" "My ticket? Oh, yes, I'm the one who has it. It's in my purse." He looked at the ticket I handed him, found the flight number and guided me to a flight-announcement monitor. After finding the gate number, he told me to follow that number in the corridor until I arrived at my departure area.

My connecting plane had been hours late, and my arrival in Venice wasn't until after midnight. Instead of a committee, a lone

Festival representative met me and took me by motorboat to the Excellsior on Lido Beach where, because of the hour, I was shown directly to my suite. Exhausted from the trip, I was also extremely restless and slept poorly. For one thing, I was bitterly disappointed in myself for not having made more of an effort to communicate with that nice man who had escorted me to the hotel. He'd been the first person, outside of the family, whom I'd had an opportunity to talk to since ending my self-imposed confinement. I'd been reticent and had failed that initial test miserably. Also, I was worried because I hadn't asked him for any information, and consequently I didn't know what would be expected of me the following day or even at what time to be ready.

So I got out of bed early in the morning, ordered a continental breakfast, showered, dressed in my bikini and matching beach skirt, and waited. After breakfast, I began pacing up and down in my rooms, glancing at the beach and the ocean, agonizing over when someone might call for me.

As the sun began to rise higher in the sky, so did the happy sounds of people emerging from the veranda below. When, in heaven's name, would someone contact me? Maybe they didn't want to disturb me; if so, I would have to make the first move. Oh, God, the idea of making any bold first move seemed terrifying. Where would I find that sort of courage? I'd been withdrawn for so long.

Was I strong enough to accept a rejection? If I received even the slightest rebuff, would I withdraw again? What if I were snubbed, or someone accused me of being a "has-been" with no right to my invitation as special guest of the Festival? Certainly the press were capable of saying that or something equally cruel.

The morning was slipping away and the telephone hadn't rung. I had no idea whom I should contact. Too much time was passing. I would have to overcome my fear and step out alone. Well, I'd have to do it, I hadn't gotten this far to stay shut up in my hotel suite. And hadn't I been locked away for long enough?

I was becoming jittery and nervous but I had to will myself to be calm. After great deliberation, I hadn't packed a single tranquilizer. This was, after all, my one chance to heal. It was my new beginning. And now I had to find the courage to emerge unsupported by drugs.

But what could I possibly do on my own? Well, first of all, I had to get out of that suite!

Maybe someone would come up to me in the lobby and give me my schedule and instructions. But what if they didn't? Well, I'd keep on moving, that was the important thing. Remember, keep on moving ahead and never sink back! Move, but in which direction? Toward the beach. Yes, toward the beach like everyone else.

I stepped out my front door and quickly slammed it behind me so I wouldn't be tempted to change my mind. My room was one flight up from the lobby. Should I walk down the staircase or ring for the elevator? If I walked the circular stairs, I'd be on view for an agonizingly long time before I reached the level. On the other hand, I had to give any Festival officials milling about in the lobby time to recognize me. It was no good dashing unseen from the elevator to the veranda.

Suddenly I panicked! I panicked at the thought of facing a crowd of curious strangers, and I ran back to my front door. But I pulled myself up sharply. No! Only go forward! If it is too difficult to walk to the staircase, then go down in the elevator—but go!

As the elevator doors opened onto the lobby, every head turned toward me. People nudged one another, whispered my name. For the moment I froze. But I didn't run. Then, all at once, my years of training returned and took control. Like a show pony bred for the arena I remembered my instructions: tilt head slightly back and prance with confidence for the judges. I had never intended to cross the whole of that room, I just automatically found myself moving as if to take center stage. I marched across the entire length of that elegantly grand lobby to the concierge. As I handed him my key, he and everyone else working in the reception area nodded and greeted me warmly. Once that first stiff silence had been broken, the guests in the lobby openly smiled at me and made a sort of path for me as I glided toward the open doorway onto the veranda.

People there paused in their conversations to stare at me, but no one approached me, and I continued to walk toward the beach. There were private cabanas all along the perimeter of the wall beneath the hotel steps. I moved slowly but again no one approached me. I seemed somehow like an intruder, so I continued down to the water's edge, now feeling very self-conscious.

I kicked off my sandals and waded in a few inches and began playing in the surf with my toes. How I wished that someone friendly—above all, kind—would speak to me and make me feel a part of the festivities. Being there alone on the beach was so hard for me, but I had to begin to *confront* things head on.

I'd known I had to come to Venice alone. To get away from Jack for a while, with his systematic undermining of my confidence. And there hadn't been the money to hire a secretary to accompany me. Anyway, I had to learn how to take charge of things for myself now.

But what would I do if no one introduced themselves all day? Never mind. I would stand there until I was burned to a crisp. I'd promised myself that even if I spent the entire day without talking to a soul, I would not turn back.

All at once the chords of a guitar struck up behind me and a vibrant male voice began crooning the popular "Quando, Quando, Quando?" At first I felt too shy to look around. But then I made out the words, "Dedicated to you, Miss Carolin-a Baecker," injected into the lyrics. I turned and saw a charming young man with a radiant smile singing in my honor. I accepted his song gratefully and unashamedly.

Other bathers began drifting in our direction, sunbathers rose from their chairs and walked from their cabanas down to the water's edge, photographers scurried in to photograph us, and within minutes all the life and excitement of the Lido was surrounding Carolin-a Baecker and her handsome serenader.

The organizers, of course, found me and escorted me to the cabana reserved for official guests. And thereafter I ceased to be lost. I was wined and dined, and given a place of honor at all their official functions. My serenader had been Toni Renis, the famous singer-composer. I never again had to feel an instant of loneliness in Venice, not from the moment Toni, my adorable friend Toni for whom I shall always have the greatest affection and gratitude, sang to me his wonderful "Quando, Quando, Quando?" When, When, When? If you ask me when, I would have to say right then—right then I began my love affair with Italy and her people. I realized that the Italians had been waiting all along with outstretched arms to accept, admire, and even coddle me. It struck me that the world did not consist only of a few square, palm-treed blocks. Perhaps we would find the world to be limitless, if only we could venture out of ourselves in search of our maker's vast, divine generosity.

It was also at the Festival that I was given the opportunity to scale yet another imprisoning wall—unemployment. The highly acclaimed Italian director, Marco Ferrari, was about to film a movie entitled *Her Harem* and he had not yet cast his leading lady. We met at a luncheon party and he chose me on the spot! I was able to stay on in Europe and to experience the great freedom and joy of working again in a movie, a fascinating movie at that, and of having paychecks actually placed directly into my hands.

I'd made the breakthrough into European films, and I felt that if I had a career and a future at all, across the ocean was where it lay. My next giant step was to go back to L.A. to face Jack. I needed live in Europe, and I wanted to take the children with me. Whatever adjustments the children would have to make, I knew their struggle would be better than living in a world without a sane mother.

I thought I could never bring myself to tell Jack that I was leaving.

However, when I did say it, Jack's reaction bowled me over. After I stammered through my intentions, he expressed what appeared to me to be not one ounce of concern over the breakup of our family. He became, in my opinion, only concerned with his own financial well-being. It seemed like he wasn't the least bit emotionally upset about our parting. Could he be that cold and calculating? Or maybe he just was fed up living with an emotional cripple.

Anyway, he insisted upon an immediate legal separation so that the community property could be divided forthwith. Then he began pressuring me for a written commitment as to the division of the Paramount monies (the five future pictures which were involved in the contract dispute) in the event the courts were to rule in my favor.

I was stunned by his callous attitude, but I hadn't yet completely broken the yoke of his dictatorial influence, and his demands confused me and left me feeling somehow strangely guilty. What did I owe him? I wasn't sure. The California community property law was clear-cut: fifty-fifty on all existing assets. But what were my legal obligations about future monies, and the deeper question: what were my moral obligations to my husband of twelve years and the father of my children?

It was his driving insistence to have a contract overnight without giving me time to think that aroused my suspicions and led me to be cautious. Also we had a mutual law firm, and I'd heard about the need to always seek independent legal counsel. I agreed to the separation with its division of community property. But I was wary of entering into any written agreement about future earnings until I'd had the time to consider it carefully with a lawyer. So I postponed that decision. I think that if Jack had not so urgently and energetically pressed me, I would —because of my feelings of guilt for wanting to leave him—have been far too unrealistically generous and forfeited my future earnings to him, to the detriment of the children and myself.

There was a mountain of debts, and these debts were also legally considered to be fifty-fifty under California law. I knew that I would one day pay off my share, even if it took me a lifetime. I was hoping that one day I would also be in a position to help Jack with his share of the debts, as a way of soothing my unreasonable conscience.

During three years of unemployment Jack had not allowed me to forgo the services of our expensive publicity and business managerial firms, and the fees owed to each of them mounted monthly and by four figures! Jack was still adamant about retaining these services, even after our separation, for what he termed "both of our benefits." But I was desperate to put a stop to this disastrous habit of living on borrowed money and at the same time permitting the bills to escalate. A week before we went to court to request the legal separation, I took a strong, independent stand. From my *Harem* earnings I paid a tiny sum toward each debt, and at the same time called a halt once and for all to any further or future deficits. Jack protested, but at least in this matter, suddenly my resolve matched his. I signed documents releasing me from all mutual commitments. Finally, finally, I had accomplished my first act of real personal self-assertion.

The children had six weeks of their school term to finish, and then there would be their camp, which had become the highlight of their summers. The agreement was for the children to come to Europe at the end of August, in time for me to enroll them in a new school.

As far as material possessions were concerned, I left behind every stick of furniture, book, ornament, and an entire room of press clippings, photographs, and memorabilia. I couldn't afford to transport my possessions such a long distance, and I had no established home. Anyway, I thought it might be better not to be tempted to reminisce or cry over the past. I had a future, now.

Besides my personal wardrobe (my jewelry was all in hock), I had a check for my share of the community property. Once I had agreed to let Jack keep the furnishings, there was no other community property except the house. My check, which represented my half of the profit on its sale, amounted to just eight thousand dollars.

It wasn't much capital with which to establish a foreign residence. It would have been foolhardy to take such a risk had there been any other alternative, but there was none, and so I simply had to find a way to make do. Obviously my children's welfare was my main concern. They had to have a roof over their heads, they had to have food, medical attention when necessary, and of course an education. So I spent seven of the eight thousand dollars for them to study and live for one school year at a Swiss boarding school.

I had thought to stay in Geneva, perhaps somewhere near the school, because it was a central location with easy access to most foreign capitals where I might find work. If I were filming in Madrid or London, Rome or Paris, I could be home on the weekends within two hours.

When I flew to Geneva, there were two prospects of work: one was a movie in London and the other was a movie in Rome. The children weren't due to arrive for a few more months, and I found Switzerland to be an overly quiet, lonely, and rather expensive country. After six weeks, I was desperate with boredom and sick at heart because my money was disappearing much too rapidly.

When I was nearly at my wit's end, the Italians made me a firm offer. One day I had been shivering on a park bench in Geneva counting my Swiss francs to decide if I could afford a hot broth to accompany my cold sandwich, and the next day I was basking in the sun on the Via Veneto savoring an enormous plate of spaghetti!

How can I describe a spring day in Rome or fully express just how glorious it made me feel? Even if one were a millionaire, what could be more delicious or more satisfying than freshly made pasta and a glass of Italian red wine? Who could be less than joyful while ogling everything and everyone on the Via Veneto or in one of Rome's fabulous piazzas? Who could fail to be awestruck by that majestic city's monuments, and sculptures, and terra cotta buildings?

The one-room apartment I rented was modest, actually it was even a bit stark. But church bells rang out all around me to greet each new day, and when I raised my shutters, I faced the Piazza Navona and a Michelangelo fountain, one of its sculptured fingers pointing as if to indicate the Bernini Church. The neighborhood children used to call out to me because I often skipped rope with them, and one of the waiters at the sidewalk cafe directly below my windows would always offer to bring up my morning cappucino.

The film I made was the story of a wealthy American divorcée on a recuperative vacation in Italy, and what happens when a group of hippies invades her rented villa and destroys her hitherto conventional attitudes toward society. It was quite an interesting movie, but I think I can be forgiven for having been thrilled mostly (as well as relieved) by the healthy salary. I was freed from my financial nightmare.

As all Italian films are dubbed and provided with an entirely new sound track after filming is completed, I was able to act my role in English. But I had to have an interpreter to translate for me, because I couldn't communicate with the director or any of the people on the set. So a member of the production staff was assigned to me for that purpose. Her name was Benedetta Vigano, and I was overjoyed when she turned out to be a girl after my own heart, for what I most needed then was a real friend and confidante.

Benedetta had descended from a long line of nobility, and Vigano was still one of the "best old names" of Florentine society. But during the Second World War, like so many aristocratic families, the Viganos had lost their vast estates along with most of their family fortune. Her parents, nonetheless, had provided Benedetta with a remarkable education, and she spoke five languages fluently, among them a flawless English. She had an elegance and simplicity that comes no doubt from breeding and would be almost impossible to affect. With it all she was also totally *simpatica.*

Like me, Benedetta was in her mid-thirties. Our backgrounds were so completely different and yet we had a meeting of the minds that made us like sisters. We were both women of a newly liberated generation, struggling to make an independent foothold for ourselves.

She was seeking a career on the production side of films, and she had already declined numerous offers of marriage to pursue her goals. My entire existence, for as long as I could remember, had been controlled by chauvinistic men: from a strict father to mad Louis Ritter, to power-orientated studio executives and producers, to my cripplingly submissive relationship with Jack Garfein. Never had I been able fully to express my own personality. The time had come to take the reins in my own hands and discover what I could do on my own. But like the cliché (once uttered only by men), "I couldn't live with them, and I couldn't live without them." I longed for male companionship—just no more relationships with puppet strings attached!

Love seemed to be everywhere, and I yearned to be a participant. My dread of physical love seemed to melt away. It was impossible to stay frigid in the warmth of the Mediterranean sun, and the heartfelt songs she inspired, and the romantic sons she nurtured. I was stirred to the depth of my womanly feelings by my renewed ability to accept affection and return it in equal measure.

No doubt I would have fallen prey to numerous celebrity-seeking playboys and perhaps even a gigolo or two, if Benedetta had not been there to point them out and steer me away. All the young men I met looked devastatingly handsome to me and altogether irresistible—it was like letting a deprived child loose in a candy store!

How many Latin lovers did I have? How many times was I swept off my feet and lost in passionate encounters? Well, I didn't keep a little black book, and my memory would have to be exceptional to have kept score. Let's just say that I didn't let another moment of my prime sexual years slip by unfulfilled.

My heartthrob during one of those years, Franco Nero, telephoned me in London not so long ago to say hello and to catch up on my latest news. When I told him that I was writing this book, he said, "I hope you don't tell them, Carroll, that I go to bed with my socks on!" I had completely forgotten—thank you for reminding me, Franco!

After the movie and for what remained of that summer of '68, Benedetta got us invited as house guests to some of the most spectacular homes in Italy. We spent a fairy-tale weekend living like queens at Palazzo Antinori, as guests of that famous wine-growing family. The Palazzo appeared to own all the sea to its right, and to its left the endless vineyards and olive groves of that Tuscan paradise. We traveled and dated, dated and traveled, stayed in opulent surroundings and went to lavish parties from Naples to Portofino, from Venice to Capri.

In Stresa, Benedetta even introduced me to a prince: Prince Carlo Borromeo! He was thirty years old, handsome, heir to the territory and treasures of the Borromeo Islands off Stresa, and considered to be the most eligible bachelor in all Italy. He became my conquest for some breathtaking weeks, but I was never tempted by his eligibility. I was having far too much fun playing the field, discovering the *mirabila,* or the marvels of courtship.

I'd had the most divine summer of my entire life, and all without spending a cent of my own money. So by the end of August I decided to splurge on a few lovely days of holiday for my family.

The children were due to arrive, and my mother was going to accompany them on the plane trip. I thought it would be super to have mother and the children arrive on the French Riviera and then to show them Rome before going on to Geneva.

When I met them at Nice Airport, Mother's luggage had been lost, Blanche and Herschel both had forgotten their shoes at camp and were barefoot, and their luggage consisted of a filthy duffel bag each with a cat in a travel box and a turtle in a bowl.

Which was how we checked into the elegant Hotel Carlton in Cannes! I don't think the management wanted us as guests. At least they tried to discourage me from registering by making me accept, instead of two rooms and a bath, three rooms and two baths—the extra room for the purpose of accommodating

Cleopatra, the cat, and the bath for the private use of Yurtle the turtle!

We cut our stay in Cannes short and moved on to Rome, which we all found to be the most enjoyable part of the vacation. The absolute highlight of mother's trip, and perhaps even of her life, was being received along with other pilgrims at Casa Gondolfo, the Pope's summer home. He stood over her and blessed her, and mother quickly held forth an arm strung with dozens of rosaries. She still has some of them, since she gives them only to very, very special people. You will know that my mother treasures you above all others if she presents you with one of her rosaries blessed by the "Papa" of their church and ours.

Once I'd put mother on her plane for Florida and settled the children into their school, it was time for me to begin fretting again over my future. I was having great difficulty finding an apartment for myself in Geneva, one which was halfway livable and yet reasonably priced. I had only one job prospect, which was for a television show in London and would pay very little. My savings had to be used sparingly for the kids and myself, and still hanging over my head were those enormous unpaid debts.

Then an incredible thing happened: the lawyers for Paramount made a gigantic boo-boo! Had they merely continued to defend themselves against my lawsuit, I surely would have lost because the consensus of opinion from my legal advisors was that we had presented a very weak case indeed. But Paramount changed their tactics, and my lawyers were flabbergasted at their obvious miscalculation in judgment. They counter-sued me, claiming that my revised contract had only been "an agreement to agree."

The court ruled that, as they had utilized my services in *Harlow* under that revised contract, it was more than just an agreement to agree in the future: it was a binding commitment. Paramount was ordered to pay me every cent for every film under that contract for the next five years, and overnight that ruling made me a wealthy woman!

The first thing I did was to pay up completely each and every hateful debt, both my share and Jack's. Then I rented an adorable unfurnished place in Rome, and began to purchase some extraordinary luxuries like my very own bed and chest of drawers. Now I had the money to have the children with me in a home of our own. Until their school finished and I was able to move them, I could afford to fly to Geneva every weekend.

In the heady bliss of my new circumstances, I had overlooked my one last ordeal: the final parting with Jack. Divorce is always an unpleasant business, so perhaps I wanted to postpone it as long as possible. Well, our divorce was more than simply unpleasant; it was both messy and degrading. Our fight brewed, bubbled, and spat bile for months on end. Then we sat in the courtroom for six weeks of utter hell, where the proceedings tore up the roots of our life together and thrashed and ground them into pitiful grains of gall.

Jack had initiated the divorce action, at the same time suing me for one half of my future income. Prior to the court action, we had made a strenuous effort to arrive at a cash settlement. However, Jack's lawyer always found our offers too low, and my lawyer always found their demands too steep. Ironically, in the end, I had to pay my lawyer the huge sum, almost to the cent, that I had been willing to settle on Jack.

The court denied every single one of Jack's petitions, and I won hands down. Just before the final ruling, the judge called our attorneys into his chambers and requested that Jack withdraw some of his claims so that he might save face, and the judge might see his way clear to awarding Jack his legal costs. But Jack, as stubborn as always, flatly refused to budge an inch. Maybe he was still thinking of winning through an appeal, but the judgment left his case without credibility.

I am so truly sorry for both of us, and for our children, that we could not have agreed on a cash settlement out of court, and spared ourselves all that pain—a pain which still persists and perhaps always will. And for that, again, I am so very, very sorry.

Ever since those most eventful years of '68 and '69, when I began my quest for independence, I have never wanted for work. Neither have I wanted for enough peace of mind, or a reasonable assertiveness, plus my share of healthy self-confidence. I've made more than twice as many movies in Europe than I made in America. And recently I've even appeared again in some excellent American films. So far the locations haven't called for me actually to film my scenes in Los Angeles, but who knows, one day I might turn the page to find the word Hollywood written there. The absolutely fascinating thing about life is that one never knows.

My children have both turned out splendidly, and I am so proud of them. They both were accepted into top colleges, Herschel has just received his Master's degree in music, and Blanche is now a successful actress in her own right.

By the way, Joe Levine and I finally kissed and made up—what the hell! And Jack Garfein? Well, Jack runs the highly respected Actors' and Directors' Lab in New York. I understand that he still hasn't learned what laundries are for and continues to send his socks and undershorts out to be drycleaned.

Now then, that brings us to Baby Doll: whatever happened to her? Well, if we speak of the Baby Doll of the movies, not a damn thing, actually. Why, that stupid little thumb-sucking brat is alive and well and seething still in the imagination of more than a generation of movie-goers. Oh, no thanks to me—for more than twenty-five years, I have devoted myself to her destruction. And I've grown so weary of the struggle, that my once maniacal resolve to eliminate her has gradually faded to a rather impotent wish. She, however, has retained every bit of her strength, and she remains as firmly implanted in my career world as ever.

But, having thoroughly probed the soft spots of the baby doll within me, I will never again permit myself to be treated like a toy. Finally, finally, this Baby Doll has found her way toward growing up. For one thing, I've matured and outgrown my devotion to *la dolce vita*. I now live in London. You see, I finally found the one fellow I know I want to be with exclusively. He is my husband, the British actor and writer, Donald Burton.

I do cherish my new life, and certainly London has always been one of my very favorite cities. But I must admit that I always become weepy when someone plays "Arrivederci Roma." There is a special place in my heart for the Eternal City, for her spiritual as well as her physical beauty. And I shall forever be grateful to the Italian people for the overwhelming understanding, generosity, and affection they have shown me. It was they who helped me to discover that here and now is all important; this breath, this sip of wine, this smile, this friend, this joy: this very moment.

Open Letter to Jack Garfein

Dear Jack,

I am sorry, most of my account must seem grossly unfair to you, one-sided —which of course it is—but I can only tell this story from my point of view. I hope you'll write your own book one day, and tell it your way.

I know that I am not without blame, that often in your efforts to please me—when you couldn't find doors, you inadvertently pushed down walls.

We were kids when we met. And I did love you. We were both inexperienced and unprepared for and overwhelmed by the events of our lives. And we got lost.

But we also must have done some things right—I mean, just look at our Blanche and our Herschel.

As ever,
Carroll

THE FILMS OF CARROLL BAKER

EASY TO LOVE. MGM, 1953. *Charles Walters.* Esther Williams, Van Johnson, Tony Martin.

GIANT. Warner Brothers, 1956. *George Stevens.* Elizabeth Taylor, Rock Hudson, James Dean, Mercedes McCambridge, Jane Withers, Fran Bennet, Earl Holliman, Sal Mineo, Jill Wills, Dennis Hopper.

BABY DOLL. Warner Brothers, 1956. *Elia Kazan.* Eli Wallach, Karl Malden, Mildred Dunnock.

THE BIG COUNTRY. United Artists, 1957. *William Wyler,* Gregory Peck, Charleton Heston, Jean Simmons, Chuck Connors, Burl Ives.

THE MIRACLE. Warner Brothers, 1958. *Irvin Rapper.* Roger Moore, Vittorio Gassman, Kattina Paxinou, Walter Slezak.

BUT NOT FOR ME. Paramount, 1959. *Charles Lang.* Clark Gable, Lilly Palmer, Lee J. Cobb.

SOMETHING WILD. United Artists, 1960. *Jack Garfein.* Ralph Meeker, Mildred Dunnock.

BRIDGE TO THE SUN. MGM, 1961. *Etienne Perier.* James Shigeta.

HOW THE WEST WAS WON. MGM, 1963. *Henry Hathaway, John Ford, George Marshall.* Karl Malden, Agnes Moorehead, Carolyn Jones, Debbie Reynolds, Jimmy Stewart, George Peppard, John Wayne, Henry Fonda, Eli Wallach, Richard Widmark, Robert Preston, Spencer Tracy as narrator.

STATION SIX SAHARA. British/German co-production, 1964. *Seth Holt.* Peter Van Eyck, Denholm Elliot, Ian Bannen.

THE CARPETBAGGERS. Paramount, 1964. *Edward Dmytryck.* George Peppard, Allan Ladd, Bob Cummings, Martha Heyer, Elizabeth Ashley, Lew Ayres, Martin Balsam.

CHEYENNE AUTUMN. Paramount, 1964. *John Ford*. James Stewart, Richard Widmark, Delores Del Rio, Sal Mineo, Ricardo Montalban, Gilbert Roland, Arthur Kennedy.

SYLVIA. Paramount, 1965. *Gordon Douglas*. George Maharis, Peter Lawford.

THE GREATEST STORY EVER TOLD. United Artists, 1965. *George Stevens*. Max Von Sydow, John Wayne, Sidney Poitier, Dorothy Maguire.

MR. MOSES. United Artists, 1965. *Ronald Neame*. Robert Mitchum, Alexander Knox, Orlando Martins, Ian Bannen Bad, Raymond St. Jacques, Perry King, Susan Tyrell.

HARLOW. Paramount, 1967. *Gordon Douglas*. Angela Lansbury, Red Buttons, Peter lawford.

BAD. *Andy Warhol*, 1977.

WATCHER IN THE WOODS. Walt Disney Productions, 1979. *John Hough*. Bette Davis, David McCallum, Lynn Holly Johnson.

STAR 80. The Ladd Company, 1983. *Bob Fosse*. Mariel Hemingway, Eric Roberts, Cliff Robertson.

RED MONARCH. Gold Crest Productions, 1983. *Jack Gold*. Colin Blakely, David Sushet.

Between 1968 and 1977, CARROLL BAKER lived abroad and appeared in many European films.

Index